Essentials of Psychiatric Assessment

A psychiatric assessment is a structured clinical conversation, complemented by observation and mental state examination, and supplemented by a physical examination and the interview of family members when appropriate. After the initial interview, the clinician should be able to establish whether the individual has a mental health problem or not, the nature of the problem, and a plan for the most suitable treatment. *Essentials of Psychiatric Assessment* provides the resident or beginning psychiatrist with a complete road map to a thorough clinical evaluation.

Mohamed Ahmed Abd El-Hay is Professor of Psychiatry at Tanta University, Egypt, where he teaches psychiatry and psychology to medical and nursing students at under and post graduate level. He also practices psychiatry at Tanta University, with special interest in child and adolescent psychiatry. Professor Abd El-Hay has published numerous scientific papers and books on psychiatry, psychology, and social psychology.

Essentials of Psychiatric Assessment

Mohamed Ahmed Abd El-Hay

Routledge
Taylor & Francis Group

NEW YORK AND LONDON

First published 2018
by Routledge
711 Third Avenue, New York, NY 10017

and by Routledge
2 Park Square, Milton Park, Abingdon, Oxon, OX14 4RN

Routledge is an imprint of the Taylor & Francis Group, an informa business

Library of Congress Cataloging-in-Publication Data
A catalog record has been requested for this book

ISBN: 978-1-138-55236-4 (hbk)
ISBN: 978-1-138-50236-9 (pbk)
ISBN: 978-1-315-14813-7 (ebk)

Typeset in Goudy
by Florence Production Ltd, Stoodleigh, Devon, UK

Contents

Preface

Throughout the twentieth century, a variety of views governed the field of psychiatry, with psychoanalytic theories dominating at one time, and behavioral, cognitive, and biological theories dominating at others. These changes have had a great effect on the aims and techniques of the evaluation of psychiatric patients, where it takes the form of either intensive study of the patient's life and his/her surrounding environment or of brief evaluation of symptoms that do not consider the complexity of human behavior.

During the middle of the nineteenth century, psychiatric evaluation focused on developing a dynamic understanding of patients derived from psychoanalytic concepts. Many such formulations were ideological as opposed to clinical. With the exception of serious depression or psychosis, treatment was uniform, regardless of the diagnosis. However, the extremism of the psychoanalytic era has been replaced by the recording of the observable symptoms at the expense of their meaning. This has led to improving the reliability of psychiatric diagnosis, although it has detracted from, rather than enhanced, psychiatric practice, and has led to the misunderstanding of patients. It seems impossible to treat a suffering individual without having an awareness of history, symbolic meaning, conflict, ambivalence, social context, and existential concerns.

The idea of this book dates back to my residency period, about 25 years ago, when I was searching for a book that would provide a simple, concise yet comprehensive idea about clinical psychiatric assessment; one that considers the complexity of human behavior and consequently the complexity of psychiatric diagnosis. Since then, a lot of suitable materials and clinical experience have accumulated to provide the basis of this work. This book is therefore indebted to other similar works that represent the frame for this work, and to my patients who taught me the actual meanings of psychiatric symptoms, and the most suitable way to assess them.

When writing this book, I tried to provide an approach that stresses the importance of critically evaluating the patient's history, and carefully observing and evaluating their mental state. Careful observation of the patient's history and symptoms is the roadway for good clinical psychiatric practice; it leads to assembling a characteristic profile of the patient that could be used to classify it according to one of the prevailing diagnostic systems, with the advantage of considering the patient's characteristics in treatment planning.

Although there is overlap and controversy about the meaning of terms used to discuss psychiatric symptoms, this book tries to include all possible psychiatric symptoms in a simple language that avoids ambiguous descriptions and explains vague ones. I hope this manual will help mental health professionals to develop clinical skills in psychiatric interviewing and assessment, and be useful for all persons working in the field of mental health.

Mohamed Abd El-Hay, M.D.

1 Introduction

At the beginning of work with psychiatric patients, students and residents have already learned much about the process of medical evaluation. They know how to detect signs and symptoms of illness by taking history and performing a physical examination. They have also learned how to use a laboratory test and to appreciate the relevance of these findings to diagnosis and treatment. These skills are all necessary, though insufficient, in evaluating psychiatric patients.

Psychiatric assessment includes a structured clinical conversation, complemented by observation and mental state examination and supplemented by a physical examination and the interview of other informants when appropriate. After the initial interview, the clinician should be able to establish whether the individual has a mental health problem or not, the nature of the problem, and a plan for the most suitable treatment.

Many of the difficulties of learning to be a psychiatrist reside in the differences between mental and physical illnesses. The traditional educational approach in psychiatry encourages students to ignore or minimize these differences and to emphasize similarities between all illnesses. Though that approach is assuring to students, it can retard or inhibit their capacity to grasp issues that are critical for psychiatric evaluation and management. This requires the psychiatrist both to become more thorough and skillful in using traditional medical methods of evaluation and to develop new skills that are unlikely to be learned in the process of traditional medical evaluation. *The psychiatrist must have the following skills*:

1. Helping the patients to communicate their inner experience. Thoughts, feelings, and perceptions are private phenomena, and many patients are unwilling or unable to discuss them with the physician. One of the first skills that psychiatrists must master is how to ask questions about inner experiences that the patients can understand and answer.
2. How to obtain accurate descriptions of abnormal behavior from the patient and other observers.

3. How to make direct observations of the patient's current behavior. Skills in detecting current behavioral aberrations are essential; in particular, patterns that appear during the process of evaluation.
4. Taking an extensive history that focuses on past behavior and experience.
5. Testing for disorders of perception, thought, and feelings.
6. Determining how behavioral and experiential difficulties may be related. Sometimes inner experience can be inferred by observing deviant patterns of behavior; e.g., patients who are withdrawn and tearful are likely to feel sad. The reverse is also true: behavior may be predicted by learning about inner experiences; e.g., patients with uncontrollable feelings of anger are at greater risk of behaving violently than those who do not experience these feelings.
7. Detecting inaccurate history: the accuracy with which a patient reports or reveals experience. It is usually difficult to understand why some patients would voluntarily or involuntarily seek to create or exaggerate symptoms.
8. Stress tolerance: working as a psychiatrist can at times be stressful. Sometimes the stresses are intense, such as a patient who unexpectedly becomes extremely agitated.

INFORMATION NECESSARY TO BE OBTAINED

The psychiatric interview should always have some structure or form; however, it may differ in the degree of structuring, running on a continuum from a poorly structured to a completely structured. The interviewer should always have a scenario for how the interview ideally will proceed, including the rationale for when to speak and when to keep silent and a sense of what the goals of interaction are. *The aims of data collection in general psychiatric evaluation are as follows:*

1. To collect data sufficient to permit a case formulation, and to establish a psychiatric diagnosis.
2. To understand how the patient experiences his/her difficulties and inner world.
3. To understand what events in the patient's life might have contributed to the current difficulties.
4. To build up an initial treatment plan, with special attention to immediate interventions that may be necessary to ensure the patient's safety.
5. To revise the treatment plan considering follow-up findings if the evaluation is a reassessment of a patient in long-term treatment.

The information obtained from the patient varies according to the availability of time, purpose of assessment, seriousness or urgency of the problem presented by the patient, and site of evaluation. These factors should be considered when ascertaining that certain settings meet the patient's needs to get a satisfactory evaluation of acceptable speed, safety, accuracy, and confidentiality. *In ordinary situations, the following information is usually obtained:*

1. Why the patient has requested or has been sent for evaluation at this particular time. Some outpatients are in urgent need for care and may come or are brought involuntarily to emergency rooms; others come to regular clinics, either voluntarily or involuntarily. Inpatients may be admitted voluntarily or involuntarily, or seen in medical or surgical wards. Patients may also be brought for forensic evaluation.
2. The sequence of events that precede and follow the patient's complaints, and their seeking help. This information is referred to as "history of the present illness." It is essentially a chronology of what has happened (or more precisely, how the patient has interacted with the environment, usually in a maladaptive manner) from the time just preceding the symptoms until the present.
3. The patient's current living environment (social, vocational, financial, academic), with an emphasis on how it contributes to the patient's symptomatology.
4. The patient's current and past psychiatric and medical history and treatment. It is also convenient to consider the family health history (i.e., mental and physical health of the extended family) under this heading.
5. The patient's personal history including childhood development, educational experiences, work and military experiences, and patterns of relating to others. The family relationship and family history of physical and mental disorders are also included here.
6. The predominant personality traits. This information helps to clarify how the patient's difficulties had developed, and how the patient is with them.

Again, the type and amount of information to be obtained from the patient can be modified according to the time available for the interview. *When time is available*, detailed information is obtained about the patient's present and past psychiatric and medical history, personal history, personality and mental state assessment. *When time is limited*, as in emergency settings, the evaluation should focus on essential information that is critical to management (see later).

A general evaluation usually takes about 45–90 minutes to complete; it depends on the complexity of the problem and the patient's ability and willingness to work cooperatively with the psychiatrist. Data collected from the interview should be integrated with that gathered from other parts of the evaluation, such as history from collateral sources, review of medical records, a physical examination, and diagnostic tests (American Psychiatric Association, 2006). Sometimes, several meetings with the patient may be necessary to reach a final conclusion about the patient's symptoms and best management plan. Circumstances often dictate that the assessment is not completed in a single interview and the interview time needs to be shortened or extended.

SITE OF THE CLINICAL EVALUATION

The scene of psychiatric evaluation is variable, and is a critical factor in the process of evaluation; evaluation of inpatients may extend for several hours, a matter that is not feasible in an outpatient setting.

Inpatient Settings

The nature of inpatient population determines the extent, time, and depth of inpatient evaluation, while the goals of the hospitalization and the role of the inpatient unit should be considered within the system of mental health service. For example, a general hospital psychiatric unit specializing in patients with combined medical and psychiatric illness will necessarily do a relatively rapid general medical evaluation of all admitted patients. The evaluation of stable, chronic general medical conditions in a long-stay setting for the chronically mentally ill might proceed at a slower pace than in a psychiatric–medical specialty unit in a general hospital.

When a patient is admitted by someone other than the treating psychiatrist, the reason for hospitalization should be carefully assessed and alternative treatment settings should be considered.

From the outset, inpatient evaluations should include consideration of discharge planning. The assessment must recognize both patient variables and community resources that are pertinent to a possible management plan and identify the problems that may hinder an appropriate disposition. If the patient was referred to the hospital by another clinician, the inpatient evaluation should be viewed in part as a consultation to the referring source. Special attention is given to unresolved diagnostic issues requiring data collection in an inpatient setting.

Outpatient Settings

The intensity of psychiatric evaluation of outpatients usually differs from inpatient evaluation; because of less frequent interviews, less involvement of other mental health professionals, and less availability of immediate laboratory services and consultants from other specialties. In outpatient settings, the psychiatrist has less opportunity to directly observe the patient's behavior or to execute necessary protective interventions. Hence, it is critical to continually assess outpatients during interview about their need for hospitalization and whether unresolved questions about the patient's general medical status entail more rapid assessment. The patient's current mental status and behavior is definitive in deciding to change the setting for continued evaluation (American Psychiatric Association, 2006).

Advantages of the outpatient setting include less financial cost, greater patient autonomy, and the potential for a longer longitudinal perspective on the patient's symptoms. However, the lack of continuous direct observation of behavior limits the obtainable data on how the patient's behavior appears to others. The involvement of family or significant others as collateral sources in the evaluation process deserves consideration. When substance use is suspected, data from collateral observers, drug screens, and/or determination of blood alcohol levels may be especially important.

Other Settings

Evaluations conducted in other settings, such as partial hospital settings, residential treatment facilities, home care services, nursing homes, long-term care facilities, schools, and prisons, *are affected by a number of factors*:

1. The level of behavioral observations available and the quality of those observations.
2. The availability of privacy for conducting interviews.
3. The availability of general medical evaluations and diagnostic tests.
4. The capacity to conduct the evaluation safely.
5. The likelihood that information written in facility records will be understood and kept confidential.

METHODS OF OBTAINING INFORMATION

Collecting information about a patient can be done through *one or more of the following approaches*:

1. Psychiatric interview
2. Patient observation
3. Interview of collateral sources
4. Working with multidisciplinary teams.

Psychiatric Interview

The psychiatric interview is the main tool in evaluating patients who complain of symptoms that were assumed to be due to mental disorder. The traditional formal examination outline of general medicine has been replaced by encouraging patients to tell their story in their own words. The question and answer technique leads to brief and sterile responses and failure to elicit an elaboration of their background. A psychiatric assessment differs from other medical interviews in that more attention needs to be paid to the patient's psychological and social influences. Accordingly, patients' cultural and spiritual backgrounds; important relationships; significant life events and their reactions to them; and their attitudes, values, and beliefs about themselves, other people, and the world may all be explored in the course of an assessment. The psychiatrist needs to consider not only the implications of conscious realistic statements but also the unconscious or transference aspects. Transference refers to the way patients "transfer" feelings from important persons in their early lives onto the psychoanalyst or therapist. *In general, there are four goals of any interview:*

1. **Establish a relationship**: interviewing is an interpersonal process. The quality of information that the patient reveals to the interviewer is a function of the trustworthiness that the patient experiences with the interviewer. Patients will not reveal the personal, intimate, and diagnostically important details of their experience to someone they do not trust. Rapport is the spontaneous, conscious feeling of harmonious responsiveness that promotes the development of a constructive therapeutic relationship. It implies that there is an understanding and trust between the psychiatrist and his patient (Sadock & Sadock, 2007).
2. **Obtain information**: information could be divided into factual and emotional information.
3. **Assessment of psychopathology**: every diagnostic interview includes assessment of the presence of psychopathology, including not only the formal mental status testing but also the inferences and conclusions that an interviewer draws as the interview is conducted.
4. **Provide feedback**: patients are usually concerned to know the opinion of the psychiatrist after the first interview about their symptoms or history. Though giving a definitive answer is not usually possible at the end of the first interview, considering these concerns tactfully is essential to deepen rapport with the patient.

For trust and rapport to develop, the clinician must display tact, empathy, and genuine respect for the individual's dignity throughout the interview. During the initial interview, the patient is usually anxious and may find it difficult to talk even under the best conditions. A **private** setting is crucial with comfortable seating and ambience and freedom from interruptions. *A number of factors contribute to the development and maintenance of a trusting relationship:*

1. **Respect** for the patient regardless of their appearance or socioeconomic state.

2.   **Compassion** for the patient's suffering and distress.
3.   **Positive regard** (warmth) for the patient, showing interest, concern, and even curiosity devoid from judgmental evaluation.
4.   **Genuineness** through a mixture of spontaneity, consistency, and authenticity. The patient should experience the interviewer's genuineness as directly responsive to his or her personhood or behavior.

Patient Observation

The second method of obtaining information about patients is observation. Systematic observations of patients' behavior by staff are a diagnostic asset of controlled settings, such as hospitals, partial hospital settings, residential treatment facilities, and other institutions. In these settings, the psychiatrist may suggest to other team members specific observations that may be particularly relevant to the diagnosis or treatment plan. *Several types of observations may be recorded, according to the patient's specific situation.*

1.   **General observations**: these are relevant to all patients in all settings and include notes on patients' behavior, cooperativeness with or resistance to staff, sleep/wake patterns, and self-care.
2.   **Diagnosis-specific observations**: these are observations relevant to confirming a diagnosis or assessing the severity, complications, or subtype of a disorder. Examples include recording of signs of withdrawal in an alcohol-dependent patient and observations during meals for patients with eating disorders.
3.   **Patient-specific observations**: these are observations aimed at assessing a clinical hypothesis. An example is observation of behavior following a family meeting for a patient in whom family conflicts are suspected of having contributed to a psychotic relapse.
4.   **Observations of response to treatment interventions**: examples include systematic recording of a target behavior in a trial of behavior therapy, observations of the effects of newly prescribed medications, and nurse-completed rating scales to measure changes after behavioral or psychotherapeutic interventions.

Interview of Collateral Sources

The third method of obtaining information about patients is interviewing friends, family members, and any relevant others. Relatives and friends are good sources of objective information. Often, they will accompany the patient to the emergency room or walk-in clinic. If the situation is less critical and they are not present, they may be willing to talk to the doctor by phone or to come in for an interview if requested. It is reassuring when the accompanying person confirms the patient's description of the present illness and even adds details that the patient may not have noted or may have forgotten. Difficulties arise when the patient and the accompanying person provide contradictory information about what has been happening to the patient, and neither changes his or her story.

Collateral information is particularly important for patients with impaired insight, in addition to those with substance use disorders or cognitive impairment, and is essential for treatment planning for patients requiring a high level of assistance or supervision because of impaired function or unsuitable behavior.

Nonetheless, the confidentiality of the patient should be respected, except when immediate safety concerns are paramount. Family members, other important people in the patient's life, and records of prior medical and/or psychiatric treatment are frequently useful sources of information.

The extent of the collateral interviews and the extent of prior record review should be commensurate with the purpose of the evaluation, the ambitiousness of the diagnostic and therapeutic goals, and the difficulty of the case.

Working with Multidisciplinary Teams

The fourth method of obtaining information about patients is through professionals of other specialties. Multidisciplinary teams participate in general evaluations in most institutional settings and in many outpatient clinics. When working with a multidisciplinary team, the attending psychiatrist integrates both primary data and evaluative impressions of team members in arriving at a diagnosis and case formulation. It is crucial that the psychiatrist's diagnosis and case formulation rely on documented data recorded in the medical record.

METHODS OF INTERVIEWING

The two commonly used interview styles by mental health professionals include insight-oriented and symptom-oriented interviewing. Both approaches have advantages and can be integrated to develop an interview style that will elicit information from the patient on many different levels.

Insight-oriented (Psychodynamic) Interviewing

The insight-oriented interview with an interpretative approach tries to explain signs, symptoms, and behaviors. Insight-oriented interviewing originates from the concept that deep-seated, often infantile conflicts that become chronic pathogens of the mind and interfere with the patient's actions distort his/her perceptions and lead to symptoms of maladjusted behavior and suffering.

Insight-oriented interviewing attempts to uncover unconscious conflicts and to bring them into the patient's awareness with the expectation that this may resolve his/her problems or complaints. The patient often resists this unraveling by using what have been termed "unconscious defense mechanisms." The interview has a dual purpose: diagnosis and therapy. *The methods employed by the insight-oriented interviewer include*:

- interpretation of the patient's free associations and dreams;
- detection of the patient's anxieties;
- confronting the patient with his/her interpersonal behavior toward the therapist and others;
- identification of defense mechanisms and analysis of the patient's behavior.

Symptom-oriented (Descriptive) Interviewing

This approach originates from the concept that psychiatric disorders manifest themselves in a characteristic set of signs, symptoms, and behaviors; a predictable course; a somewhat specific treatment response; and often a familial occurrence. The goal of symptom-oriented interviewing is to classify the patient's complaints and dysfunctions according to defined diagnostic criteria. Such a diagnosis helps to predict the future course and to empirically select the most effective treatment, but may not allow conclusion about its etiology.

In the symptom-oriented interview, the role of the clinician is to observe the patient's behavior and to motivate the patient to describe his/her problems in detail. The interviewer translates his/her perception into signs and symptoms for a descriptive diagnosis. The interviewer includes the evaluation of the patient's general medical conditions, adjustment, and coping skills, and the patient's personal way of dealing with his/her disorder, psychosocial and environmental problems, global assessment of functioning, and defensive functioning. The symptom-oriented interview with a descriptive approach classifies signs and symptoms into disorder categories.

Both insight-oriented and symptom-oriented approaches are compatible and can be used effectively in conjunction with one another. Bleuler (1972) was the first prominent psychiatrist to integrate the two approaches. Mental health professionals seem to agree that they can best understand the patient's personality, conflicts, and problems of living by a psychodynamic approach, but that major psychiatric and personality disorders are best assessed by the descriptive method. A synthesis of interpretation and description can bridge the different points of departure. For instance, when a patient has both major psychiatric disorder and personality disorder, as well as unconscious conflicts, the interviewer diagnoses the major psychiatric disorder and personality disorder according to DSM-5 by means of symptom-oriented interview. If, after treatment, interpersonal conflicts persist or surface, the interviewer may switch to an insight-oriented interview as a second step, thus complementing his/her symptom-oriented interview.

INITIATING AN INTERVIEW

There is no uniform approach to begin a psychiatric interview. The only rule of thumb is that physicians should begin by introducing themselves and saying something about their status, followed by greeting companions if the patient is accompanied. A polite, respectful, understanding, and tolerant attitude on the part of the psychiatrist helps to put the patient at ease. The emphasis is on developing a good relationship, since the relationship determines to a great degree the kind of information the patient will give and the psychotherapeutic interaction depends on the rapport established.

Some clinicians may prefer to start the interview by inquiring about the demographic data such as the patient's age, occupation, marital state, and residence. This is to attempt to decrease the patient's initial hesitancy and fears. As the interview unfolds, more questions aiming at clarifying symptoms and their evolution are used.

Perhaps the majority of patients respond best to straightforward inquiry about what is troubling them—this allows patients to explore their own thoughts, feelings, and behaviors—or asking about the chief problems that brought the patient to the clinic or hospital. When possible, the interviewer should help patients follow their own leads and make their own discoveries (Meier & Davis, 2011). This is especially true of voluntary patients who may be eager to seek help. The patient can then be encouraged to tell the story of his present illness. Listening carefully is a major part of the psychiatric interview; it lessens the patient's anxiety, which leads to blocking and silence.

In the case of involuntarily hospitalized patients, a straightforward inquiry may elicit annoyed or defensive responses in the patient. The patient usually best responds to questions such as: "How can I help you?" "Do you have any problems?" or questions about sleep and appetite. The answer may set the stage for more specific information.

Note-taking

Documentation of the psychiatric history is a usual practice, where the data are recorded in a meaningful chronological order. This will enable the psychiatrist to notice any information that may have not been satisfactorily covered, and any questions that may still lack answers. It also indicates areas that the patient may have avoided or that the psychiatrist him/herself may have unconsciously omitted. Also, a written history is a source of information to others; this is especially true in hospitals where psychiatrists work for only limited periods. Many therapists and writers have discussed note-taking (Benjamin, 1987; Hartley, 2002; Pipes & Davenport, 1999).

Although some experts recommend that interviewers take notes only after a session, others point out that interviewers don't have perfect memories and thus an ongoing record of the session is desirable (Shea, 1998). In some cases, note-taking may offend clients. In other cases, note-taking may enhance rapport and interviewer credibility. Note-taking should be delayed at the outset until the patient feels that he or she has the clinician's attention, and notes should not be so extensive as to interfere with the free flow of the patient's talk. If the patient is highly anxious, agitated, hostile, or paranoid, it may be sensible to defer note-taking until after the interview, and limit the amount of factual information at the first interview. When notes are not taken during the interview, the data should be recorded immediately after the patient leaves. In this case, there is danger that the interviewer's own personal reactions will extensively contaminate the patient record.

Reassurance of the patient that the notes are confidential should be given at first, especially with patients who feel uncomfortable about them. If the patient objects to note-taking, it is best to discontinue it. Do not write notes that are not accepted by the client. If clients ask to see what you've written, they are allowed to read the notes and express their concerns. This means sticking to the facts (Sommers-Flanagan & Sommers-Flanagan, 2014).

There is no one correct form for eliciting or recording the psychiatric history. However, it is important for a student to have a form so that he/she learns to cover the important developmental areas. Over time, the student will gain experience that enables him/her to modify whatever form he/she has learned to suit his/her own personality and own approach.

STRATEGIES TO GET THE PATIENT'S RAPPORT

The first-time psychiatric patient is often doubtful, apprehensive, and anxious. He/She has overcome the stigma of seeing a mental health professional, but the taboo about psychiatric and psychological problems still troubles him/her. He/She is unsure of the people who are involved in such matters and does not know what to expect. He/She has rarely verbalized what troubles him/her before this visit. This is why it is important to establish rapport with the patient. The importance of developing a positive relationship with clients before using interventions is an area of agreement among clinicians and psychotherapists from virtually every theoretical perspective (Ackerman et al., 2001; Chambless & Ollendick, 2001; Norcross & Lambert, 2011). Some theorists refer to this as rapport, others use the terms "working alliance" or "therapeutic relationship" (Bordin, 1979, 1994; Sommers-Flanagan & Sommers-Flanagan, 2007).

In most interviewing situations, non-directive listening is the first step to get rapport, where the clinician speaks very little and uses open-ended questions or open-ended statements in an effort to get the patient talking (Shea, 1998). Being prematurely active and directive carries the risk of being insensitive and non-therapeutic (Strupp & Binder, 1984). The therapist should resist the compulsion to do something, especially at those times when he/she feels under pressure from the patient (and him/herself) to intervene, perform, reassure, and so on. *Common strategies to get the patient's rapport include the following:*

- putting the patient and yourself at ease
- recognizing signs
- responding to signs
- finding the suffering
- showing expertise
- establishing leadership
- balancing the roles
- dependence on the interviewer's leadership.

Putting the Patient and Yourself at Ease

The interviewer should convey to patients that he/she feels their doubts and concerns, respects them, and that he/she will help them. If fears and hopes are ignored, reservation and frustration will prevail.

When the patient arrives, it is often best to put him/her at ease by introducing yourself, asking the patient about his/her name and its proper pronunciation, and whether he/she prefers to be addressed by his/her first or last name. Then, the interviewer might want to engage in small talk with the patient, e.g., how did you find your way to the clinic? or ask him/her about his/her area of geographical origin. This break of easy conversation will help to settle both the patient and the interviewer, and initiate an initial rapport. However, some patients, e.g., patients with anxiety disorders, may want to get to the point, and some obsessive patients may feel that these questions waste time by not going straight to the assessment.

The importance of positive attending behaviors to successful interview is recognized across various disciplines and theoretical orientations; it is out-standingly uncontroversial (Akhtar, 2007; Cormier et al., 2012; Wright & Davis, 1994). Attending behavior is primarily non-verbal. In clinical inter-viewing, it is likely that if verbal and non-verbal messages are in conflict, the client will believe the non-verbal message. This is why being aware of and effectively using non-verbal channels is so important when communicating with clients (Birdwhistell, 1970).

Recognizing Signs

A sign is the non-verbal language of the face, body, and voice that is often hard to control. Signs are of a different nature: behavioral, emotional, or verbal. Understanding and decoding the patient's signs makes the patient feel comforted and helps him/her to express his/her state of mind.

Responding to Signs

There are different ways of responding to signs:

- Simply observe the patient and give him/her the time and space to express him/herself more and to relax, but always monitor the patient's signs.
- Draw the patient's attention to his/her signs and discuss their meaning with him/her.
- In many cases, it is best to respond in kind—with or without reflecting on them. This response is often the most effective, e.g., when the interviewer faces a patient who avoids him/her, the interviewer may move slowly toward the patient to show that he/she is concerned about his/her well-being and make inviting gestures. In the case of an intrusive patient, the interviewer can make gestures to stop this intrusion and follow up verbally (Othmer & Othmer, 2002).

Finding the Suffering

There are usually two aspects to the patient's problems; the facts and the associated emotions. The facts may be symptoms such as loss of appetite and early morning awakening, or stressors such as the death of a child or job loss. The emotions are the feelings that these facts stir up in the patient and make him/her suffer. Patients may hide this aspect because of fear of being ashamed or embarrassed. The clinician could intensify rapport if he/she could bring out not only the facts but also the suffering. This could be achieved by assessing the suffering and responding with empathy.

Assessing the Suffering

1. Ask the patient about what is bothering him/her (this is called the chief complaint).
2. Ask the patient to describe his/her distress and feelings in words: in the early phase of the interview, it is more important to allow the patient to talk about his/her suffering rather than to list his/her symptoms. Giving the patient the opportunity to talk freely about his/her suffering and bringing the patient's affect to his/her awareness accomplishes two goals:
   - It allows the clinician to judge the patient's affect and mood and to detect the underlying quality, such as depression, anxiety or anger.
   - It shows the patient that the clinician has an interest in his/her feelings, which brings both of them closer to each other and deepens rapport.

Responding with Empathy

Among the criteria used to choose a physician, empathy was rated as the second most important criterion after expertise (Hill & Garner, 1991; Yassini et al., 2010). When the patient reveals his/her suffering, tell him/her that you understand, show empathy, and express compassion.

Showing Expertise

People rank competence highly in choosing a physician. To establish your expertise, you need to show the patient that you are competent to handle his/her problem. *This could be reached through*:

- putting the illness into perspective—make the patient aware that he/she is not alone with his/her problem;
- showing knowledge—communicate to the patient that you are familiar with his/her illness;
- dealing with doubt—address his/her doubt about your professional skills, or the presence of beneficial treatment;
- instilling hope about the patient's future.

Establishing Leadership

Leadership originates from the clinician's ability to motivate and guide the patient. This could be reached through taking control of the interaction with the patient, expressing an interest in his/her welfare, and motivating him/her to change.

Some interviewers overstep their authority; they perceive the patients as subordinates who should obey. Some patients accept this demanding or even punitive behavior, and feel strongly guided rather imposed on. Obviously, such interaction fosters dependence. Most authoritarian interviewers are unaware of their lack of empathy or willingness to explain. They are often insecure and hide their self-doubt behind an authority role. If your patient responds to you with resistance or anxious obedience, examine whether you were too threatening or demanding.

Sometimes the patient pushes the clinician to take an authoritarian role even against the clinician's will, then the patient may protest against the authority he/she has endowed the clinician with. Make the patient aware of his/her attempts to push you to take an authoritarian role and point out to the patient the unrealistic expectations, thus countering his/her false expectations that will possibly be followed later by disappointment.

Grandiose and suspicious patients and persons with antisocial personality often defy your leadership, try to disarm you, and demonstrate disrespect: attitudes that disturb rapport.

Balancing the Roles

Patients and clinicians enter the interview with a set of expectations. In some cases, the patient wants the clinician to assume a role, such as the authoritarian or empathic listener. If the clinician is aware of the roles that the patient asks of him/her, he/she will be able to gauge how to respond. The skillful interviewer balances the roles of empathic listener, expert, and leader throughout the interview. Ideally, the interviewer switches these roles according to the patient's needs. Rapport is achieved when the interviewer and the patient balance their changing roles and act accordingly. If the interviewer or the patient reject each other's adopted role, conflict arises. The interviewer should monitor the emerging roles and react accordingly.

The Roles of the Patient

These roles include:

- **Carrier of an illness**: patients see themselves only temporarily impaired. They put a distance between themselves and the disorder, e.g., they will say it is their sleep not themself that is disturbed. They put the problem into quarantine so that it cannot infect the rest of them. Other than the disturbance, the patient tries to live a normal life and does not demand special privileges, or crave sympathy, but expects only expert medical management.
- **The sufferer**: such patients are the opposite from the carrier of an illness. They are consumed by their disturbance and suffering. They exaggerate the disability and crave comfort, sympathy, and understanding rather than expert advice. They force the clinician to set firm limits. Chronic depression and some personality disorders favor the development of this role.
- **The VIP**: some patients see themselves as very important, privileged, and entitled to attention at any time of day or night. They expect preferential treatment. They search for the very best in the field, the star psychiatrist or psychologist. Establishing rapport with such patients may become complex and limit setting is unavoidable. The VIP attitude can be adopted by anyone, from the very successful to the least privileged.

The Roles of the Interviewer

These roles include:

- **The empathic listener**: the empathic listener puts his/her patients at ease, is sensitive to their suffering, and expresses his/her compassion. Being empathic does not mean being overly lax or behaving like a permissive mother with a spoiled child. When you recognize that you over-emphasize empathy, start to set limits, take the leadership, and bring your expertise to bear whenever it appears in the best interest of a well-run, economic, yet informative interview.

- **The expert**: the expert should be sensitive to the patient's suffering and communicate empathy to the patient. Some experts neglect this and consider it a waste of time, though this has serious consequences for the patient.
- **The authority**: the interviewer should avoid being overly empathetic or authoritarian. Some points may refer to the inappropriate style of the interviewer's role, e.g., the patient opposes you, becomes reluctant, grins or makes undermining remarks, or may contradict you, become very obedient, or become uncomfortable and monosyllabic, anxious, or insecure.

Dependence on the Interviewer's Leadership

A patient's dependency needs may be as disturbing as a rejection of the interviewer. The patient attempts to put the interviewer in the role of an advice-giving authority. So, avoid giving advice to the doubting patient who is suffering from depression and instead offer empathic listening. In contrast, it is sometimes therapeutic for a patient if you do accept the authority role; e.g., when the patient is pondering a realistic plan but is still filled with self-doubt because of depression, your support and encouragement for his/her plan may make the difference.

In conclusion, for good rapport, good clinicians should be able to:

1. put an anxious patient at ease;
2. gain sufficient trust to encourage an unwilling or suspicious patient to discuss relevant issues by displaying tact, patience, and encouragement;
3. be comfortable, tolerant, and empathic when a patient becomes tearful during the interview;
4. recognize and respect patient–clinician boundaries especially with dependent, disinhibited, overfamiliar, or adulatory patients;
5. know how to set limits if patients become angry, hostile, or abusive;
6. politely interrupt and refocus talkative patients, explaining that because of time restraints it may be necessary to break into their flow of conversation from time to time to concentrate on the points that are important for planning treatment;
7. rapidly identify patients who are demented, disorganized, disoriented, intoxicated, grossly psychotic, or dysphasic and for whom other informants will be imperative, and become aware of and monitor their own countertransference responses to particular patients;

8. be aware of your own prejudices, weaknesses, blind spots, and personal vulnerabilities, and recognize when patients arouse strong feelings of anger, boredom, or sexual excitement; in doing this, you are accordingly less likely to react inappropriately to them.

TECHNIQUES TO GET INFORMATION

The patient who comes voluntarily to a mental health professional has a reason for his/her visit—usually a problem with his/her functioning, with personal interaction, or self-satisfaction. When he/she talks about these problems, the interviewer should recognize the suffering behind the words. The patient usually expects empathy for his/her suffering and expertise to identify the source of the problem, that is, the patient expects to get a diagnosis and a treatment plan.

Patients show varying abilities to cooperate. Some are very compliant in revealing their complaint. Others actively obstruct their psychiatrist's effort to find out their problems—they may feel ashamed, hostile, or scared. Still others unwittingly distort their perceptions and revelations of their problems. *The following are possible strategies to deal with different patients:*

*   Techniques that deal with cooperative patients who openly describe most of their problem.
*   Techniques that deal with patients who conceal part of their problems from the interviewer.
*   Techniques that deal with patients who unknowingly distort their perception of themselves and others.

Techniques that Deal with a Cooperative Patient

To reach an appropriate diagnosis and to be in a position to recommend a treatment plan, *professionals need three sets of techniques to accomplish these goals:*

1. Opening techniques to elicit all complaints;
2. Clarification techniques to translate the patient's complaints into symptoms, long-term behavioral traits, or problems of living;
3. Steering techniques to cover the territory and move from one set of complaints to another.

Opening Techniques

Allowing the patient to tell his/her story without constraints may result in an endless interview full of unnecessary details, while asking the patient specific questions may distort his/her story. So, a psychiatrist should find a balance between letting the patient tell his/her story in his/her own words and obtaining information necessary for a diagnosis.

1. **Open-ended, patient-centered questions**. Using broad, open-ended questions (e.g., "Why you are here today Mr./Ms. X?" "How can I help you?") allows the patient to present his/her problem in his/her own words.) Broad, open-ended questions are the least suggestive and allow the patient to emphasize and elaborate what he/she sees as important. However, open-ended questions can elicit answers that are lengthy, unreliable, vague, and incomplete. So, using open-ended questions alone may result in a flood of information yet still lack the details needed for diagnosis.

2. **Closed-ended questions**. The interviewer asks yes or no questions, getting information about a circumscribed topic. This approach generates quick, clear, reliable answers about a topic; however, it will never reach the chief complaint. Thus, the closed-ended approach collects small details but is unable to assemble a clinical picture or a diagnostic impression. Closed-ended questions may force false positive answers and inhibit the patient's freedom to express him/herself.

3. **Interviewer-directed questions**. The best approach is to combine questions along the continuum of broad to sharply focused questions. Introduce a new topic with a broad open-ended question; follow up with targeted ones; and finish with a series of narrow, sometimes closed-ended questions—the yes/no type. Yes/no questions can be used to verify, specify, or challenge a response. If you want to avoid closed-ended altogether, use sharply focused but open-ended questions.

Clarification Techniques

Some patients answer questions clearly; others are narrow, disjointed, vague, or circumstantial in their response. In such situations, the interviewer needs to help the patient to explain him/herself more clearly (Othmer & Othmer, 2002). *There are various techniques to encourage the patient's clarity of response:*

1. **Specification**: when the patient's answers are vague or a one-word response, switch to closed-ended questions to elicit accurate answers. The validity of these answers has to be judged in the context of the total interview.

2. **Generalization**: sometimes a patient will provide specific information when the interviewer needs an account about an overall recurrent pattern of behavior. If the patient complained of a sexual problem, or sleep or eating problems last night, the interviewer should ask questions to discover a time perspective by using terms such as "usually," "regularly,"

"most of the time," or "often." If the patient again refers to specific circumstances or situations, the interviewer should explore each situation to appreciate the overall problem.

3. **Checking symptoms**: this approach is sometimes the only way that allows you to collect diagnostically useful information within a reasonable time frame. When the patient provides a vague story, the interviewer can present a list of symptoms to help the patient in detecting any psychopathology. If an anxious patient continues to give vague answers, the interviewer may suggest some symptoms and ask him/her to agree or disagree. It is always wise to verify symptoms captured this way to avoid being suggestive.

4. **Leading questions**: the interviewer subtly prompts the patient to answer in a particular way. Leading questions are generally undesirable as they result in false or distorted information. For example, "Of course, you never considered suicide, did you?" or "You never heard voices, did you?" Such formulation of questions may lead to approval of symptoms in some patients, even if they did not in fact have the symptom. On the other hand, leading questions may provoke a contradiction in oppositional patients who have or have not considered the symptom but feel offended by the interviewer's suggestion or lead. Properly selected leading questions can elicit a valid and trustful answer, or conversely they may influence the patient in a specific direction. If you plan to provoke the patient's compliance with the treatment plan you may say: "You will try to take the medication as prescribed, won't you?" or "You will try to go to a crowded mall and see if you experience panic, won't you?" Conversely, if you plan to provoke the patient to contradict your assertion, you may formulate the leading question accordingly. Thus leading questions can be considered neither good nor bad, but rather suitable or unsuitable to accomplish a particular purpose.

5. **Probing**: in some patients who give a confusing significance and meaning to their experiences without explaining why, asking probing questions is a strategy for finding out more detail. Probing questions are usually open-ended, i.e., their answer is not directed to a specific response, and it could be one of variable responses. Questions that begin with "what," "why," or "how" are the most probing questions, e.g., when the patient admits to a psychiatric symptom such as a delusion or hallucination; if a patient answers a query about having heard voices with "Yes," get the precise time, place, and frequency of its occurrence. Thus, probing is used on many levels: from determining the patient's degree of insight into their symptoms (e.g., delusions), to finding out more about a topic that the patient seems to want to hide. Probing is an essential tool for helping the patient to tell his/her story without feeling confronted. It helps to detect the underlying logic of his thinking by exposing misinterpretations

(e.g., "I don't know why I am here; the police brought me"; in this case, ask, "Why do you think they brought you?" If the patient heard voices, ask "Do you think these voices are real?") Ask about the exact time and place and frequency of occurrence. Probing is not limited to the patient's interpretation of events, but it is a handy tool to elicit emotional responses to other life events. For example, in situations where the patient talks about his/her marriage problems, conflicts at work, or difficulties with his/her children in a somewhat distant way, jump out of the groove of collecting further information and ask the patient directly about his/her emotions regarding these events.

6. **Interrelation**: the patient is asked to explain the seemingly unconnected or distorted elements in his/her speech (e.g., "Wait, I don't understand what A has to do with B"). Such intellectual interrelation may reveal disordered thinking or emotional interrelating disordered affect.

7. **Summarizing**: restating the main ideas of the interview, reflecting back to the patient what the you think the patient has said. Summaries are useful for patients whose response is vague or circumstantial, shows loose association, or flight of ideas. It is useful to use the patient's vocabulary. Be aware that summaries can lead the patient and put words in his/her mouth.

Steering Techniques

These techniques offer a way to keep the interview on a desired course. It helps to redirect the patient from one topic to another without suppressing him/her.

1. **Continuation technique**: it encourages the patient to go on with his/her story and indicate the course is right. This includes gestures, nodding, keeping eye contact, and statements such as "What happened then?" "Tell me more," "Anything else?" "Go on," "Keep on talking." This allows the patient to talk about him/herself in his/her own words, choosing his/her order of importance rather than that of the interviewer, no symptoms are suggested.

2. **Echoing**: the interviewer repeats certain part of the patient's speech, on which he/she wants a more elaborate answer. In this technique, the interviewer selectively emphasizes certain elements of the patient's statements, thus directing him/her to follow the highlighted parts rather than any other. The echoing technique is useful in distractible patients.

3. **Redirecting**: when patients ramble, get lost in irrelevant details or discuss other people problems, it is useful to redirect the course of the interview and to ask the patient to return after he/she has moved away from it. *Redirection could be accomplished through different ways:*

- **empathic interruption**: the interviewer adds an empathic statement to soften the interruption; "I can guess that this situation's been really hard for you to deal with. Have you been drinking lately, to cope with it?";
- **delaying interruption**: the interviewer assures the patient that his/her topic is important and that he/she will come back to it later;
- **educating interruption**: this incorporates a structuring statement in which the interviewer educates the patient about the sorts of questions he/she wants to ask and the time constraints. Usually, this is done only after you've used the other two interruptions several times with no results.

4. **Transitions**: during an interview, many topics have to be covered within a brief period. The interviewer has to encourage the patients to change topics. The manner of change depends on the patient's mental state. Skilled interviewers are able to change topics without repelling their patients and use various transitions to turn the interview into a cooperative inquiry. An attentive patient may focus better if a new topic is accentuated, whereas a paranoid patient may become suspicious. *Transition strategies include*:

- **Smooth**: smooth transitions lead easily from one topic to the next by giving the impression of their connection. *There are two types*:
    - **Cause and effect relationship** (e.g., substance abuse and its effects, life events and their consequences, or a physical illness and its impact) may affect the patient's functioning. A cause and effect transition motivates the patient to answer, since his/her view of problems is accepted by the interviewer.
    - **Temporal relationship**: the transition between symptoms is smoothed by relating symptoms to the same point in time.

- **Accentuated**: accentuated transitions emphasize a shift in topic and are best introduced by summarizing what you have learned before switching to the new topic. Accentuated transitions revive the patient's attention and make him/her aware of how many different topics have been covered.
- **Abrupt**: abrupt transitions introduce a new topic with little warning. They are often clumsy and awkward and usually ill advised. However, abrupt transitions are useful with patients who lie or simulate symptoms in that they catch them off-guard. Abrupt transitions have the effects of cross-examination. They prevent the patient from keeping track of what he/she wants to portray. They reveal inconsistencies. They are the lie detectors of an interview.

Techniques that Deal with Patients Who Seem Resistant or Conceal Part of Their Problem from the Interviewer

It is usually difficult to understand why some patients would voluntarily or involuntarily seek to create or exaggerate symptoms when such behavior provides them no apparent gratification. *There are many reasons for psychiatric patients to withhold, to minimize, exaggerate, or even fabricate information:*

1. The patient lacks the cognitive or expressive capacities to communicate essential data to the evaluator.
2. Some patients with dissociative disorder experience difficulty in recalling important personal events.
3. Some patients perceive the interview as a stressful situation, the stress of the interview diminishes the capacity of some patients to think and communicate clearly.
4. In the initial interview, most patients try to present themselves in a good light, and do not want to embarrass themselves, or be judged as crazy. Some patients intentionally withhold information to maintain self-image and to avoid humiliation due to uncertainty about the interviewer's response to the disclosure of senseless obsessions, silly fears or strange hallucinations, and fear of the interviewer's rejection, fear of mental illness, and concern about stigmatization.
5. Memory loss may be accompanied by an attempt by the patient to hide this deficit.
6. The patient wishes for more attention.
7. The patient seeks for some form of excuse from responsibility, often leading to inaccurate reporting.

Therefore, the psychiatrist should develop skills and competence to determine when patients are presenting misleading information. *Cues that alert the clinician that the patient is withholding or providing inaccurate information include the following:*

1. The clearest form is refusal to answer questions.
2. An indirect form of resistance is the patient's attempt to distract the interviewer from pursuing a topic.
3. The patient may answer questions briefly even when asked to expand on these answers or not answer at all.
4. The patient starts talking intensely about something else, or he/she is vague, shows reluctance in his/her facial expression, or pauses before answering.
5. The patient may try to sidetrack the interviewer with expressions such as "This really does not bother me," "It is not one of my main concerns," and "There are more important things to worry about."

6. The patient may change the subject or show changes in the attitudes toward the interviewer.
7. The patient may give statements of ignorance or amnesia when asked about certain topics, e.g., "I do not know," "I do not remember."
8. The patient may give contradictory information.
9. The patient may try to take control of the interview by insisting on limiting disclosures only to subjects that he or she chooses. The patient may simply state that there is something that he or she is unwilling or unable to discuss.
10. The patient may be obviously exaggerating, e.g., "When I have this head-ache I go blind for hours at a time."
11. Patients may deny the existence of experiences or events that would be easily inferred from their behavior, e.g., patients who bursts into tears while insisting they are feeling fine.
12. Patients change their information in response to suggestions by the clinician.

Multiple useful strategies are available to deal with resistant patients:

Expressing Acceptance

This is useful to overcome a concern about being ridiculed, which is what may make a patient reluctant to talk. To help the patient to overcome his/her resistance, encourage him/her and express understanding of the patient's symptoms (thoughts, feelings, and behavior). Expressing acceptance should mean neither condemning nor praising the patient.

Confrontation

It highlights the patient's awareness of the resistance and invites an explan-ation. This technique is used when the interviewer observes behavioral clues of resistance. In patients who stubbornly refuse to interact with the inter-viewer to get a result, the interviewer tells the patient that his/her behavior will delay this wish; the patient may then start to cooperate (confrontation with consequences).

Shifting Focus

In patients who do not want to talk about or reveal a certain topic, it may be beneficial to approach this topic from another direction, instead of forcibly pursuing one line of questioning. It is like coming through the back door. Shifting the point of view often frees the patient and gets him/her ready to discuss that topic.

Exaggeration

This refers to an overestimation statement about something either in a worse or better direction, in contrary to what it actually is. It is used to help patients who are reluctant to admit to minor wrongdoings or failures because of a fear that the interviewer will reject them if he/she becomes aware of their character flaws, e.g., if a patient is reluctant to elaborate on shoplifting a candy bar when a child, you can say "you did not steal a diamond." By comparing the patient behavior to major harm or crime, the patient usually feels relieved and experiences that he/she has not reached your tolerance level where he/she has to fear rejection, but feels assured instead and can overcome his/her reluctance to talk more.

Shame Attenuation

When the interviewer notices that the patient is reluctant to give details of incidents that may affect his/her image, the interviewer uses statements that nullify or express acceptance of such behaviors; e.g., when a patient resists talking about his/her school troubles, the interviewer may challenge him/her with "were you a good fighter?" or when a patient is lying and cheating but tries to conceal these traits, the interviewer may encourage him/her by saying "you seem to be like a fox." This strategy may diminish the patient's prohibitions about talking on such topics.

At a later stage, the interviewer will have to explain to the patient that accepting patients' problems neither means that the interviewer encourages the patient to further continue such acts nor that the interviewer excuses and likes what the patient has been doing. It just means that the interviewer is willing to give the patient enough space and attention to allow the patient to tell his/her story with the affect typical of his/her personality.

Techniques that Deal with Patients Who Unconsciously Distort Their Perception of Themselves and Others

Defense mechanisms are specific cognitive processes; ways of thinking that function in part to avoid painful feelings. In general, all people, including patients, employ defense mechanisms to hide awareness of feelings and memories that could provoke anxiety. Thus, it is logical to find a patient who unconsciously recollects data about him/herself and his/her environment in a distorted manner, due to excessive use of defense mechanisms.

In an insight-oriented therapeutic interview, the therapist attempts to make the patient aware of his/her defenses, their underlying mechanism, and their unconscious origins, with the expectation that the patient will replace his/her defensive behavior with a more reality oriented behavior. However, in a diagnostic interview based on signs and symptoms, defense mechanisms do not seem to belong in a discussion of diagnosis, yet being familiar with defense mechanisms helps the clinician to understand some of the content and meaning of the patient's psychopathology. In such diagnostic interviews, the interviewer needs to handle defense mechanisms to the extent that they interfere with rapport and history taking. The first step of dealing with defense mechanisms is to recognize reality distortions followed by the use of suitable strategies to handle such defense mechanisms. *Strategies to handle defenses include*:

Bypassing

Sometimes, it is wise to bypass or ignore discussing a defense mechanism with the patient; e.g., for the diagnosis of the depression of a widow who claims that her husband was the best and one wouldn't find a second like him, even though the record shows that he was an alcoholic and physically abusing her, it may not be essential to confront her with her denial and idealization, at least in the first interview. It would better to bypass or ignore her defenses. Her defense mechanisms may, however, be discussed in the report of her mental state examination.

Reassurance

Instead of assessing and discussing a defense mechanism with the patient, the interviewer supplies the patient with support. Reassurance attempts to decrease the patient's anxieties and suspicions and to increase his/her self-confidence by offering support. This empathic approach will give the feeling of having support. It is most effective when patients appear overwhelmed by their problems.

Confrontation

Confrontation is used to draw the patient's attention to a particular behavior, with the expectation that he/she will recognize and correct it during the interview. Choose a point of view for your confrontation that helps the patient understand his/her inappropriate behavior and at the same time makes him/her feel your empathy.

Interpretation

Interpretation refers to the interviewer's understanding of the patient's defensive behavior. The interviewer suggests to the patient the meaning of his/her thoughts or the intent of his/her behavior. Usually interpretation follows confrontation, as the patient should be aware first of his/her behavior before he/she can understand its interpretation. A correct interpretation explains the patient's behavior satisfactorily in the context of all other behaviors. Unfortunately, there is no sure way to be correct.

The interpretation is made when the patient recognizes his/her behavior as irrational and starts to wonder about it. The best time of an interpretation is usually easy to judge. When a patient becomes curious about his/her own behavior, he/she is ready to explore its meaning. In a patient with rejection of authority figures, the interviewer confronts the patient first with the common thread that runs through different situations. The patient recognizes the similarities in his/her problems with others. He/She starts to wonder about it him/herself by raising questions about his/her behavior. This is the time to attempt an interpretation of the patient's rejection of authority figures. He/She can then continue to talk about difficulties in following rules and of possible feelings of revengefulness and vindictiveness.

The way you deliver an interpretation is important. An interpretation from the interviewer's point of view may make the patient feel criticized, annoyed, angered, and compelled to resist. An interpretation, from the patient's point of view, is more likely to be accepted provided that it is correct (Othmer & Othmer, 2002).

2 Signs and Symptoms in Psychiatry

Clinical medicine makes a clear distinction between signs and symptoms. Symptoms refer to the patient's complaints, e.g., feeling agitated and uncomfortable in hot weather in a case of hyperthyroidism. Physical signs are elicited on examination: soft goiter with audible bruit, loss of weight, rapid pulse and exophthalmos.

This clear distinction is not usually made with the phenomena of the mental disorders. The patient's description of an abnormal mental phenomenon is usually called a symptom, whether the patient is complaining about something that distresses him/her, or simply describing a mental experience that appears pathological to an observer. In his/her account about his/her experiences, both of these are therefore considered as symptoms. When these symptoms are aggregated, they may be regarded as the signs of whatever diagnosis is indicated. *Determination of a psychiatric symptom is usually identified by*:

1. **The nature of the symptom per se**, e.g., commenting or commanding auditory hallucination. Any psychiatric symptom has a form and content; the form of a psychiatric symptom refers to its structure in phenomenological terms, e.g., a delusion, hallucination, and obsession. Content is the coloring of the experience, e.g., the belief of being followed by the CIA. While the patient is distressed only with the content, the clinician should be concerned by both the form and content.
2. **The opinion of society**, usually important in determining conduct problems and cultural beliefs. Certain behaviors accepted in one culture may not be accepted in another culture.
3. **Comparison of the patient's symptoms** with his/her previous beliefs, mood, or behavioral background. It is very important to compare the patient's thoughts, mood and behavior with his/her own previous ones; this will illustrate changes that may be important in the assessment of the mental state and the patient's condition in general.

The following signs and symptoms will be discussed in the next sections:

1. disturbed consciousness
2. general appearance abnormalities
3. disturbance in behavior
4. disturbance of language and speech
5. disturbance of mood and affect
6. thought disorders
7. perceptual disorders
8. disturbance of orientation
9. disturbance of attention and concentration
10. memory disturbance
11. abstraction abnormalities
12. intellectual abilities abnormalities
13. abnormal insight and judgment
14. cortical function abnormalities (agnosia and apraxia)
15. gender and sexual problems
16. disturbance of self.

DISTURBED CONSCIOUSNESS

Philosophers and scientists have long discussions and debates about the nature of consciousness. Consciousness could be defined as the state of being awake, alert to what is going on around you, and being aware of one's own self and environment. The awareness of internal stimuli involves physiological states such as feelings of pain, hunger, and thirst, and psychological states such as awareness of own thoughts and emotions; while the awareness of external stimuli includes the outside world, such as feeling the hotness or coldness of weather, seeing people and places around you, and hearing the voice of a friend. Thus, consciousness encompasses two dimensions: arousal (vigilance or wakefulness; i.e., levels of consciousness), and awareness (i.e., content of consciousness).

Arousal is essentially a function of the brain stem and thalamus. Vigilance means the faculty of deliberately remaining alert—contrary to being drowsy or asleep. This is not uniform or unvarying, but fluctuating. Factors inside the individual that promote vigilance are interest, anxiety, extreme fear, or enjoyment; whereas boredom encourages drowsiness. Environmental factors and the way the individual perceives them affect this dimension of consciousness (Vigilance–drowsiness/wakefulness–sleep dimension).

Awareness is a conscious perceptual process that involves cognition, past and present experiences, and intentions. It is subdivided into awareness of the self and environment, and is supported by the cerebral cortex.

- **Awareness of self** means the ability to experience self, that is being aware of our existence, and aware of things inside us, a process that does not essentially need external stimuli.
- **Awareness of the environment** means our ability to consciously perceive external environmental stimuli at a certain time, and to the knowledge we have about our own social and cultural history. It is called lucidity-clouding dimension. It may be clear or clouded.

Thus, appropriate response to external and internal stimuli necessitates being both awake and aware. In the medical field, attention is usually given to any disturbance in wakefulness or arousal (it is a medical emergency), while psychologists always give attention to awareness and its contents. The Freudian view about levels of mind was no exception; *Freud divided the mind into three different levels of awareness*:

1. **The conscious mind**: a collective term that involves all things that we are aware of. It includes mental processes through which we rationally think and talk. Memory is not completely part of consciousness, as it involves another part that can be retrieved easily into our awareness from what Freud called it preconscious.
2. **The preconscious mind**: the part of the mind that represents memories of events and facts of which we are not consciously aware at a given time, but can be retrieved easily into consciousness. Otherwise they lie in the background of the mind just beyond the boundary of consciousness, until needed.
3. **The unconscious mind**: the main storage place of unacceptable or unpleasant feelings, thoughts, desires, urges, and memories that are kept away from conscious awareness as they would be threatening if brought to consciousness. Freud supposed that the unconscious mind influences our behavior and experience, though we are unaware of its influence.

Consciousness comes at the top of cognitive functions, hence the importance of its assessment at the first contact with any patient. Any quantitative impairment in the level of consciousness will be detrimental in directing the evaluation of patients, as disorders of consciousness are associated with disturbance of cognitive functions such as perception, attention, attitudes, thinking, registration, and orientation. So, evaluating level of consciousness is a first step before concluding the cause of cognitive dysfunction.

Neural Basis of Consciousness

The level of consciousness is a function of an intact ascending reticular activating system (ARAS) and cerebral cortex. The ascending reticular activating system lies in the brain stem; extending from the lower border of pons to the ventromedial thalamus. It projects to the whole cerebral cortex, and receives collaterals from the spinothalamic and trigeminal thalamic pathways. So, a small lesion to ARAS can impair consciousness, while a diffuse cortical lesion is needed to produce the same effect.

Disturbance of Consciousness

A variety of adjectives are used to describe states of decreased arousal, but there is no clear consensus on the precise definition of these terms or on the differences among them. In approximate order of increasing severity, these terms include drowsy, lethargic, obtunded, stuporous, and comatose. These states must be differentiated from normal sleep, from which patients can be fully aroused. Disturbance of consciousness is classified in various ways; the following is a simple classification.

Quantitative Changes in Consciousness

Quantitative changes in consciousness affect essentially arousal or wakefulness of the patient, with subsequent changes in awareness.

Heightened Arousal

Occasionally, patients will be overly alert, a state that is termed hypervigilant or hyperaroused. Hypervigilant persons may restlessly scan the room and attend to every noticeable sound or change in visual stimuli; and they may be easily startled. Hypervigilant individuals appear anxiously attentive, and do not relax. This condition can be caused by mania, anxiety, paranoid delusions, as well as some medical conditions such as hyperthyroidism. It may also be the effect of ingestion of sympathomimetic drugs (cocaine, amphetamines, etc.).

Quantitative Lowering of Consciousness

Consciousness may be considered a continuum from full alertness to coma. *The following terms are usually used to describe different levels of quantitative lowering of consciousness:*

1. **Drowsiness**: diminished alertness and attention that is not under the patient's control. It is a mild degree of lowering of consciousness in which the person is unable to sustain a wakeful state without the application of external stimuli; the person can be aroused to full wakefulness through voice. It is more or less synonymous with sleepiness or hypersomnia

and is characterized by yawning, and a tendency to fall asleep if left without sensory stimulation. A drowsy patient is slow in his/her actions, has slurred speech, sluggish in attention and sleepy on subjective description. Drowsiness occurs in patients suffering from organic brain disease, metabolic disorders, overdose of drugs with CNS depressant effect, and toxic states.

2. **Confusion**: traditionally referred to as "clouding of sensorium." It denotes inability to think with customary speed, clarity, and coherence, accompanied by some degree of inattentiveness and disorientation. Confusion results most often from processes that influence the brain globally, such as toxic or metabolic disturbance or a dementia.

3. **Delirium**: acute state of disturbed consciousness in which there is reduced ability to direct, focus, sustain, and shift attention, disorientation, disturbance in memory, language, visuospatial ability, and/or perception (e.g., visual hallucinations). There may be periods of hyperactivity during which the patient is agitated, talkative, and irritable. Alternatively, there may be hypoactive periods with hypersomnolence and inverted sleep–wake rhythm.

4. **Coma**: an un-arousable unresponsiveness state in which the person cannot respond appropriately to stimuli even with vigorous stimulation. The patient lies with the eyes closed, may grimace in response to painful stimuli, and limbs may demonstrate withdrawal responses, but the patient does not make localized responses or discrete defensive movements.

5. **Persistent vegetative state**: sleep–wake cycles are present, and the open eyes may follow moving objects, which may give an inaccurate impression of consciousness. However, the patient cannot otherwise respond to

Table 2.1 Glasgow Coma Scale

Best Motor Response	1	No movement
	2	Abnormal extension
	3	Abnormal flexion
	4	Withdraws to pain
	5	Localizes to pain
	6	Obeys commands
Best Verbal Response	1	No sounds
	2	Incomprehensible sounds
	3	Inappropriate
	4	Confused conversation
	5	Oriented and appropriate
Eye Opening	1	No eye opening
	2	To pain
	3	To speech
	4	Spontaneous

the environment, and mental activity appears to be entirely absent. Neurologic lesions that prevent motor or vocal expression may result in a state that appears similar to a persistent vegetative one, but in which the patient presumably retains consciousness; it is called locked-in syndrome.

A well-defined classification of lowered consciousness is the Glasgow Coma Scale (see Table 2.1). It depends on the patient's best motor and verbal responses as well as eye opening.

Etiology of Quantitative Lowering Consciousness

Structural Brain Lesions

1. *Large supratentorial brain lesions* (causing brainstem dysfunction), e.g., extradural/subdural hematomas, intracerebral hemorrhage, cerebral infarction, brain abscess.
2. *Subtentorial brain lesions* compressing/destroying the reticular formation, e.g., cerebellar abscess, cerebellar infarction, cerebellar hemorrhage/tumor.

Systemic Disorders

1. diabetic coma
2. hepatic coma
3. respiratory failure
4. fluid and electrolyte imbalance
5. concussion and postictal states
6. drug overdose or poisoning: e.g., sedatives, analgesic, alcohol, carbon monoxide poisoning
7. inflammatory brain diseases: e.g., meningoencephalitis.

Clinical Approach to a Comatose Patient

Alteration in arousal is an acute life-threatening emergency that aims at stabilizing vital functions, and then understanding and dealing with the underlying cause. On arrival at the emergency room, immediate attention is given to Airway, Breathing, Circulation, establishing IV access. Blood should be withdrawn for estimation of glucose, other biochemical parameters, and drug screening. Intravenous thiamine (at least 100 mg) and 50 percent dextrose in water (25 g) is given empirically to prevent Wernicke's encephalopathy. In suspected cases of opiate overdose, intravenous naloxone hydrochloride is given in doses of 0.4 up to 10 mg.

GENERAL EXAMINATION OF A COMATOSE PATIENT

1. **Signs of trauma**: a) Raccoon eyes, b) Battle's sign, c) CSF rhinorrhea or otorrhea.

2. **Blood pressure evaluation**:

   - **Hypotension** suggests:

     - significant blood loss due to external or internal hemorrhage;
     - serious cardiac diseases, e.g., myocardial infarction, cardiac tamponade, dissecting aortic aneurysm;
     - intoxication: with alcohol or other drugs (especially barbiturates);
     - some endocrinal disorders, e.g., Addison disease.

   - **Hypertension** suggests:

     - subarachnoid and intracerebral hemorrhage;
     - hypertensive encephalopathy;
     - increased intracranial pressure: it may lead to reflex hypertension associated with bradycardia and respiratory irregularity (Kocher-Cushing or Claude Bernard reflex).

3. **Heart rate**:

   - **Bradycardia** can result from the effects of certain drugs such as the beta-blockers, myocardial conduction blocks, and from certain intoxications.
   - **Tachycardia** can result from fever, hypovolemia, anemia, hyperthyroidism, and certain toxins and drugs including cocaine, atropine, and other anticholinergic medications.

4. **Respiration**:

   - **Decreased respiratory rate** can result from intoxication or drug overdose with central nervous system depressants, and a lower brain stem lesion, e.g. due to stroke.
   - **Increased respiratory rate** can result from fever, sepsis, hypoxia, hypovolemia, acidosis, hepatic disease, toxins or drugs (salicylates), pulmonary embolism and in some cases with psychogenic unresponsiveness.

5. **Temperature** (measured with a rectal probe in a comatose patient):

   - **Hyperthermia** suggests a) systemic infection, b) Meningoencephalitis, c) heat stroke, d) anticholinergic drugs abuse. Neurogenic hyperthermia is a rare condition that may result from hypothalamic dysfunction due to infarction or cerebral vasospasm in cases of subarachnoid hemorrhage.

- **Hypothermia** can lead to altered consciousness regardless of its cause. *Common causes include*:
  - alcohol or barbiturate intoxication
  - peripheral circulatory failure
  - cold exposure
  - hypothyroid coma, hypopituitarism
  - advanced tubercular meningitis.

6. **General symptoms:**

   - **Vomiting**: it may result from increased intracranial pressure, drug overdose, and metabolic or toxic causes.
   - **Incontinence** of urine or feces may follow loss of consciousness due to any cause.
   - **Cachexia**: it usually suggests debilitating diseases such as cancer, chronic inflammatory disorders, Addison disease, or hyperthyroidism.
   - **Signs of liver cirrhosis** including gynecomastia, spider nevi, testicular atrophy, and decreased axillary and pubic hair.

7. **Head and neck examination:**

   - **Signs of trauma** should be explored carefully, including Raccoon eyes and Battle sign.
   - **Neck stiffness (meningismus)** is an indication of meningeal irritation due to infectious, carcinomatous meningitis, subarachnoid hemorrhage, and central or tonsillar herniation.

8. **Eye examination:**

   - **Edema** of the conjunctiva and eyelids may result from local eye diseases (usually unilateral) or congestive heart failure (usually bilateral).
   - **Scleral icterus**: yellowish discoloration of the sclera usually denotes hyperbilirubinemia.
   - **Kayser–Fleischer** rings in cases of Wilson disease.
   - **Papilledema** in cases of increased intracranial pressure.
   - **Subhyaloid** hemorrhages in subarachnoid hemorrhage.

9. **Ear examination:**

   - **Hemotympanum or CSF otorrhea** may result from fracture base of the skull involving the petrous ridge.
   - **Exploration for signs of infections** of the middle ear, mastoid, and paranasal sinuses; infections in these areas constitute the most common source of brain infection and may result in brain abscess.

10. **Oral examination:**

- The odor of the breath may indicate alcohol intoxication, diabetic ketoacidosis (acetone odor), uremia, and hepatic encephalopathy (fetor hepaticus).
- Pustules on the nose or upper lip may spread bacteria to the cavernous sinus leading to cavernous sinus thrombosis.
- Tongue biting during seizure disorder may result in lacerations on the tongue.
- Herpetic vesicle may suggest herpes infection as etiologic factor.

11. **Skin examination:**

- Hot dry skin is seen in cases of heatstroke.
- Sweaty skin is seen in cases of hypotension and hypoglycemia.
- Bullous skin lesions usually result from use of barbiturates but also may be caused by lamotrigine and carbamazepine.
- Petechial skin rash suggests meningococcemia, staphylococcal endocarditis, typhus, or Rocky Mountain spotted fever (RMSF).
- Diffuse petechiae suggest thrombotic thrombocytopenic purpura (TTP), disseminated intravascular coagulation (DIC), or fat embolism.
- Skin manifestations as seen in cases of acquired immunodeficiency syndrome (AIDS) including Kaposi sarcoma, anogenital herpetic lesions, or oral candidiasis.

NEUROLOGICAL EXAMINATION OF A COMATOSE PATIENT

A **structural** brain lesion is suggested as a cause of coma if there is any focal neurologic sign. These include unequal pupils, facial asymmetry, unilateral hypo/hypertonia, asymmetric deep reflexes, unilateral motor weakness, unilateral extensor plantar response, and unilateral focal fits. Multifocal myoclonus almost always indicates metabolic disorder.

Patients' responsiveness can be assessed by observing response to verbal stimulus, e.g., calling their name, or to noxious stimuli, e.g., supraorbital or sternal pressure. Glasgow Coma Scale is a standardized rapid assessment tool that also allows the clinician to track the level of consciousness changes over time.

Posture in comatose patients:

1. **Decerebrate rigidity** (extensor posturing): consists of opisthotonus, clenching of jaws, stiff extension of limbs with internal rotation of arms and plantar flexion of feet. It arises in a variety of settings: midbrain compression, cerebellar lesions, metabolic disorders, drug intoxication etc.

2. **Decorticate rigidity**: consists of flexion and adduction of arms and extended legs. It usually results from lesions above the brainstem.

Respiratory patterns in comatose patients:

Characteristic abnormalities of respiratory rate and pattern may occur in patients with variable brain lesions resulting from different causes.

- **Cheyne-Stokes respiration**: repeated cycles of abnormal breathing that are characterized by a gradual increase in depth of breathing, followed by gradual decrease, that ends by a period of apnea where breathing temporarily stops. It occurs in cases with bilateral hemispheric lesions, increased intracranial pressure, and in patients with heart or renal failure.
- **Slow, shallow, regular breathing**: it occurs in drug intoxications, e.g., benzodiazepine, and metabolic disorders, e.g., severe hypothyroidism.
- **Central neurogenic hyperventilation**: characterized by deep and rapid respiration, at least 25 breaths per minute. It occurs in brainstem lesions.
- **Apneustic breathing**: the essential characteristic of this abnormal pattern of breathing is the presence of a prolonged inspiratory phase followed by pauses in the respiratory cycle at full inspiration. It usually occurs at a rate of about 1.5 breaths per minute. It is caused by lesions in lower pons and upper medulla.
- **Biot's breathing**: respiration has clusters of fairly rapid respirations, nearly of equal depth followed by regular periods of apnea that last 15–120 seconds. It occurs in lesions of dorsomedial part of medulla.
- **Ataxic breathing**: markedly irregular breathing pattern interposed with irregular and unpredictable periods of apnea. It is usually caused by lesions of the medulla. It indicates a poor prognosis.
- **Agonal gasps**: not breathing, but isolated or infrequent gasping in the absence of other breathing in an unconscious person. It occurs after cessation of heart beating.

Pupil size and reactivity in comatose patients:

Normally, pupils are equal in size and about 2 to 6 mm in diameter. *Abnormalities may indicate one of the following*:

- The presence of symmetrically reactive round pupils excludes midbrain damage.
- A unilateral dilated and unreactive pupil (>5 mm) may occur in ipsilateral intrinsic midbrain lesion.
- When an aneurysm, other compressive lesion, or temporal lobe herniation is the cause of third nerve palsy, the pupil will almost always (95–97 percent of the time) be dilated, since the parasympathetic fibers run on the outside of the nerve.
- Bilateral dilated and unreactive pupils may occur in cases with severe anoxia as seen after cardiac arrest, or anticholinergic drugs toxicity, e.g., atropine and tricyclic antidepressants. Bilaterally dilated reactive pupils

may result from intake of cocaine, amphetamine, or other sympathetic nervous system agonists.

- Metabolic encephalopathies or thalamic hemorrhages may cause bilaterally reactive small but not pin point pupil (1–2.5 mm).
- Opioid or barbtiturate overdose, organophosphate poisoning, or bilateral pontine hemorrhage may cause very small but reactive pupil (less than 1 mm).

Ocular motility in comatose patients:

- **Roving eye movements**: this refers to slow ocular conjugate deviations in random directions. It occurs in coma due to metabolic or toxic causes or bilateral lesions above the brainstem. It is a sign of intact ocular motility function in the brainstem.
- **Spontaneous nystagmus**: this is unusual in coma; it suggests an irritative or epileptogenic supratentorial lesion.
- **Ocular bobbing**: conjugate eye movement that begins with a brisk downward movement followed by a slow drift back to the midline. It may occur with lesions in the pons, usually secondary to infarction or hemorrhage. Horizontal eye movements are usually lost in bilateral pontine lesions.
- **Ocular dipping**: slow downward movement is followed by faster upward movement (inverse bobbing) in patients with normal horizontal gaze.
- An initial fast upward deviation that is followed by a slow return to primary position is referred to as **reverse ocular bobbing**; while a slow initial upward movement followed by a fast return to primary position is referred to as converse bobbing, or reverse ocular dipping. Ocular dipping and reverse bobbing have no localizing value. They indicate hypoxic-ischemic encephalopathy and drug intoxication.
- **Dysconjugate ocular deviation**: this usually indicates cranial nerve palsy. Adducted eye at rest results from sixth nerve palsy. If it is bilateral it is a sign of increased intracranial pressure. Abducted eye at rest result from third nerve palsy.
- **Conjugate lateral eye deviation**: this indicates ipsilateral hemispheric or lesion in contralateral pons. In focal seizures, eyes deviate toward the convulsing side.

Testing of reflex ocular movements in comatose patients:

Oculo-cephalic reflex (Doll's-eye movement): this is elicited by rapidly turning or tilting the head. In coma due to metabolic causes or bilateral hemispheric structural lesions, both eyes move in the opposite direction. This response (positive response) is indicative of intact oculomotor, abducent, midbrain and pons, but there is loss of cortical inhibition on brainstem that normally inhibits these movements. **Absent reflex (loss of Doll's-eye movement)** indicates lesion in the brainstem, though it may occur in overdose of sedatives or anticonvulsants.

Oculovestibular reflex (caloric test): the head is elevated to 30 degrees above horizontal, and the external auditory canal is irrigated with 200 ml of cold water; this normally causes slow conjugate movement of the eyes toward the irrigated ear, followed within a few seconds by compensatory nystagmus (i.e., fast component away from irrigated ear). This test assesses the integrity of the brainstem, so, loss of conjugate ocular movements indicates a lesion in the brainstem. In cases of metabolic or bilateral hemispheric structural lesions, fast corrective nystagmus is lost and eyes are tonically deflected to side irrigated with cold water and this position may be held for 2–3 mins.

LABORATORY STUDIES AND IMAGING IN COMATOSE PATIENTS

- Toxicology screen is ordered to identify the presence and levels of illegal drugs, and confirm intoxication with drugs or toxic substances.
- Random blood sugar, complete blood count, electrolyte panel (levels of sodium, potassium, chloride, and bicarbonate), and arterial blood gas analysis.
- Renal and liver function tests.
- CT or MRI brain imaging in suspected cases of structural brain lesion.
- Lumbar puncture to assess possibility of CNS infection.
- Electroencephalogram (EEG): to evaluate brain activity. It is mainly ordered in suspected cases of seizure activity.
- Electrocardiogram (EKG): to evaluate possible cases of cardiac arrhythmia and ischemia.
- Chest X-ray: to evaluate the lungs and heart.

Qualitative Changes in Consciousness

Qualitative changes in consciousness imply mainly changes in awareness without significant changes in arousal level. Terms that describe qualitative changes in consciousness are confusing, with the same term being used to denote different meanings, while similar phenomena are being described by different terms. States of altered awareness of consciousness differ from one another in important ways, *but they share the following common characteristics*:

1. **Distortions of perception**: this often involves visual, auditory, and tactile domains. The passage of time may be experienced differently, and the body may seem distorted.
2. **Intense positive emotions**: experiences of being joyful, euphoric, loving, or profoundly tranquil are usually described by persons who have qualitative alteration of consciousness.
3. **Sense of unity**: this refers to the experience of being unified or blended with nature, with the universe, or with a spiritual force.
4. **Illogical**: the person may have some illogical experiences as judged by the standards of everyday logic, e.g., experiencing that one is a separate person, though unified with the universe.

5. **Indescribable**: the nature of the experience of altered states of consciousness cannot adequately be expressed in words.
6. **Transcendent**: this means perception that goes beyond ordinary conceptions of space and time limitations; thus going beyond the limits of ordinary experience.
7. **Self-evident reality**: new convictions and intuitions are experienced and felt to be real in a way that requires no proof (ultimate reality).

Given these qualities (particularly the euphoric emotionality of experiencing self-evident revelations), our evaluation of the insights obtained through altered states of consciousness depends on the perspective we take. From the standpoint of science, we can say only that altered states of consciousness are different from everyday waking consciousness. No scientific claims can be made that one "reality" is more "real" than another. Consciousness may be altered during meditation, psychoactive drug use, intense sexual orgasm, or moments of religious conversion. *The following is a summary of commonly described states of qualitative changes in consciousness.*

Dream-like Changes of Consciousness

1. **Daydreams** are normal commonly experienced conscious states of thinking and feeling, not bound by logic or reality. In daydreams, attention turns inward to memories, expectations, and desires, often with vivid mental imagery. Most people report daydreaming when they are about to fall asleep, when they are alone, relaxed, or engaged in a boring or routine task.

2. **Twilight state** is a general term that is used to describe dreamy states lacking touch with present reality, occurring in epilepsy, dissociation, and narcotics use and schizophrenia. It is better to be avoided as its precise definition and causes are vague and overlap with other concepts.

3. **Lucid dreaming** is a rare dissociated state, which may be defined as the conscious awareness that one is dreaming while dreaming; i.e., a lucid dream is a dream in which, during the dream, you are aware that you are dreaming. In normal dreams, your self-awareness is shut down. That's why they often feel indistinct and distant. In lucid dreaming, the dreamer has a sense of being consciously aware of being in a dream. The dreamer may be able to direct the events that occur in the dream.

4. **Trance** is a term given to any state of consciousness in which the person has a narrow focus of attention. Persons in a trance behave as if asleep but are still able to hear and understand what is said to them. Trance states are elicited or experienced during hypnosis, meditation, mindfulness, and mystic states.

A. **Hypnosis** is an artificially induced trance state resembling sleep. This state of artificially induced modification of consciousness is characterized by focused attention and reduced peripheral awareness and an increased capacity for response to suggestion. *This hypnotic state differs from individual to individual but typically has the following characteristics:*

   (i)   **Relaxation**: the hypnotized person experiences a sense of deep relaxation and peacefulness. It is usually accompanied by distinctive body feelings, such as floating or sinking.
   (ii) **Hypnotic hallucinations**: the person may develop altered perceptual experience; seeing, feeling, or hearing things in altered ways or may even experience things that are not present, e.g., smelling a flower that is not present.
   (iii) **Hypnotic analgesia**: one of the most confirmed features of hypnosis is the reduced sense of touch or pain in some region of the body. This feature led to the use of hypnosis in surgery, dentistry, and childbirth.
   (iv) **Hypnotic age regression**: the person may feel that he/she can go back into an earlier stage of life. However, most hypnotists do not believe that hypnosis improves the recall of childhood events.
   (v)   **Hypnotic control**: hypnotized individuals may appear as if they have lost control over their own body, e.g., when a lady is told that her arm can move, the arm may move in the suggested direction.

B. **Meditation** means focusing attention on a single target (such as the breath or a repeated sound) as a way to increase awareness of the moment. A meditative state is not a qualitative state of consciousness, as evidenced by EEG recordings of newly practicing meditators. However, EEG recordings of expert meditators may represent a unique state of consciousness. Meditative states are associated with an increase in alpha and theta brain waves, and physical indicators of relaxation such as slowed pulse and breathing. An individual can perform meditation alone without the interaction of a therapist.

   Although there are a number of different techniques in use, the central feature of all meditation is clearing the mind in order to achieve a state of relaxed awareness and focus. In spite of having their roots in some religious practices, the use of meditative techniques has gained popularity among alternative medicine practitioners.

C. **Mindfulness** is the state of focusing one's conscious awareness completely on what is going on at the present, e.g., a father returning home from work would be taught to focus entirely on his children, who greet him at the door, rather than on thinking about the complaints he got from his biggest customer that afternoon or his plans to pay bills that evening. Mindfulness is a variation of meditation, but the meditator's attention is focused on some internal process or an external object. In mindfulness training, one is taught to acknowledge thoughts about things that are not present, but are constantly entering one's consciousness, and to calmly leave those thoughts and return one's complete awareness to the present moment. The goal is to experience life as it unfolds to the fullest extent and minimize concerns about the future and past.

5. **Mystic state** is a term used to denote an altered state of consciousness resulting from attempts to be united with or absorbed into the Deity or the absolute through contemplation and self-surrender in states of spiritual ecstasy. It is supposed to be the absolute state of pure consciousness and realization of truth, which involves an alteration of the self-process and freedom from symbolic thinking. There are different names for mystic experience according to the origin of mystic traditions; Hindus call it samadhi, Buddhists call it nirvana, Christians call it pneuma and Muslims call it Sufism. The highest mystic experience is supposed to be go beyond time and space.

6. **Fugue** is a state in which the patient has apparently purposeful travel or bewildered wandering that is associated with amnesia of identity and/or other important autobiographical information (see later).

7. **Stupor** is a syndrome characterized by a marked reduction or complete loss of motor activity leading to a state of immobility and lack of or reduced responsiveness. Response to spoken commands is either absent or slow and inadequate. Vigorous repeated stimuli are necessary to arouse stuporous patients. Restless or stereotyped motor activity is common in stuporous patients and there is a reduction in the natural shifting of positions. Reflexes are normal and resting posture is maintained, though it may be awkward. When left unstimulated, these patients quickly drift back into a sleep-like state. *Causes of stupor include:*

    A. Psychiatric disorders:

    (i) **Depressive stupor:** stupor usually follows a period of increasing motor retardation and withdrawal; the patient may still radiate a sense of melancholy by facial expression and by passive turning away from offered assistance. The refusal to eat or drink may represent a total lack of interest, though it may arise from abnormal beliefs such as disappearance of gut, so food he/she has eaten will enter the abdominal cavity and kill him/her. It may be also a means for suicide.

(ii) **Manic stupor**: stupor may supervene on the excited disturbances of mania where extreme hyperactivity gives way to a state of mute immobility. In this state, some signs of the previous gross overactivity may remain in brief outbursts of motor restlessness.

(iii) **Schizophrenia**: stupor may supervene on a catatonic schizophrenia. Muscle tone is increased, the patient is like a block of wood, and the sternomastoids are contracted (psychological pillow). The face is stiff and devoid of expression. Response to painful stimuli is absent. Incontinence of urine is the rule and fecal incontinence may occur. The stupor could be interrupted by intravenous amylobarbitone. Retrospectively, schizophrenic patients may give a detailed account of the happenings during the period of stupor and on occasions will give explanation of their immobility, e.g., they are directed by God or under some external control.

(iv) **Dissociation**: this is not common. The patient usually has secondary gain, incontinence of urine is rare if it ever occurs. The patient tends to eat when no one is observing them.

(v) **Severe fright**: stupor can follow extreme stress, as during severe bombardment. The patient may be paralyzed by fear and unable to retreat from danger. In less severe cases, the patient may be mute but not completely motionless and may at times wander about slowly in a small area in a very bewildered way. This stupor can be terminated by an anxiolytic drug sufficient to induce sleep.

B. **Neurological conditions**: such as Petit Mal Status and brain lesions in the area of the third ventricle, diencephalon, upper brainstem, frontal lobe, and basal ganglia may produce a stuporous state in which eyes are open, the patient appears to be alert, reacts slightly to painful stimuli and is uncooperative (akinetic mutism).

C. **Some metabolic disorders**, e.g., hypercalcemia.

GENERAL APPEARANCE ABNORMALITIES

This is generally the most neglected part of mental state examination, perhaps due to the lack of distinct categories of abnormality in appearance and behavior. However, the ability to observe is an absolute prerequisite for doing mental state examination well. Observation is an active process; the interviewer has to be able to notice what is there. A lot of valuable clues to a person's mood, cognitive state, self-awareness, thought disorder, motor condition, and general physical health can be inferred from his/her appearance. Assessment of appearance during mental status examination involves evaluation of a patient's state of consciousness, physical characteristics (shaved head, tattoos, etc.), approximate height and weight, apparent age in relation to chronological age, eye contact, facial expression in relation to affect and thought content, posture, personal hygiene, dress and grooming, and manner of relating to examiner. Obvious physical stigmata and general state of physical health are to be noted. In some cases, these observations will reveal a little about the mental status.

Apparent Age

This refers to correspondence between the patient's age and his/her appearance. This judgment by the examiner is based on factors such as hairstyle and hair color, skin condition, vigor, mode of dress, and so on. When patients appear older than their actual age, it may indicate poor physical health due to medical illness, alcohol abuse, depression, or perhaps a lifestyle full with excessive hardships, such as homelessness. Premature graying or baldness may affect self-esteem.

Some patients may purposely attempt to appear older or younger than they actually are, e.g., an adolescent whose pseudo-maturity is due to inadequate parenting. A commonly used description is: "appears as stated age," "appears older than," or "younger than stated age."

Facial Expression

Facial expression displayed during interview can provide information about mood (elation, fear, or anger). Appropriateness of the facial expression and its consistence with the subject under discussion should be observed. Patients with little or no facial expression (mask face) may have depression, a neurologic syndrome (e.g., Parkinson's disease, minor hemisphere stroke), or a drug-induced parkinsonian syndrome. In some medical diseases, the patient looks ill, a matter that should alert the interviewer to an etiological or associated medical condition.

Eye Contact

The degree to which a patient makes eye contact with the examiner often indicates his or her level of comfort in the interview. Suspicious and shy persons may avoid eye contact, as will those who are wishing to deny the situation or their emotions. In some cultures, such as Islamic culture, it is considered rude to make direct eye contact, especially between opposite sexes. Hostile patients may stare to scare the examiner, whereas confused or intellectually impaired patients may stare because of lack of self-awareness. Lack of eye contact is a cardinal feature in autism, and cases of social phobia may avoid eye contact with unfamiliar persons. Depressed patients often look downward. Hallucinating patients may look in unexpected directions in response to their own internally produced visual or auditory stimuli. In first encounters, it is usually appropriate to follow the patient's lead; for example, an examiner's fixed stare could unnerve the patient who is overtly avoiding eye contact.

Position and Posture

Position of the patient refers to the location of the patient's body in space (relaxed, lying, sitting, kneeling, stiff and guarded, limp, or sprawled in the chair, etc.), whereas posture refers to the arrangement of the patient's body parts (e.g., cross-legged, leaning, arms akimbo, etc.).

Position and posture should be observed, and any abnormality recorded, e.g., if a patient is rigidly erect, lying on one side because of pain, or wheel-chair-bound. Every posture may have significance, particularly when integrated with other mental state examination information, such as affect and attitude. Position and posture are important non-verbal clues to the patient's mood. Keeping arms and hands tightly crossed against the body may indicate anxiety, whereas sprawling with arms over the back of furniture suggests confidence or even arrogance. A change in the patient's position may reflect an underlying emotional response to the topic of conversation, and so should be noted.

Abnormal posture may be induced by others (catalepsy), or assumed spontaneously by the patient (posturing):

1. **Catalepsy**: a condition of diminished responsiveness characterized by maintenance of postures imposed by the examiner for a long period of time. It occurs in organic or psychiatric disorders, or under hypnosis. It is usually accompanied by waxy flexibility.
2. **Waxy flexibility**: the patient shows slight even resistance while moving limbs into imposed positions that are maintained for long periods of time.
3. **Posturing**: purposeless, voluntary assumption of inappropriate or bizarre postures that are maintained for long periods of time.

Physical Characteristics

Striking physical characteristics such as tattoos, needle marks, scars from prior suicide attempts or self-mutilation (particularly common on the anterior fore-arms), skin lesions or discoloration, unusual facial markings, obesity or thinness, sweating, handicaps, and amputated limbs should be noted.

The examiner should note any odors coming from the patient, including that of alcohol, feces, or urine; those produced by medical causes (e.g., fetor hepaticus, ketone breath, anaerobic cellulitis); or foul body odor from lack of bathing. These give obvious clues to the patient's physical condition and self-care. Clues to physical problems may also be found in sounds made by the patient, such as wheezes, coughs, or teeth grinding. Hair changes or baldness may reflect nutritional abnormalities, radiation or chemotherapy, or tricho-tillomania. Cigarette-induced yellow or brown discoloration and burns of the fingers are common among the chronically mentally ill, and are a clue to smoking habits and self-care.

Dress and Grooming

Grooming is the things that people do to make their appearance clean and neat, e.g., brushing hair, or dressing in clean and neat clothes. The subject may dress in an unusual manner or do other strange things to alter his/her appearance, e.g., he/she may shave off all his/her hair or paint parts of his/her body different colors. The patient's clothing may be quite unusual, e.g., he/she may choose to wear some outfit that appears generally inappropriate and unacceptable. A patient may dress in a fantastic costume representing some historical personage or a person from outer space. Similarly, other patients may wear clothing completely inappropriate to the climatic conditions, such as heavy wool in the midst of summer. Patients with histrionic personality disorder may have seductive dress, while demented and intoxicated patients may have soiled and stained clothing.

The examiner should note hairstyle, cleanliness, nails, facial hair, clothing, and, if applicable, oral hygiene and body odor. Poor personal hygiene may be associated with extreme poverty or the rejection of conventional societal standards, but it may also be a sign of serious mental or physical illness. Clothes and grooming may also reflect socioeconomic status, occupation, self-esteem, interest in life, socialization, and the motivation or ability to present oneself in an appropriate way.

Expectations for clothes and grooming must be modified depending on the context of the examination; being unshaven, un-combed, and dressed in pajamas may be expected in medically ill inpatients but not in outpatients coming for elective evaluation. One should note any peculiarities in dress and grooming, while avoiding a judgmental tone, e.g., it would be appropriate to note "hair is oily and fingernails are long and dirty," or "the patient wore a green sock on one foot and no sock on the other," or "clothing was threadbare and torn," but not appropriate to write "he looks like a hippie," or "her clothing is cheap."

Bizarre make-up or haircuts may indicate psychosis. Clothing that seems incongruous for gender may indicate sexual identity issues or even psychosis. Dirty bodies and soiled clothing are sometimes encountered in outpatient and emergency settings and generally indicate self-neglect (e.g., due to dementia or severe psychosis) or significant deprivation (e.g., homelessness).

DISTURBANCE IN BEHAVIOR

Behavior of the patient during interview and in the ward may provide an invaluable diagnostic clue. Behavior of the patient includes motor behavior, social and sexual behavior, attitude toward the examiner/interview behavior, and behavior exhibited on the ward. Assessments of overall behavior during interview necessitate careful observation of qualitative and quantitative abnormalities, its appropriateness to the situation, and its frequency and effect on the patient's and others' lives.

I. Psychomotor Behavior

Psychomotor behavior includes all non-verbal behavior by the patient evident during the interview. Psychomotor behavior can reveal information regarding a person's mood, energy level, muscle strength, coordination, general medical condition, and potential adverse effects of medication. Description of activity and behavior should provide a mental image of the person during the interview. Psychomotor behavior may provide evidence of a person's ability to maintain normal control. Agitated, restless behaviors suggest one clinical picture whereas frozen posture with a lack of eye contact suggests an entirely different clinical situation. Activities and behaviors that need to be documented during the mental status examination involve abnormalities in the activity level, involuntary movements, or abnormal behavior, and significantly excessive, repetitive, or characteristic activity. It is important to describe the actual behavior (e.g., constantly wringing hands, tapping foot repeatedly, and sighing deeply) rather than simply stating your interpretation of the behavior (e.g., appears anxious).

Classification of Psychomotor Disorders

Normal human behavior is variable and complex. Abnormal behaviors show more and more variations and complexity, that no simple classification will be satisfactory. The following classification adapted from Fish (1967) is just a comprehensive frame that gathers psychomotor disorders.

A. Disorders of Adaptive Movements

DISORDERS OF EXPRESSIVE MOVEMENT

Expressive movements involve face, arms, hands, and the upper trunk. The extent of the expressive movements varies with emotion, and the range of emotional expression is very different in different cultures and among individuals in the same cultures. In some countries, expressive movements of the hands are natural accompaniment of speech and certain verbal expressions are accompanied with gestures. In other countries, the use of the hands in speech is considered vulgar, or at least a mark of a foreigner. In some countries, depressed men are unlikely to weep. *Examples of disorders of expressive movements include*:

- In depressed patients: there are diminished body movements and gestures.
- In mania: there are exaggerated expressive movements. The patient is unnaturally cheerful, uses wide expansive gestures.

- Excessive grimacing and facial contortions are features of catatonia: these are disorders of expression but are best regarded as stereotypes or the result of parakinesia. *Grimacing*: defined as a sharp contortion of the face, can be expressive of pain, contempt, or disgust. It is abnormal when excessive and causeless.
- Snout spasm: rounded lips thrust forward in a tubular manner; seen in catatonia.
- In schizophrenia, especially catatonia: expressive movements are often disordered. The catatonic patient has a stiff expressionless face and the expressive movements of the body are scanty.

DISORDERS OF REACTIVE MOVEMENTS

These movements are immediate automatic adjustments to new stimuli, such as responding to a threat or turning toward the source of a novel sound. These movements give rise to a general impression of alertness and adaptation to environment, so that when they diminish or become lost the patient appears to be stiff and unresponsive in a way that is difficult to describe. Reactive movements are increased in anxiety and manifest as enhanced startle response. They are decreased in neurological disorders such as parkinsonism, and are usually affected by obstruction in catatonia.

DISORDERS OF GOAL-DIRECTED MOVEMENTS

1. **Hyperactivity**: hyperactive patients show marked increase in goal-directed activity; it is seen in patients with mania or hypomania, and ADHD.
2. **Psychomotor agitation**: there is excessive motor activity that is usually repetitive, and not goal-directed (e.g., ringing fingers, rubbing hands, fidgeting feet, finger and foot tapping, frequent change of posture, rhythmic leg movements, frequent standing to walk around, unexpected leaving of the room) and associated with a feeling of inner tension that may appear in raising voice or shouting, and raising hands. Agitation may be found in mania, psychosis, anxiety, agitated depression, ADHD, stimulant intoxication, and in delirium.
3. **Excitement**: an extreme degree of motor hyperactivity that is frequently associated with irritability and destructiveness. It occurs in epilepsy, catatonia, mania, dissociation, and delirium.
4. **Psychomotor retardation**: a generalized reduction of physical and emotional reactions, in which there is lack of initiation and reduction of spontaneous movement. It shows all gradations up to stupor (see before). *It is seen in patients with depression, catatonia, some frontal lobe syndromes, parkinsonian syndromes and delirium*:

    - In depressed patients with psychomotor retardation there is subjective feeling that all actions become more difficult to initiate and carry out. In more severe degrees, movements become more slow and dragging. In the mildest degrees, there is only lack of expression, with furrowed eyebrows, and the eyes are unfocused.

- *Obstruction*: the equivalent in the flow of action to thought blocking in the flow of speech. While carrying out a motor act, the patient stops still in his/her track. After a pause he/she continues with the act or may proceed to do something else. Usually he/she cannot account for his/her obstruction, but may do so in passive terms: "my actions were stopped."

- Individual variations in the execution of goal-directed movements may become so pronounced that the movements are odd, although still obviously goal-directed. Unusual repeated performances of goal-directed motor action or the maintenance of an unusual modification of an adaptive posture are known as mannerisms. Examples of these are unusual hand movements while shaking hands, when greeting others, and when writing. The strange use of words, high-flown expressions (showy, grandiose, or fancy words or phrases that are intended to sound important and impressive), movements and postures, which are out of keeping with the total situation, can also be considered as mannerisms. Mannerisms can be found in relatively normal subjects, abnormal personalities, schizophrenia, and in neurological disorders. Mannerisms in non-psychotic persons are likely to be a means of attention-seeking. In the psychotic patient, they may result from delusional ideas or be regarded as expressions of catatonic motor disorder.

B.   *Non-adaptive Movements*

SPONTANEOUS INVOLUNTARY MOVEMENTS

These include tremors, tics, spasmodic torticollis, chorea, dystonia, and athetosis.

1.   **Tremors** are involuntary trembling or shaking, nearly rhythmic movements, that lead to to-and-fro movements of one or more body parts. They result from muscle contraction and relaxation around the corresponding joint. They are the most common type of involuntary movements. Tremors mostly affect the hands, but may affect the arms, head, face, voice, trunk, and legs.

2.   **Tics** are repeated, irresistible and purposeless movements that involve a few muscle groups, e.g., blinking and grimacing.

3.   **Spasmodic torticollis** is when cervical muscles undergo repetitive or sustained contraction, causing sustained twisting of the neck to the left, right, upward, or downward.

4. **Chorea** is a rapid jerky, non-rhythmic involuntary movement that affects chiefly the face and extremities.

5. **Dystonia** is a movement disorder in which muscles contract involuntarily, causing twisting movements or abnormal fixed postures.

6. **Athetosis** is involuntary movement characterized by slow, wormlike, twisting movements of the fingers, hands, toes, and/or feet. Occasionally, it affects arms, legs, neck, and tongue. It is usually a manifestation of extrapyramidal lesion.

ABNORMAL INDUCED MOVEMENTS

1. **Automatic obedience** refers to uncritical or mechanical compliance with requests, suggestions, or commands of other individuals. The patient obeys commands automatically and without question, even if it is unusual and difficult to do.

2. **Echopraxia** (repetitions of actions seen) and **echolalia** (repetition of words heard). Echo reactions occur in transcortical aphasia, severe mental subnormality, clouded consciousness, catatonia, and autism spectrum disorder.

3. **Waxy flexibility** is when the patient shows slight resistance while moving limbs into imposed positions that are maintained for long periods of time.

4. **Perseveration** is senseless repetition of a goal-directed action that has already served its purpose. It is found in catatonia and organic brain syndrome.

5. **Forced grasping** is when the patient shakes (grasps) hands whenever a hand is offered, even though you have instructed him/her not to do so. It is found in catatonia, dementia, and frontal lobe lesions of the opposite side.

6. **Magnet reaction** is when the patient gropes after an object that has stimulated the palm of the hand. The patient's hand follows the examiner's fingers when the examiner rapidly touches the palm and then steadily withdraws his/her finger. It can be seen in catatonia, dementia, and frontal lobe lesions.

7. **Mitgehen** represents an extreme degree of cooperation; the patient moves a limb in the direction of the slightest pressure by the examiner, regardless of the given instructions to resist the pressure.

8. **Gegenhalten (Opposition)** refers to an involuntary resistance to passive movement of the extremities. It may occur as a symptom of catatonia, dementia, or diffuse forebrain dysfunction. The patient, even though instructed to allow you to move his/her limbs, resists movements with a force proportionate to the applied force.

9. **Negativism** is motiveless resistance to all interference and may or may not be associated with an outspoken defensive attitude. It may be passive

when the patient resists all interventions, and orders are not carried out (resistiveness); e.g., keeping looking straight when asked to look up, or active when the patient does the exact opposite of what he/she is asked to do; e.g., looking down when asked to look up.

10. **Ambitendency** is when the patient alternates between opposite movements when he/she is expected to carry out a voluntary action, e.g., putting out the arm to shake hands, then withdrawing it, extending it again and so on, and does not reach the intended goal.

C. *Abnormal Complex Patterns of Behavior*

1. **Non-goal-directed complex patterns of behavior**:
    - **Impulsive actions** may be regarded as non goal-directed complex patterns of behavior. Impulsive actions refer to sudden outbursts of activity with little or no provocation, without considering their consequences.
    - **Abulia**: this refers to loss or impairment of the ability to act or to make decisions and is associated with indifference about consequences of actions; it may be a symptom of schizophrenia or other mental disorders.
    - **Stereotypy**: aimless monotonous repetitive behavior, such as touching the nose or pacing up and down the room.
    - **Mannerisms**: repetition of a behavior for hours or days, which are in keeping with the personality or the mental illness.
    - **Hoarding**: a patient has a strong desire to save items and possessions, and becomes distressed with discarding them. This leads to difficulty discarding property and continually collecting items regardless of their actual value.
    - **Acting out**: the expression of unconscious wishes or impulses in actions rather than words. The individual typically behaves in impulsive and unrestrained ways such as tantrums, and other attention seeking behavior.
    - **Restlessness**: the inability to sit or stand for long periods.
    - **Akathisia**: a subjective feeling of muscular tension, which can cause restlessness, pacing, repeated sitting and standing. It is usually due to the use of antipsychotic drugs.
    - **Catatonia**: a syndrome characterized by stupor, catalepsy, waxy flexibility, mutism, negativism, excitement (agitated purposeless motor activity that is not influenced by external stimuli), posturing (voluntary assumption of a rigid posture that is held against all efforts to be moved), mannerism, stereotypy, grimacing, echolalia and echopraxia (American Psychiatric Association, 2013).

2. **Goal-directed abnormal patterns of behavior**:

  • **Compulsive rituals**: repetition of an act as part of obsessive compulsive disorder, either in response to obsessions or on its own.

  • **Behaving in a childish spiteful way** to others: e.g., pulling a chair away from another patient, is seen in some schizophrenics usually of disorganized type. Also, manic patients may play practical jokes, e.g., one patient would creep behind a nurse in the ward.

  • **Aggression**: hostile or angry feelings, thoughts, or actions directed toward an object or person, which may be verbal or physical. Harsh and aggressive behavior is usually socially determined. On the whole, aggression is not very common in chronic psychiatric disorders.

  • **Disinhibited behavior**: may occur in organic brain diseases, mania, and schizophrenia. The patient lacks restraints customarily exhibited in social situations, leading to tactless, rude, or even offensive behavior.

3. **Grossly disorganized behavior**:

Patients with grossly disorganized behavior have difficulty formulating and producing goal-directed behavior. They are often found wandering about, disheveled, malnourished, talking to themselves, and exhibiting unpredictable agitation. Grossly disorganized behavior is a manifestation of impaired reality testing and hence is a sign of psychosis. Disorganized behavior may manifest as repetitive behavior, aimless wandering, task interruption by a change in focus, unexpected violent behavior, or meaningless response (words or gestures). The patient might show task derailment (defined as task interruption by change in focus). Derailment of task performance appears as a behavioral equivalent to derailment of speech. It is this behavior that usually prompts family members, friends, or the police to bring a patient to the emergency department. *Grossly disorganized behavior can show up in a variety of ways*:

1. A person may be unkempt, completely neglecting his/her hygiene, or may wear clothes in a bizarre or grossly inappropriate way, e.g., a person may dress in multiple layers of clothing in hot weather or in light clothes during cold weather.
2. A person be easily agitated with little or no provocation, or act in a silly and childish manner.
3. A patient may not shower or eat for extended periods of time.
4. Sexual behavior in public.

II. Social Behavior

Humans are social creatures; without social support of caregivers, no infant would survive. Even when we become capable of living independently, very few people seek to live in isolation.

Social behavior describes the general conduct exhibited by individuals within a society. Social behavior is determined and governed by doing what is supposed to be acceptable by a person's peer group, and avoiding behavior that is characterized as unacceptable. While social conduct is often modeled to create a comfortable social environment, antisocial behavior, such as aggression, scapegoating, and group bullying, may also be defined as negative social behavior, particularly in instances where other individuals within a peer group all behave accordingly.

Lacking social conformity or appropriateness is usually considered abnormal as judged by social norms. Subjects may do things that are considered inappropriate according to usual social norms, e.g., public masturbation, urinating or defecating in inappropriate places, talking to people whom they have never met before about their personal life, dropping on their knees, praying and shouting, or taking an unusual position when in the midst of a crowd.

III. Sexual Behavior

Sexual behavior is a largely private complex activity that affects all facets of human life. It is subject to varying degrees of social, cultural, religious, moral, and legal norms and constraints. Risky sexual behaviors can have deleterious effects on family, relationships, and health. There is a growing recognition among clinicians that any type of sexual behavior can become pathologically impulsive or compulsive. Culturally unaccepted sexual behavior may be observed in a wide variety of psychopathological and non-pathological conditions. Inappropriate sexual display or remarks to strangers, and social sexual behavior in the workplace, are usually considered as deviant, harassing in nature, and inappropriate.

IV. Interview Behavior

The relationship between the patient and the examiner, and the patient's reactions to the interview process reflect the patient's attitude toward the interviewer. This attitude may influence the validity and content of information elicited during the interview. In addition, the patient's general attitude at the time of the initial examination may be a guide to his/her capacity to work constructively with a therapist to form a therapeutic alliance, which is important to treatment planning. The patient's manner of approaching the examination includes a lot of descriptions: cooperative, uncooperative, evasive, bemused, arrogant, apathetic, friendly, passive, ingratiating, seductive, obsequious, hostile, assaultive, or guarded, which requires judgment, inference, and observation.

The patient's attitude can be judged based on a summary of observations made by the examiner in the course of the interview (facial expressions and posture, completeness of answers, tone of voice, willingness to cooperate, attentiveness, degree of evasiveness in responses, and the fantasies and wishes of the patient as they relate to the interview process).

Cooperative attitude describes the individual who is alert and attentive, and tries to communicate relevant information to the examiner, including answering questions. Normal assertiveness (e.g., identifying a topic as painful or interrupting the interview to answer the telephone) should not be interpreted as a lack of cooperation. Resistance is the conscious or unconscious attempt by the patient to withhold information or affect from the examiner. In psychodynamic psychotherapy, the term *resistance* describes any attempt by the patient, subtle or overt, conscious or unconscious, to avoid the exploration of sensitive or conflicted material.

During an interview, it is expected that some patients are cooperative, relate easily with the examiner, and reveal information freely; while other patients are suspicious and guarded in revealing information, and may require frequent reassurance that the content of the interview is confidential. Hostile patients may embarrass or humiliate the examiner, while manipulative patients try to get the interviewer on their side, by repeatedly praising the competency and character of the examiner. The interviewer should document the reported conclusion about the patient's attitude, explaining how it was reached, documented with specific examples of the patient's behavior.

The patient's attitude toward the examiner and the interview context may be greatly affected by the circumstances of the examination, e.g., one might expect more resistance during the initial evaluation of an involuntarily hospitalized patient than in the office-based interview of an outpatient who is known to the examiner. The causes of lack of cooperation are variable; it may result from incompetent or insensitive interviewing or from multiple pathological conditions including impaired alertness, impaired attention, impaired memory, impaired judgment, anger, and personality and mental disorders.

Concerns about confidentiality may underlie the patient's negative feelings, and this may also need to be discussed specifically with the patient. Patients may be reluctant to cooperate if they are concerned that sensitive material will be discovered by others from whom they wish to conceal it.

Although assessment of the patient's manner does not provide direct diagnostic clues, it often helps the clinician to confirm the presence of certain personality traits, e.g., an antisocial patient often appears charming but may circumvent answering certain questions that would reveal illicit drug dealing or other illegal behaviors. A histrionic patient may be seductive toward the examiner as a way to gain control of the interview. Excessive praise of the examiner and statements demeaning of previous caregivers may confirm the examiner's own feelings but, especially during the initial interview, may represent the idealization and devaluation commonly seen in borderline personality disorders. Splitting is the term used to describe the inability of a person to recognize good and bad features simultaneously in another individual (or institution). Patients with borderline personality disorder may seem strikingly variable in their attitude toward the therapist because of splitting. They have difficulty tolerating mixed or ambiguous feelings and so vacillate between all-positive feelings (idealization) and all-negative feelings (devaluation). Patients with developmentally primitive personality disorders, such as borderline and narcissistic, may lump (i.e., split) clinicians into all-good or all-bad status, and thus may be uncooperative after deciding the psychiatrist is all bad. Comments such as "you are the only doctor who can help me—you're not like all the others" signal that the patient may be idealizing the current physician.

Assessment of the patient's attitude also provides clues to the possibility of eminent violence. Suspicious, restless, and uncooperative patients have a higher potential of being violent and should be interviewed in a tactful and non-challenging manner. Regressed patients may revert to dependent behavior in which they rely on others to take care of them, e.g., a patient may adopt the sick role to receive special attention and exemption from responsibilities as though they were children. A guarded patient avoids self-disclosing statements. A vigilant patient may be hyperalert, warily looking about the room. A suspicious patient not only avoids self-disclosure but may also question the examiner (instead of the reverse). A hostile patient may communicate anger by appearance, words, or deeds.

The patient may bring feelings to the interview that relate to past personal or family experience with psychiatry, or the patient may be inexperienced with the actual practice of psychiatry. These feelings may cloud or interfere with compliance during the interview—that is, may lead to resistance. If the patient exhibits a negative attitude toward the examiner, this may need to be explored before continuing the interview, as it is likely to affect adversely the information gathering efforts of the examiner.

V. Behavior in the Ward

The behavior of the patient in the ward can display a lot of abnormalities:

- The patient may show indifference to events and may be out of contact with surroundings, leading to impaired awareness of the environment, which may manifest as a confused expression, aimless wandering, restlessness or repetitive stereotyped behavior.

- The patient may show reduced level of competence over daily life activities, e.g., dressing, undressing, and matters of hygiene.
- The patient's response to various events and situations may reveal defects not previously suspected, e.g., paranoid ideas or delusions may be revealed only during interaction with others. Also, the patient may be seen reacting to hallucinatory experiences not previously disclosed.
- Subtle symptoms of dementia can occasionally be revealed in a patient with a good social manner, e.g., disordered feeding habits. Incontinence of urine along with the patient's reaction toward it may also be noted.

DISTURBANCE OF LANGUAGE AND SPEECH

Language is the process through which thoughts and ideas become spoken. It involves a whole system used to communicate a meaning including words and symbols, written, spoken, or expressed with gestures and body language, i.e., language is what we speak, write, read, and understand, and is communicated through verbal or nonverbal means. Verbal language is shaped by socially shared rules that involve: semantics (the meaning of words), syntax (the way words are joined together to form sentences through the rules of grammar), and pragmatic speech (social suitability of the speech).

The language that one learns first is the one that is more "automatic" or "over-learned" and, consequently, better preserved if one is rendered aphasic (**Ribot rule**). However, the language most recently learned and used may be the one that is best preserved in aphasia (**Pitres' law**). Receptive language disorder refers to difficulties in understanding others, while expressive language disorder refers to difficulties in verbal communication of thoughts, ideas, and feelings.

Speech refers to the process of articulation and pronunciation; i.e., speech is the motor process resulting in sound production. It involves the bulbar muscles and the physical ability to form words. It depends on a respiratory input, and using the muscles of the tongue, lips, jaw, and vocal tract in a very precise and coordinated way to produce the recognizable sounds that make up language. Speech consists of **articulation** (how speech sounds are made), **voice** (use of the vocal folds and breathing to produce sound), and **fluency** is the flow of speech. Fluent speech is smooth, unhesitant, and effortless. Any break or irregularity that affects the flow of speech is called dysfluency. Occasional dysfluency is common in normal persons, especially when one is stressed, nervous, excited, or tired. The average person may have dysfluencies at a rate between 7 percent and 10 percent of their speech. These dysfluencies are usually word or phrase repetitions, fillers (urn, ah), or interjections. Dysfluencies at a rate greater than 10 percent of speech are indicators of speech disorder.

An individual may have either speech or language disorders, or may have both disorders simultaneously. Assessment of language includes all of its components: fluency, comprehension, naming, repetition, reading, writing, and prosody.

Prosody refers to intonation, stress pattern, loudness variations, pausing, and rhythm. We express prosody mainly by varying pitch, loudness, and duration. We also may use greater articulatory force to emphasize a word or phrase.

Aprosodic speech is monotonic and without inflections. It typically follows minor right cortical hemisphere lesions, in an area that corresponds to Broca's area in the left hemisphere of the brain, which may lose their ability to encode emotion into speech. Right temporoparietal lesions are associated with comprehension dysprosody. To evaluate this function, the examiner speaks the same words but with different intonations, which the patient is asked to identify (i.e., happy, sad, surprised, angry, and questioning tones). Any stock phrase can be used, such as "Richard and Linda Thompson performed well." Quite different meanings can be conveyed by emphasizing a given word in the sentence in a particular way. Patients with dysprosody cannot distinguish such differences in meaning. Patients with motor dysprosody cannot convey different meanings when asked to articulate the same sentence in the manner described.

Writing is the other form through which ideas and thoughts are transformed into written words or shapes. **Agraphia** is the inability to write dictated material in the absence of weakness in the arm or hand. It is caused by posterior perisylvian lesions, and it rarely occurs alone. The inability to write is usually associated with other types of aphasia. A writing sample of aphasic patients often contains spelling and grammatical errors. **Dysgraphia** is a less severe degree than agraphia that is observed usually in children with neuro-developmental specific learning disorders. However, agraphia and dysgraphia are sometimes used as synonym disorder, of different degrees of severity.

Language and Speech Abnormalities

Aphasia

Aphasia refers to a disturbance of language that is not caused by motor abnormalities of speech or articulation. It manifests in spoken language, auditory comprehension, written language, and reading:

1. **Spoken language**: observing speech is the simplest way to detect inadequate or inappropriate use of language. Observation of spoken language may show one of the following:

- **Anomia**: means difficulty in word finding. The patient has difficulty in retrieving or recalling a particular word. It is most evident in the case of nouns. Some patients talk around or about the specific word, or substitute another word, phrase, or gesture to communicate the meaning of the word. Circumlocutions, or substitutions of object description (e.g., snow/soft, white/cold) and instrumental function (e.g., watch/knowing the hour) can be observed in those patients.
- **Paraphasias**: a correct word is substituted by an incorrect one. It arises from breakdown at word-retrieval process. Thus, it is a common symptom within anomia. There are several subtypes of dysphasia:

  (i) **Phonemic paraphasias**: means substitution, addition, or re-arrangement of speech sounds of a word. This can lead to a variety of errors, including formal ones, in which one word is replaced with another phonologically related to the intended word, e.g., pike/pipe.
  (ii) **Verbal paraphasias**: the word is substituted with another one that is related to it (e.g., wife/husband; talking/hearing car for van). Different types of verbal paraphasias are identified:

  – *coordinate semantic paraphasias*: the target word is replaced with another one from the same category, e.g., replacing orange for apple or tiger for lion;
  – *associate semantic paraphasias*: the target word is replaced with another one that is related to the target word but is not of the same category, e.g., replacing gloves with hand;
  – *superordinate semantic paraphasias*: a specific target word is replaced with a more generalized group, to which the target word relates, e.g., replacing apple with fruit;
  – *subordinate semantic paraphasias*: the target word is replaced with one that is more specific, e.g., replacing flower with rose;
  – *part–whole semantic paraphasias*: the whole is used interchangeably with the part, e.g., using finger for hand; or, conversely, using leg for foot;
  – *visual semantic paraphasia*: the target word is replaced with a word that shares visual features with the target word, e.g., such as knife for nail.

  (iii) **Neologistic paraphasias**: words that are invented by the patient, e.g., nosto/car; mabos/door.

- **Jargon**: a fluently articulated speech that makes little or no sense to the listener. It usually results from neologistic and semantic paraphasias:

(i) **Neologistic jargon**: consists of neologistic paraphasias.

(ii) **Semantic jargon**: consists of unrelated verbal paraphasias (content words).

2. **Auditory comprehension**: patients have difficulties in the comprehension of spoken language and in understanding what is being said. The problem tends to become worse in lengthy or complex speech. These deficits manifest clinically as failure to follow an instruction correctly, or irrelevant responses to questions.

3. **Written language**: aphasic writing usually exhibits patterns of writing that are similar to the speaking impairment. Impairment in writing is called agraphia. It can be obscured by associated motor weakness.

4. **Reading**: impairment in reading is called alexia/dyslexia. The dyslexias are observed during reading silently or aloud.

Speech Sound Disorders

Speech sound disorder is an umbrella term referring to any difficulties in productive speech that interfere with communication, and produce impairment in functioning, and distress. In speech sound disorder, phonemes, or the basic units of speech, can be added, omitted, distorted or changed, or substituted in a manner that makes the speaker difficult to understand. Sometimes, it is not possible to determine the underlying cause of a speech sound disorder or to differentiate articulation from phonological etiology.

Dysarthria

Dysarthria is a motor speech disorder that encompasses a wide variety of neurogenic speech disorders that result from alterations of the range, speed, strength, or coordination of the speech mechanism. The physiological systems involved in the production of speech (i.e., respiration "breath support"; phonation "voice production"; articulation "pronunciation of words"; resonation "nasal versus oral voice quality"; and prosody "rate, rhythm, and inflection patterns of speech") may be variably affected. The specific nature of the speech impairment is largely determined by the manifestation of one or more pathophysiological processes, including spasticity, rigidity, flaccidity, ataxia, dysmetria, and tremor, resulting from different neurological disorders. A dysarthria subtype partially derives its name from the main characteristics of the underlying movement disorder (DeLassus, 2014). *Several types of dysarthria were described*:

SPASTIC DYSARTHRIA

Spastic dysarthria is caused by bilateral damage of corticobulbar tracts. It is commonly caused by spastic cerebral palsy, multiple sclerosis, amyotrophic lateral sclerosis, multiple strokes, and closed head injuries. Speech in spastic dysarthria is slow, labored, and has a harsh vocal quality and excessive nasal resonance. Articulation is imprecise with slurred sound productions and periods of speech unintelligibility. Other neurological manifestations of UMN damage are usually evident in individuals with spastic dysarthria.

UNILATERAL UPPER MOTOR NEURON (UMN) DYSARTHRIA

Unilateral UMN dysarthria results from focal unilateral pyramidal tract lesions that carry impulses to the cranial and spinal nerves that supply the speech muscles, due to strokes or mild to moderate head injuries. Speech may show imprecise articulation, slow rate, harsh phonation, decreased loudness, and nasal resonance.

ATAXIC DYSARTHRIA

The cerebellum plays a major role in regulating the force, timing, rhythm, speed, and overall coordination of all bodily movements. Ataxic dysarthria may result from a large number of neuropathologies and a variety of focal or diffuse lesions of the cerebellum or its connections to the cerebral cortex or brain-stem, which results mostly from cerebral palsy, multiple sclerosis, and closed head injuries.

HYPOKINETIC DYSARTHRIA

Hypokinetic dysarthria is characterized by imprecise articulation of sounds, harsh-hoarse voice quality, and abnormal bursts of speech that sound like the individual is tripping over his or her tongue. It may result from extrapyramidal system affection, particularly Parkinson's disease, parkinsonian syndromes, progressive supranuclear palsy, and multiple system atrophy. The hypokinetic dysarthria results from features of these disorders that include widespread rigidity, hypokinesia, tremors, and incoordination of the tongue, lip, jaw, and voice box musculature.

HYPERKINETIC DYSARTHRIA

Hyperkinetic dysarthria is associated with some disorders of the extra-pyramidal system, particularly dystonia and chorea. Hyperkinetic dysarthria is also associated with tremors, athetosis, myoclonus, action myoclonus, and tic disorder. These abnormal movements interfere with normal speech production.

In spasmodic dysphonia, the vocal cords experience sudden involuntary movements (spasms) that interfere with the ability of the folds to vibrate and produce voice. It gives the voice a tight, strained quality, and results in voice breaks that occur once every few sentences. However, the disorder may be severe and spasms may occur on every other word, making it difficult for others to understand.

FLACCID DYSARTHRIA

Flaccid dysarthria results from lower motor neurons damage; i.e., affection of cranial nerves, or spinal nerves to diaphragm and abdominal muscles. The chief muscles responsible for speech production, namely, the jaw, lips, larynx, and palate, and tongue are supplied by cranial nerves V, VII, X, and XII respectively. The diaphragm is innervated by the cervical spinal nerves, and the chest and abdominal wall muscles are innervated by the thoracic spinal nerves. regardless of the cause or severity of flaccid dysarthria, the most common speech signs observed include articulation imprecision, hypernasal voice, hoarse and breathy vocal quality, and slow-labored speech rate.

MIXED DYSARTHRIA

Mixed dysarthria results from damage to both upper and lower motor neurons, and cerebellar lesions, e.g., in cases of amyotrophic lateral sclerosis, multiple sclerosis, and severe head injuries. The characteristic features will depend on the exact mixture of neurological damage affecting upper and lower motor neurons. In amyotrophic lateral sclerosis, the patient usually suffers from mixed spastic-flaccid dysarthria. While in multiple sclerosis, patients often present with mixed spastic-ataxic dysarthria.

Aphonia and Dysphonia

Voice disorders include aphonia and dysphonia. Aphonia is abnormal phonation in which there is loss of the ability to vocalize; the patient talks only in a whisper. In dysphonia, there is impairment with hoarseness, but without complete loss of function. Voice disorders may be: organic, functional, or psychogenic.

Organic voice disorders refer to conditions in which there is impediment to the function of the vocal cords. *Organic voice disorders are divided into neurogenic and structural disorders:*

- *Neurogenic disorders* are related to problems of the nervous system, including paralysis or weakness of the vocal cords, tremor, or other neurologic conditions.
- *Structural disorders* include problems involving the tissue or fluids of the vocal cords, e.g., nodules, polyps, ulcers, or other lesions on the vocal

cords. These lesions can impair the normal vibration and function of the vocal cords which causes hoarseness.

A **functional disorder** means the physical structure is normal but there is muscle tension due to improper use or strain when vocalizing, which prevents normal voice production.

In **psychogenic voice disorder**, the voice is usually lost suddenly, or becomes of poor quality when people are under stress. It important to notice that the psychogenic component is commonly present in other types of voice disorder.

Dysfluency

Dysfluency refers to a speech that is not smoothly delivered or grammatically well formed. Dysfluency becomes more evident when one is asking questions or when someone else asks a question.

Speech dysfluency can be a part of normal speech, especially in 2–7-year-old children. Those persons rarely notice that they have speech dysfluency. Physical symptoms such as eye blinking or frustration are usually absent in these cases. Normal speech dysfluencies have no apparent cause, and do not follow a particular pattern. Disordered fluency includes stuttering, stammering, and cluttering.

Stuttering

Stuttering typically has its origins in childhood. Most children who stutter, begin to do so around 2 ½ years of age. Approximately 95 percent of children who stutter start to do so before the age of 5 years. Stuttering can greatly interfere with school, work, or social interactions. Children who stutter may report fear or anxiety about speaking and frustration or embarrassment with the time and effort required to speak. Children who stutter may also be at risk of experiencing bullying. Stuttering can co-occur with other disorders, such as intellectual disabilities; articulation or phonological disorder; and language disorders. The frequency and severity of stuttering may change day to day, or according to the speaking situation. Thus, it could be expected that the severity of stuttering frequently increases if there is pressure to communicate, e.g., giving a report at school or interviewing for a job.

PRIMARY SIGNS AND SYMPTOMS OF STUTTERING

- Monosyllabic whole-word repetitions, e.g., "But-but I don't want to go," "Why-why-why did he go there?"
- Phrase repetitions or revisions, e.g., "This is a—this is a problem."

- Hesitations: such as silent pauses, interjections of word fillers, e.g., "The color is like red," and non-word fillers, e.g., "The color is uh red."
- Words produced with an excess of physical tension or struggle.
- Part-word or sound/syllable repetitions, e.g., "Look at the b-b-baby."
- Prolongations of sounds, e.g., "Ssssssssometimes we stay home."
- Blocks, i.e., inaudible or silent fixations or inability to initiate sounds.

SECONDARY SIGNS AND SYMPTOMS OF STUTTERING

- Distracting sounds, e.g., throat clearing, insertion of unintended sound.
- Facial grimaces, e.g., eye blinking, jaw tightening.
- Head movements, e.g., head nodding.
- Movements of the extremities, e.g., leg tapping, fist clenching.
- Sound or word avoidances, e.g., word substitution, insertion of unnecessary words, circumlocution.
- Reduced verbal output due to speaking avoidance.
- Avoidance of social situations.
- Fillers to mask moments of stuttering.

Stammering

The term "stammering" is the same as "stuttering," which is in common use in some countries. Stammering is typically recognized by a tense struggle to get words out.

Cluttering

The speaker's rate of speech is not always measured to be greater than average, but is perceived by the listener as rapid. This is thought to be because speakers with cluttering speak at a rate that is too fast for their systems to handle, resulting in breakdown of clarity of speech. Although some with cluttering lack awareness of their difficulties with communication, many are aware that others have difficulty understanding them. People with cluttering can experience the same affective and cognitive components as those with stuttering, including communication. Cluttering may co-occur with Tourette's syndrome, autism, language disorders, and attention deficit hyperactivity disorder. *Signs and symptoms of cluttering include:*

- Rapid and/or irregular speech rate.
- Deletion and/or collapsing of syllables, e.g., "I wanwatevision," and/or word endings, e.g., "Turn the televisoff."
- Excessive revisions and/or use of filler words, e.g., "um."
- Pauses in places in sentences not expected grammatically, e.g., "I will go to the/store and buy apples."

- Unusual prosody: often due to the atypical placement of pauses rather than a "pedantic" speaking style, as observed in many with autism spectrum disorder.

Mutism

Mutism refers to a condition characterized by refraining from speech during consciousness. Complete muteness is seen in some psychiatric disorders (e.g., catatonia, elective mutism) but not in aphasia. Even patients with severe motor aphasia can phonate some sounds.

Causes of mutism

1. All causes of stupor.
2. All causes of catatonia.
3. Selective mutism in childhood: it is characterized by a lack of speech in one or more contexts or social settings that is not caused by a speech problem. It is now classified among anxiety disorders.
4. Conversion disorder (hysterical mutism).

Evaluation of the patient's speech includes the following:

1. *Intensity*: Was the patient's voice normally audible, excessively loud, or excessively soft?
2. *Pitch*: Was the voice monotonous or did it show any abnormal changes in pitch?
3. *Speed*: Did the patient speak at the usual rate of speed, very slowly, or rapidly?
4. *Ease of speech*: Did the patient speak easily, under much pressure, or hesitantly?
5. *Spontaneity*: Was the patient's speech spontaneous, did he/she respond only to questions, or was he/she mute?
6. *Productivity*: Did the patient speak with usual verbal productivity, or was he/she talkative, or laconic?
7. *Relevance*: Was the speech relevant, flighty, or easily distractible?
8. *Manner*: Did the patient speak in a pedantic, excessively formal, relaxed, or inappropriately familiar manner?
9. *Deviations*: Was there evidence of neologisms, echolalia, clang associations, or verbigeration?
10. *Reaction time*: Was it appropriate or abnormally slow? If significant, the time interval between asking the question and the answer should be determined.
11. *Vocabulary and diction*: Were the patient's vocabulary and diction consistent with his/her social and educational background?

DISTURBANCE OF MOOD AND AFFECT

Emotion is a complex state that is easily recognized, though difficult to define, in part because our emotional experiences are so varied and complex. Emotion researchers define emotion as "a pattern of response subjectively experienced as strong feeling (affect), usually directed toward a specific object." The emotional responses include physiological arousal, impulses to action, thoughts and expression of all these. The specific objects involve people's goals and needs, which could be fundamental such as food, shelter, and survival, or could be more complex, such as searching for love, ambition to win a prize or to build self-respect. Affect is transitory, responsive to changing emotional state, with relatively well-defined beginnings and endings. This is in contrast to moods, which have less specific causes and last for longer periods of time.

Until recently, the mood disorders were called "affective disorders." The DSM-III-R was the first to use the term mood disorder and the ICD-10 now employs what is apparently transitional terminology, "Mood [Affective] Disorders." In recent editions of the DSM classification, it was stated that affect is to mood like weather is to climate. This illustrates the more changeable nature of affect as compared to mood.

The above description of mood and affect explains why a patient's mood can be captured in one or two words over the course of the interview, while the patient may experience and give expression to a number of emotions. It is the capacity or limitations of a patient to vary emotional expression in concert with thought content during the interview that is meant by affect. The examiner usually infers affect from the patient's facial expression; either normal, constricted, blunted, or flat.

Assessment of Mood and Affect during Interview

Affect refers to the prevailing emotional tone during the interview as observed by the clinician. Affect is usually described in terms of its content or type, depth or intensity, range, change pattern (lability), and appropriateness to mood/context (Buyukdura et al., 2011; Iverson, 2004).

Affective content (type) involves identifying the client's affective state. Is it sadness, euphoria, irritability, anxiety, fear, anger, or something else? Affective content indicators include facial expression, body posture, movement, and voice tone. For example, if you see tears, accompanied by a downcast gaze and minimal movement (psychomotor retardation), you'll likely conclude your client has a "sad" affect. In contrast, clenching fists, gritted teeth, and strong language suggest an "angry" affect. Although people use a wide range of feeling words in conversation, affect content usually can be accurately described using one of the following: angry, guilty or remorseful, anxious, happy or joyful, ashamed, irritable, euphoric, sad, fearful, or surprised (Sommers-Flanagan & Sommers-Flanagan, 2014).

Intensity of affect refers to the strength of emotional expression displayed by the patient. It is characterized as average (euthymic), flat (complete lack of emotional expression), or blunted (reduced intensity of emotional expression).

Range refers to the amount of variation in emotion during the interview (such as enthusiasm that fluctuates with sadness).

There is a normal amount of emotional variation that patients will display during an interview, usually equivalent to that seen in everyday conversations with associates, friends, significant others, etc. Normal individuals can express very different feeling states at different times, and their affects can range from sad to happy, from satisfied to angry, or from anxious to calm, and so on. The ability of a patient to express many different emotions, in appropriate contexts, is described as a full or broad range of affect. Those people who are limited to the expression of one class of emotions (e.g., the interrelated group of anxious, worried, frustrated, and irritable) are said to have a restricted range of affect. Those that display only one type of emotion throughout the interview may be said to have a fixed or immobile affect. Restricted affect refers to a limited or decreased range of affect. Though these individuals may have intense affective expression, they do not show many types of emotion; for example, they may seem incapable of feeling happy or comfortable. If the patient demonstrates more variation in affect than is usual, this is considered an increased range of affect; e.g. if a patient expresses euphoria and then changes, within the same interview, to a deep, non-responsive depressed appearance, this would be increased rage. Finally, when there is absolutely no change in affect (as seen in negative symptoms of schizophrenia), this can be described as flat.

Emotional change pattern (lability) refers to the rate of change of emotional expression; it is characterized as stable (normal rate of change) or labile (rapid change in emotional expression, without external stimuli). Emotional lability can be thought of as rapid, extreme, brief swings of emotion followed by a quick return to normal. A presentation of labile affect would be a patient who appears sad, breaks into sudden laughter with little prompting for one minute, followed by crying for another minute, and then back to appearing depressed again.

Appropriateness of affect refers to whether the emotion is expected for the patient's current expressed thought. For example, a patient who laughs uncontrollably while recalling a sad or dreadful event is demonstrating an inappropriate affect. It is also important to examine whether the affect is congruent to mood (which is another area to assess appropriateness). For example, if a patient states he/she is "deeply depressed" and laughs, jokes, and smiles throughout the entire interview—this would demonstrate an affect that is not congruent with mood.

Whenever the patient experiences emotional disturbance, it is essential to know how that emotion is experienced, what it feels like, how severe it is perceived to be, how long it lasts, what brings it on, and what relieves it. It is critical to know that it is difficult to learn much about emotionality without considering the patient's history.

Caution is required when judging appropriateness of client affect, especially when interviewing clients with diverse cultural backgrounds (Hays, 2013). Cultural variables may complicate affect expression during interview, and hence the importance of its consideration in such assessments, e.g., a frightened patient from a minority group may give the false impression of emotional flatness through revealing only minimal information with minimal emotional involvement, because of his/her attempts to guard against giving a poor impression. A thorough knowledge of the culture or subculture in question is important when considering the role of cultural variables in explaining abnormal findings. When there is suspicion about the effect of cultural variables, definite conclusions should be suspended until there has been an opportunity to observe the patient spontaneously interacting freely with others including peers, family members, and nursing staff.

Mood is the emotional state prevailing at a given period of time (e.g., lasts 2 weeks). It is the prevailing hedonic tone that colors the person's perception of the world that is experienced and reported by the person (the patient's own assessment of his/her emotion) and observed by others. Mood self-reports do not always coincide with the affect that is observed during the interview. Mood is best described by terms that define feelings, e.g., sad, anxious, elated, euphoric, tense, or angry. Virtually no particular mood is necessarily abnormal or pathologic; rather, mood must be assessed in the context of the patient's entire history and mental state examination.

Mood is best assessed by describing four variables: predominant mood and its intensity, its duration, reactivity, and diurnal variation:

- **Predominant mood**: euthymic, anxious, depressed, dysphoric, apprehensive, happy, euphoric, angry, and irritable. One should be as specific as possible in describing a mood, and vague terms such as "upset" or "agitated" should be avoided. The depth or intensity of the prevailing mood should be stated.
- **Duration**: refers to the persistence of the mood, measured in hours, days, weeks, months, or even years. Duration is of diagnostic importance, e.g., 2 weeks of depressed mood is essential to diagnose major depressive disorder, while 2 years of depressed mood is essential to diagnose dysthymia.

- **Reactivity**: refers to whether or not mood changes in response to external events or circumstances.
- **Diurnal variation**: refers to the consistency of the mood within the course of the day, e.g., depression is present continually but is greater in the morning and lifts slightly as the day goes on.

Mood disorders usually include several components other than the mood change itself. Thus, feelings of anxiety are usually accompanied by autonomic overactivity and increased muscle tension, while feelings of depression are usually accompanied by gloomy preoccupations and psychomotor slowness, and eating and sleep problems. These other features are part of the syndromes of anxiety and depressive disorders.

In evaluating emotional state, the physician's major problem is trying to identify a private experience precisely. The interviewer may begin by asking the patient to describe the experience, and then he/she may try to help the patient to be more detailed and precise by suggesting descriptive adjectives (intolerable, frightening) or sometimes metaphors.

An important issue in assessing emotionality is the reliability of the patient's descriptions of their experiences. Some patients cannot describe their feelings very well, and often they describe them inaccurately. Here the clinician must use empathic skills and ask questions such as "Does it feel as if you want to cry?" or "Do you feel a sense of impending death?" to help patients identify the exact nature of their emotions.

Affective (Mood) Disturbances

The terminology in this area is complicated and a source of confusion, as several common usages are attached to each word, e.g., feelings in everyday use can refer to sensations, beliefs, presentiments, and considerations for others. *Disturbances of affect can be classified into:*

Quantitative Disturbances

Quantitative disturbances include a spectrum of affects, with pleasurable and unpleasurable affects as their dimensions.

1. **Pleasurable affects**:
   - **Elation**: this refers to excessive happiness. It is pathological when out of accord with the patient's actual circumstances.
   - **Euphoria**: a generalized sense of well-being (not amounting to a definite affect of gladness).
   - **Exaltation**: a feeling of happiness associated with grandeur.
   - **Ecstasy**: a feeling of happiness with mystical coloring.
   - **Expansive mood**: expression of one's feelings without restraint with overestimation of one's significance or importance.

2. **Unpleasurable affects:**

- **Sadness**: a sense of unhappiness that occurs as a reaction to the loss of loved persons, money, or status.
- **Depression**: a feeling of sadness out of accord with the patient's actual circumstances.
- **Anhedonia**: refers to the subject's difficulties in experiencing interest or pleasure. It may express itself as loss of interest in and withdrawal from all regular and pleasurable activities, an inability to experience pleasure when participating in activities normally considered pleasurable, or lack of involvement in social relationships of various kinds.
- **Anxiety**: feeling a diffuse unpleasant vague sense of apprehension, tension, or uneasiness due to anticipation of danger, the source of which is largely unknown or unrecognized. This is distinguished from fear, which is the emotional response to a threat that is known, external, and well-defined. It is often accompanied by autonomic symptoms. It is regarded as pathological when it interferes with effectiveness in achievement of desired goals, personal satisfaction, or reasonable emotional comfort.
- **Panic attack**: a relatively short-lived period (usually less than one hour) of abrupt intense fear or discomfort that reaches a peak within 10 minutes, and is accompanied by autonomic symptoms such as palpitations and tachypnea with a sense of impending death. It is accompanied by the abrupt onset of a variety of symptoms and fears, including fear of going crazy, or losing control, shortness of breath or smothering sensation, dizziness, faintness, or feelings of unsteadiness, tremors, sweating, nausea or abdominal distress, flushes, or chills, and chest pain or discomfort.
- **Irritability**: an emotional response is elicited with undue readiness, i.e., easy provocation. It is a common emotion that occurs in a variety of disorders: depression, mania, anxiety and in psychotic disorders.
- **Phobia**: a persistent irrational fear in the presence of or anticipation of a specific object or situation that results in conscious avoidance of the feared object, activity, or situation. Either the presence of or the anticipation of the phobic entity elicits immediate anxiety response or panic attack in the affected person (anticipatory anxiety) who recognizes that the reaction is excessive. The phobic stimulus is avoided or endured with marked distress.
- **Blunted affect**: a state in which externally expressed emotion is present but much diminished in its intensity, as compared to what is normally expected. The blunting of responsiveness should be distinguished from flattening of affect (see below) in which there is

no emotional expression at all, though they are used interchangeably. Blunting of affect occurs most frequently in psychotic patients. However, blunted affect may occur after a traumatic event when the person does not express the horror that he/she is expected to feel. Blunted affect may also be seen in delirium, dementia, and lesions of frontal lobes or the right hemisphere.

- **Flat affect**: a severe reduction in the intensity of emotional expression and reactivity. The patient is aware of the potential meaning of an event and the feelings it should evoke but lacks the appropriate degree of response. It could be evaluated by observation of the subject's behavior and responsiveness during interview. *It may manifest as:*

(a) **Unchanging facial expression**: the facial expression does not change or shows less than normally expected change, in the face of changes of emotional content of speech. In severe cases the face appears wooden, mechanical, or frozen. In patients receiving antipsychotic drugs, the interviewer should be careful to differentiate unchanging facial expression from a similar effect produced by these drugs (mask face) due to its extrapyramidal side effect.

(b) **Decreased spontaneous movements**: the subject shows few or no spontaneous movements or does so less than normally expected, sitting quietly throughout the interview, without shifting position or moving his/her legs or hands.

(c) **Paucity of expressive gestures**: the subject does not use his/her body as an aid in expressing ideas through such means as hand gestures, sitting forward in the chair or leaning backward, etc.

(d) **Poor eye contact**: the person avoids direct eye contact with the interviewer or others speaking to him/her, by looking in a different direction and bypassing looking at them, and having difficulty in using the eyes in nonverbal expression.

(e) **Lack of vocal inflections**: people have difficulty in showing normal vocal emphasis patterns. Speech has a monotonic quality, where important words are not emphasized through changes in pitch or volume. People also may have difficulties in changing volume when they change the topic, so they do not drop their voice when discussing private topics or raise it when discussing exciting topics or for which louder speech might be appropriate (Andreasen, 1984).

(f) **Affective non-responsiveness**: the person shows no or little affective response when prompted by joking in a way that would usually elicit a smile in a normal person.

Qualitative Disturbances

Inappropriate (incongruent) affect indicates an internal feeling state that is not culturally consistent with the conversation, thought content, or interaction (e.g., giggling when the death of a loved one is discussed; feeling happy while believing that one will be killed by one's enemies; smiling or assuming a silly facial expression while talking about a serious or sad subject; weeping while talking about events which, by objective criteria, should not cause excessive sadness).

This category must be used with caution; an anxious individual who is embarrassed by a certain event (e.g., spilling coffee at an important meeting) or a topic of their history, may defend it with a laugh. The emotional pain of loss may be overridden with a laugh. Further, it is necessary to have access to the content of thought before it is possible to comment on whether or not the affect is inappropriate, e.g., laughter at the mention of the death of a parent by an individual who disliked the parent may be appropriate rather than inappropriate. Inability to get access to the content of thought of psychotic individuals makes use of this term problematic.

Ambivalence is the simultaneous existence of contradictory emotions (love and hate) or ideas (present and absent at the same time). Thus incompatible emotions and desires coexist at the same moment. At one time, Bleuler considered ambivalence as one of the fundamental symptoms of schizophrenia.

Emotional lability (labile affect, emotional incontinence, pseudobulbar affect) is a disorder characterized by involuntary emotional displays of mood that are overly frequent and excessive. Historically, emotional lability has been used interchangeably with pseudobulbar affect that generally refers to excessive emotions that may or may not correspond with the underlying mood. Pseudobulbar affect encompasses a broader range of emotions including anger and irritability, while emotional lability generally refers only to emotions characterized by laughing and crying. Although the definitive cause is still unknown, most hypotheses point to the loss of voluntary, cortical inhibition over brainstem centers that produce the facio-respiratory functions associated with laughing and crying as the anatomical basis for this syndrome. This loss of cerebral control results in a dissociation of affective displays from the subjectively experienced emotional states.

Another similar term that is used interchangeably with emotional lability is mood swing. Mood swings refer to rapid shifts in mood over brief periods of time, i.e., the alternation among euphoria, dysphoria, and irritability. These changes of mood that are culturally excessive in the given environment occur in response to a minimal stimulus and interfere with an individual's functioning in everyday life. In contrast to the neuropathological etiology of emotional lability, mood swings may be observed in the aftermath of severe psychological trauma, intoxication, substance withdrawal, as well as schizophrenia, attention deficit hyperactivity disorder, bipolar disorder, premenstrual dysphoric disorder, and some types of personality disorders.

Common Difficulties in Distinguishing Affect

Severe Depression vs. Flat or Blunted Affect of Schizophrenia

- A patient with depressed affect is best described as being in a state in which he or she experiences mental anguish, or is unable to experience joy or pleasure. He/She will not be cheered up by reassurance or jokes; he/she cannot imagine a time when he/she will not be suffering the pain of depression.
- A patient with blunted or flat affect shows emotional impoverishment. He or she not only fails to experience joy but cannot feel sadness, anger, desperation, or any other emotion. Such emotional impoverishment, which is characteristic of schizophrenia, tends to go hand in hand with formal thought disorder and is often present throughout the course of the illness, not just during florid psychotic flare-ups.
- Apart from using the patient's history, differentiation of depression and emotional flatness on a Mental Status Examination can be accomplished as follows:
  - The facial expression of the chronic schizophrenic is typically vacant; that of the depressed patient is one of gloom, pain, and dejection.
  - The interviewer usually has difficulty empathizing with the schizophrenic except on an intellectual level ("How this person must suffer inside"), but the depressed person's dejection and pain tends to be communicated to the clinician and elicits emotional as well as intellectual empathy. Admittedly, this is a subjective criterion, but it is valuable in the hands of experienced clinicians.

Mood Swings vs. Incongruent Affect

Another difficult distinction is that between mood swings (which changes quickly, often from one extreme to the other) and incongruent affect (which is inappropriate to the thought content or the context). Both mood swings and incongruent affect should be differentiated from affective incontinence, where the patient laughs or cries for extended periods with little or no provocation (i.e., the patient loses control over emotional expression). Mood swings may be encountered in character disorders such as histrionic personalities; in mixed states of bipolar disorder where there is rapid shift from elation to irritability to depression; and in acute organic mental disorders, where the affect can quickly change from anxiety to terror to panic. By contrast, incongruent affect (e.g., laughing while relating the unpleasant details of a fatal accident) should raise the suspicion of schizophrenia. Emotional incontinence occurs most commonly in organic mental states such as arteriosclerotic dementia and multiple sclerosis.

Distinguishing Causes of Euphoria and Elation

Euphoria and elation, although characteristic of manic states, can also occur in organic mental disorders such as those resulting from systemic lupus erythematosus and multiple sclerosis. The euphoria seen in mania has warmth that is communicated to the observer, although, in the extreme, the manic patient can be irritable. A silly kind of euphoria occurs in chronic schizophrenia and frontal lobe lesions, i.e., the patient relating silly jokes. Manic euphoria tends to be contagious or infectious: "the clinician cannot help but enjoy the patient and laugh along with him or her." This is not the case with the silly euphoria found in schizophrenic and organic states. Again, these are not entirely reliable judgments but seem to carry diagnostic weight in the hands of experienced clinicians.

THOUGHT DISORDERS

The functions of thinking and speaking overlap and cannot be readily separated from each other; at the time, they are clearly different. Language closely mirrors thoughts and thought disturbance cannot be judged without language. At the same time, language without thought is meaningless. Language and speech disturbances were described separately in the language and speech section.

Thought disorders are disturbance in one's ability to generate a logical sequence of ideas, as indicated by disordered speech, writing, or sign language. It is to be noted that ideas may appear to be more or less well-connected, depending on the circumstances; a speech that a psychiatrist describes as loosely associated might in another context be considered poetry. Because disruptions of thought process are important indicators of psychopathology, these judgments should be made as carefully as possible. Difficulties with inaccuracies can be minimized by basing conclusions on as much information as possible, and by including a description of the abnormality and its associated features, and an estimate of its severity, supported by specific examples. Thought disturbance involves the form (formal thought disorders) and the content of speech (thinking).

Formal Thought Disorders

Thought process describes the manner of organization and formulation of thought. Formal thought disorders (FTD) mean an abnormality in the way by which a person puts together ideas and associations. Abnormalities in the form of thinking become evident while carrying out the interview, and suggest a disorder of thinking. Eugen Bleuler regarded FTD as central for the conceptualization of schizophrenia. Today FTD remains as one of the diagnostic criteria for schizophrenia according to the DSM-5. Since early FTD descriptions, there has been a debate on ascribing the symptom to the field of language or thought. *FTD can be divided into abnormalities of amount and form of speech:*

1. **Abnormalities concerning amount (productivity)**: these may include overabundance (pressure of speech) or paucity of ideas (poverty of speech content; laconic speech), and rapid or slow thinking, hesitant thinking, and whether the patient speaks spontaneously or only questions are asked.
2. **Abnormalities in the form (continuity of thought)**: this refers to goal-directedness or continuity of thoughts. In normal thought, a speaker presents a series of ideas or propositions that form a logical progression from an initial point, to the conclusion, or goal of the thought. Disorders of continuity tend to distract from this goal, and the relatedness of a series of thoughts becomes less clear. As the thought disorder gets more serious, the logical connectedness of different thoughts becomes weaker.

The following are brief definitions of common formal thought disorders.

Abnormalities Concerning Amount of Speech

1. **Excessive talk (talkativeness, logorrhea, volubility)**: copious, coherent and logical speech. Rapid or excessive speech may reflect cultural patterns, personality traits, or anxious patients. Such patients can usually slow down their rate of speech when asked to do so.
2. **Pressure of talk**: excessive spontaneous talking but still perfectly coherent and logical, though there is marked difficulty in stopping the stream of talk (difficult to interrupt). Patients may talk continuously as though pressured to do so. Often they acknowledge that their thoughts are racing. In the extreme form, the rapid speech of manic patients may lose coherence.
3. **Poverty of speech**: there is a general lack of additional, unprompted content. This results in restricted quantity of speech, and brief unelaborated responses. *Poverty of speech may show as:*

    *   lack of spontaneous talk;
    *   delayed response to questions;
    *   short response to questions;
    *   no response to questions in cases with mutism.

Abnormalities in the Form

It should be noted whether the patient's replies really answer the questions. Are they goal-directed and relevant, or irrelevant? Are the statements illogical, tangential, rambling, evasive, or perseverative? Is there blocking or distractibility? It encompasses distractible speech, loss of goal, derailment (loose associations), illogicality (non sequitur), and incoherence. *Abnormalities in the form may be arbitrarily classified in the following categories* (this classification is useful only in better understanding and memorizing those disorders):

1. **General changes of form of speech**: these may be reflected in the following concepts (overlap of meanings is common among different concepts, where some concepts are more general, more specific, or more severe forms of other concepts):

   - **Poverty of content of speech (laconic speech)**: although replies are long enough, and speech is adequate in amount, it conveys little information—there is a poverty of ideas that is often associated with vague, repetitive, over-abstract or over-concrete speech. The patient's speech usually contains no syntactic or vocabulary errors. This disorder is sometimes called "empty philosophizing." It differs from circumstantiality in that the circumstantial subject tends to provide a wealth of details.
   - **Woolly type of thinking and pseudophilosophical thoughts**: both refer to thoughts that are vague and ill-defined. The thoughts in pseudophilosophical thinking are full of existential questions about the goal of living or the unresolved conflict of immorality without going into deep analysis to tackle such mixed themes seriously.
   - **Interpenetration**: the patient's speech contains elements that belong to the task in hand interspersed with a stream of fantasy that he/she cannot stop (failure of filtering reality from fantasy).
   - **Over-inclusion**: this is the opposite of concrete thinking—the person loses the ability to maintain boundaries of the problem and to restrict operations within their correct limits. Over-inclusiveness expands the concept of a word (Cameron, 1964); ideas that are remotely related to the concept under consideration become incorporated within the patient's thinking. The patient is able to generalize and shift from one hypothesis to another, but his/her generalization is too involved, too inclusive, and too much entangled with much private fantasy.
   - **Thought block**: interruption of the stream of talk for a while, before a thought or idea has been completed. Blocking should only be judged to be present if the patient is unable to account for such stoppage or goes on talking about an unrelated subject, or the patient attributes it to losing thoughts or having his/her mind blank.
   - **Talking past the point (vorbeireden)**: the patient seems always about to get near to the matter in hand but never quite reaches it.

The patient understands what has been asked but deliberately gives irrelevant or approximate answers or talks about an associated topic. *It occurs in*:

- *pseudodementia*: first described by Ganser in criminals awaiting trials for serious offences who deliberately give wrong answers in a fashion that indicates that the question was understood (prison psychosis). Talking past the point is intended to give the impression of being demented or mentally insane. Pseudodementia may occur deliberately in malingering to escape from punishment or to obtain a certain goal, or it may be unconsciously produced in dissociative disorder.
- *acute psychosis*: talking past the point is an indication of a "silly facetious attitude" and can be regarded as a hebephrenic symptom. Answers are silly and do not serve a specific purpose.

- **Desultory thinking**: speech is marked by lack of definite plan or regularity or purpose—jumping from one thing to another in an irregular way. Ideas are grammatically and syntactically correct, which, if used appropriately, are quite suitable, but the patient has these ideas forcing themselves from time to time.
- **Use of idiosyncratic language (neologism)**: patients may create words that do not exist in the dictionary and use them as substitutes for conventional words.
- **Condensation**: fusion of various concepts into one.
- **Metonyms**: refers to using the name of an object or concept for another to denote another related one, or one of which it is a part, e.g., using Crown in place of a royal person, the White House in place of the American president, eyes for sight, ears for giving attention, and hands for help. Metonyms draw a contiguity between two things, in contrast to metaphors which draw a similarity between two things. A metaphor substitutes a concept with another that is similar, e.g., he was a lion in battle—the word lion is used in substitution for displaying an attribute of the person.
- **Circumstantiality**: a pattern of speech that contains excessive, irrelevant, and unnecessary details or parenthetical remarks to the central theme, which make speech indirect and delayed in reaching its goal. However, clauses remain logically connected, and the object in view at the beginning is finally reached. It is seen in major and minor illnesses, e.g., obsessive-compulsive disorder and bipolar disorder. In the elderly it may be a sign of organicity.
- **Tangentiality**: lack of the ability to have goal-directed associations of thoughts—the patient's answers miss the goal, but land in close vicinity. The patient is unable to go from desired point to desired goal. Initially, ideas seem related, and the patient seems to address the

intended point, but he/she progressively moves away from the initial topic in unrelated directions and never reaches the desired goal.

- **Irrelevant type of answer**: a lack of cause and effect relation in the patient's explanation— the answer is not in harmony with the question (i.e., outside the point) or even conveying no meaning at all.

2. **Repetition of certain sounds, words, or phrases**: this occurs particularly at the end of a thought sequence, in a senseless way. *Variable forms of repetition may be observed*:

- **Repetitive use of stock words or phrases**, even when these words do not enhance the meaning of communication. The repeated words are used in ways appropriate to their usual meaning. It may be culturally determined, e.g., the use of the phrase "you know," with the continuous repetition of phrases in a non-conventional manner. Some words or phrases are commonly used as pause-fillers, such as "you know" or "like." These should not be considered perseveration. Repetitive use of stock phrases is often associated with organic brain syndromes.
- **Echolalia**: the echoing of the words or phrases of others. It is often associated with meaningless repetition of the same words. This condition occurs in children with developmental language disorder in autism spectrum disorder, a perseverative in individuals with transcortical aphasia, and rarely in patients with schizophrenia.
- **Palilalia**: a speech in which the person repeats the same words or phrases that he/she had used in conversation with increasing rapidity. The repeated words are usually said in a whispered or mumbling tone, e.g., a person may say "I want go home," followed immediately by a decreasing volume of whisper "go home, go home, go home."
- **Logoclonia**: a near-extinct term for a variation of palilalia in which there is a meaningless repetition of the last syllables of a word or phrase, and formerly regarded by some authors as typical of pre-senile and senile dementias, general paresis and other neurological diseases, e.g., "I am all right ietietiet."
- **Glossolalia**: rarely used term for unintelligible jargon or babbling— speech is incomprehensible, non-meaningful, and is composed of nonsense words and phrases.
- **Verbal preservation**: themes, phrases, or words are inappropriately and repeatedly present in the flow of speech.
- **Perseveration**: the patient retains a constellation of ideas long after they have ceased to be appropriate, e.g., "Where do you live?", "Tanta City." However, any subsequent stimulus that demands a different response may get the same response: "What is the capital of Egypt?" "Tanta City." "Who lives with you at home?" "Tanta City." It occurs in patients with developmental language disorder, organic syndromes, and rarely schizophrenia.

3. **Loosening of associations**: a pattern of speech in which words or phrases do not seem to be meaningfully connected—the connection between associations cannot be ascertained. The themes of speech change from one topic to another in a completely unrelated way; the speech appears incoherent in severe cases. *There are varying terms that are used to describe loosening of associations:*

- **Derailment**: the themes of thought deviate either suddenly or gradually without blocking—i.e., the patient's ideas shift from one unrelated topic to another and the patient is unaware of the incongruity of this change in ideas.
- **Fragmented speech**: when words or sentences are unrelated.
- **Asyndesis**: the lack of adequate connections between two consecutive thoughts. The patient uses a cluster of more or less related thoughts in place of well-knit sequences and he/she is unable to eliminate unnecessary material and focus on the problem that he/she has to solve.
- **Clang association**: a form of derailment in which the patient changes the topic of speech because of the sound rather than the meaning of words—i.e., associations are made by the sound of words rather than by the meaning of words, e.g., "I went to the house, the mouse and louse bit me." Thus the speech becomes derived by punning and rhyming instead of logic, and loses its function as a vehicle for communication.
- **Flight of ideas**: a combination of fragmented and circumstantial communication with deviation from logical links apparently related to environmental cues. The stream of talk is rapid, continuous, but the ideas are frequently changed. The talk becomes fragmentary, the connections being determined by chance associations between the fragments, e.g., the meaning of the last word, or by chance stimuli from the environment (distractibility). Rhymes and other sorts of word play and jokes are common. In severe cases, speech may become disorganized and incoherent, but syntax and vocabulary are usually intact.
- **Incoherent talk**: a pattern of speech that is essentially incomprehensible at times. Incomprehensibility is often due to lack of logical connections between words or phrases, marked by frequent changes in subject matter due to deviation from the central topic into another unrelated one, excessive use of incomplete sentences, idiosyncratic distorted usage of words or grammar. Incoherence is the end result of severe forms of formal thought disorder.

Abnormal Thought Contents

In their invaluable review, Kiran and Chaudhury (2009, p.5) stated that "Jaspers distinguishes four forms of beliefs, i.e. four distinct modes or ways in which beliefs can be presented to consciousness. These are normal belief, overvalued idea, delusion-like idea (secondary delusion) and primary delusion."

Most of the literature distinguishes between a normal belief and an overvalued idea on one hand, and primary and secondary delusions on the other hand. This distinction emphasizes whether the belief is delusional in nature or merely overvalued.

Kiran and Chaudhury showed that the essential distinguishing factor among all forms of belief is the concept of understanding. Thus, the evolution of the normal belief and the overvalued idea can be understood and explained by the personality, life events, and psychopathological experiences, but the primary delusion differs in three ways from the other forms of belief: (a) it is unmediated by thought; (b) it is un-understandable; (c) it implies a change in "the totality of understandable connections," which is personality. The following abnormal thought contents will be discussed: magical thinking, overvalued ideas, delusions, and obsessions.

I. Magical Thinking

Magical thinking means believing in things more strongly than either evidence or experience justifies. Magical thinking is illogical, often attributing more connectedness to events than is actually the case; many superstitions are examples of culturally validated magical thinking. Individual examples might include the belief an extramarital affair was responsible for a traffic accident, or it will rain because he/she got up on the left side of the bed. Such thinking is common among children and obsessive-compulsive or schizophrenic patients, but it is not necessarily indicative of psychopathology. Sometimes a magical belief forms an overvalued idea.

II. Overvalued Ideas

Wernicke was the first to coin the term overvalued idea in order to define those solitary beliefs firmly supported and related with the personality of the individual and that differentiated it from obsessions and delusions (Santín & Gálvez, 2011). An overvalued idea is an unreasonable and preoccupying sustained belief that is maintained with less than delusional intensity (i.e., the person is able to acknowledge the possibility that the belief may not be true) and not obsessional in nature, which comes to dominate a person's life. It is overvalued in the sense that it causes disturbed functioning or suffering to the person him/herself or to others. The background on which an overvalued idea is held is not necessarily unreasonable or false. It becomes so dominant that many other ideas revolve around this idea. It is usually associated with strong affect that the person has great difficulty in expressing. The belief is not customarily accepted by other people of the person's culture.

David Veale (2002) concluded that the term overvalued idea deals with a firmly maintained ego syntonic belief (without reaching delusional intensity) that concerns the individual. It is often developed from an abnormal personality that is normally understood within the past experience and the personality of the individual; Veale concluded that the content is abnormal for the general population (but not bizarre), that it alters functioning and causes distress to the individual and others, is highly associated with affect, leads to repeated and justified actions by the individual, and may progress to delusional ideas for which the patient normally does not request help. From a cognitive perspective, Veale distinguishes between beliefs and values and defines the overvalued idea as beliefs associated with specific idealized, rigid values that are excessively identified with the self.

Delusions can be difficult to distinguish from overvalued ideas, though there is a clear connection with delusions, especially secondary delusions, where the individual has come to believe, because of circumstances and the nature of his/her personality, that people are against him/her and deliberately frustrating him/her.

III. Delusions

There is no adequate definition of delusions; however, a delusion is traditionally defined as false belief based on incorrect inference, despite what constitutes unquestionable and obvious proof or evidence to the contrary. The false belief cannot be explained by the person's cultural or religious background, level of intelligence, or the education level of the patient.

The key feature of a delusion is the degree to which the person is convinced that the belief is true. A person with a delusion will hold firmly to the belief regardless of contrary evidence (Kiran & Chaudhury, 2009).

Patients with delusions are likely to hold their belief with the same conviction and intensity as they hold other non-delusional beliefs about themselves; or as anyone else holds intensely personal non-delusional beliefs. Subjectively, a delusion is simply a belief, notion, or idea.

Jaspers (1962) regarded a delusion as an aberrant view of reality that has three characteristic components: being held with unusual conviction, not amenable to logic, and the manifest absurdity or erroneousness of the content.

There is now considerable evidence that reasoning, attention, meta-cognition, and attribution biases play a role in delusional patients. Recently, these findings have been incorporated into a number of cognitive models that aim to explain delusion formation, maintenance, and content.

The presence of delusions demonstrates the presence of a psychotic illness but does not necessarily distinguish the underlying disorder. Delusions may be a feature of any of the following mental disorders: (1) Psychotic disorders: schizophrenia, schizoaffective disorder, delusional disorder, schizophreniform disorder, shared psychotic disorder, brief psychotic disorder, and substance-induced psychotic disorder, (2) Bipolar disorder, (3) Major depressive disorder with psychotic features (4) Delirium, and (5) Dementia (Kiran & Chaudhury, 2009).

Until the end of the last century, it was felt that certain types of delusions (Schneiderian symptoms) were pathognomonic of schizophrenia. Clinical observation with careful diagnostic formulation has demonstrated that each of these Schneiderian symptoms may occur in many other types of psychosis, such as in mania or delirium. Therefore, the diagnostic meaning of the type of delusion is only relative. Schneiderian symptoms are less commonly seen in mood disorders; however, they are not enough on their own to diagnose schizophrenia or to exclude mood disorders. This understanding has resulted in the concept of mood-congruent or mood-incongruent delusions.

Although they are a hallmark of psychotic disorders, delusions may be manifestations of neurologic disease, while reduplicative paramnesias are reported in schizophrenia and other psychotic disorders, they are seen commonly also in chronic or resolving amnestic syndromes. Sometimes reduplicative paramnesia occurs in the context of identifiable brain lesions; frontal, limbic, and right-hemispheric areas have all been implicated.

Reaction of Patients to Delusions

Many schizophrenic patients have a blunted affect, and show little emotional response to their delusional beliefs. Although the deluded patient is convinced that his/her delusions are true, he/she does not necessarily act on them. However, it is not surprising that individuals can act violently on the basis of their delusions. There have been homicides by paranoid persons who kill to prevent a perceived danger; accidental deaths of those who behave recklessly because of delusions of immortality; suicides in response to guilty or nihilistic delusions; and self-mutilation because of somatic delusions. Though violent behavior cannot always be predicted, elucidation of the content of delusions may herald possible risk.

Usually, when the illness becomes chronic there is discrepancy between the delusions and the patient behavior, e.g., a grandiose patient may scrub the floor or a persecuted patient who insists that he/she is not ill, remains in hospital as a voluntary patient.

Remarks on Definition of Delusion

It is easy to demonstrate the inadequacy of different definitions of delusions; imagine two politicians with opposing beliefs. Both hold views with an "extraordinary conviction" and "an incomparable subjective certainty." Both show a very definite "imperviousness to other experiences and to compelling counter-argument." For each, the judgments of the other are "false," and "the content impossible." Obviously, neither is deluded. Both are having views that are highly valued, or perhaps overvalued, but that fulfill the above "external characteristics" of delusional belief. *Thus, the falsity and fixation of beliefs could be questioned as distinguishing points of delusions:*

1. **The reality of the delusional belief**: delusions traditionally have been considered as false beliefs. It has been shown that delusions are not necessarily false, although in some sense they are discordant with reality. A very common delusion among married persons is that their spouses are unfaithful to them. In the nature of things, some of these spouses will indeed have been unfaithful; the delusion will therefore be true, but only by coincidence. What determines being a delusion here is not being false but the mode of inference and reaching to that conclusion. A well-known pitfall in clinical practice is to assume that a belief is false because it is odd, instead of checking the facts or finding out how the belief was arrived at, e.g., improbable stories of persecution may turn out to be arrived at through normal processes of logical thinking, and, in fact, to be correct.
2. **The fixity of conviction**: delusions traditionally have been considered as fixed beliefs, however the delusional beliefs like normal beliefs may have a variable degree of conviction, and this is especially evident along the course of treatment. Thus, distinguishing the different forms of belief lies not in their conviction and certainty, not in their amenability to change and correction, and not in their impossible content but in their origins within the patient's experience.

Kendler et al. (1983) proposed the following factors as indicators of delusional severity:

1. **Conviction**: the degree to which the patient is convinced about the reality of his/her delusions.
2. **Extension**: the extent to which the delusional belief affects other areas of the patient's life.
3. **Bizarreness**: how much the delusional belief differs from culturally determined conventional reality?
4. **Disorganization**: the extent to which the delusional beliefs are internally consistent, logical, and systematized.
5. **Pressure**: the extent to which the patient is preoccupied and concerned with the delusional beliefs.
6. **Affective response**: the amount of the patient's emotions regarding such beliefs.
7. **Deviant behavior resulting from delusions**: the degree to which patients act upon their delusions.

Table 2.2 Summary of Classification of Delusions and Their Different Subtypes

Domain	Types	Characteristics
Origin	Primary	A delusion that does not occur in response to another psychopathology
	Secondary	A delusion that occurs in response to another psychopathology
Relation to mood	Mood congruent	Delusions going with the patient mood
	Mood incongruent	Delusions not going with the patient mood
Degree of organization	Systematized	Delusions form an elaborated system of beliefs
	Non-systematized	Delusions are fragmentary
Number of themes	Monothematic	Delusions are restricted to one particular topic
	Polythematic	Delusions involve multiple themes
Plausibility of occurrence in life	Bizarre	Delusions are totally implausible
	Non-bizarre	The content of delusions can occur in real life
Content	Variable contents that involve every possible and impossible idea	Persecution; love; grandeur; religious; guilt and unworthiness; negation/nihilistic, reference, poverty; hypochondriacal; infestation; sexual, somatic; influence; misidentification; thought insertion, broadcasting and reading

Classification of Delusions

There is no completely satisfactory way of classifying delusions according to any phenomenological principles. A *lot of dimensions (see Table 2.2) were considered in the literature*:

1. Primary and secondary delusions.
2. Mood congruent versus mood incongruent.
3. Monothematic or Polythematic.
4. Organization (systematized versus non-systematized).
5. Bizarre versus non-bizarre.
6. Content of delusions.

Primary and Secondary Delusions

Primary delusions denote that it is not occurring in response to another psychopathology such as other delusions or mood disorder. It appears suddenly and with full conviction but without any mental events leading to it. According to Jaspers the core of primary delusion is that it is ultimately incomprehensible.

Gruhle (1915) considered that a primary delusion was a disturbance of symbolic meaning, not an alteration in sensory perception, apperception, or intelligence, while Wernicke (1906) formulated the concept of an autochthonous idea; an idea arising without external cause. The trouble with finding supposed autochthonous or primary delusions is that it can be disputed whether they are truly autochthonous. For this reason they are not considered of first rank in Schneider's (1957) classification of symptoms.

Primary delusional experience was generally held to have particular significance for the diagnosis of schizophrenia. However, it is common in several psychiatric conditions, and may occur in a diverse range of other disorders (including brain injury, intoxication, somatic illness, and epileptic psychoses).

Secondary delusions are understandable when a detailed psychiatric history and examination is available. That is, they are understandable in terms of the patient's mood state, circumstances of his/her life, the beliefs of his/her peer group; and his/her personality. Thus, the classification of a delusion into whether primary or secondary in nature is based on delusional evidence and the reason the patient gives for holding his/her belief.

TYPES OF PRIMARY DELUSIONS

Four types of primary delusions were described in literature: (1) delusional mood/atmosphere; (2) delusional perception; (3) delusional memory/delusional ideas; (4) delusional awareness.

Delusional mood is usually a strange, peculiar mood in which the patient experiences that his/her world has been subtly altered in a threatening way but the significance of the change cannot be understood by the patient who is tense, anxious, and bewildered. The events as well as the actions and words of others seem to hint at hidden meanings that carry a personal significance; however, the precise nature of the meaning seems elusive. Finally, a delusion may crystallize out of this mood and its appearance is often associated with a sense of relief.

Delusional perception is the attribution of a new meaning to a normally preceived object, usually in the sense of self-reference, despite the absence of any emotional or logical reason. The essence of delusional perception is the abnormal significance attached to a real percept without any cause that is understandable in rational or emotional terms; it is self-referent, momentous, and urgent. The patient receives a normal perception that is interpreted with a delusional meaning and has personal significance. The new meaning cannot be understood as arising from the patient's affective state or previous attitude.

This is important in the differentiation of delusional perception from delusional misinterpretation. An example: "a woman said that every night blood is being injected out of my arms, when asked for her evidence she explained that she had little brown spots on her arms and therefore knew that she was being injected."

Delusional memory/delusional ideas—a delusion may take the form of memory—an event or idea that is clearly delusional in nature is recalled by the patient, but is projected into the past. *Thus, it is sometimes called retrospective delusion, e.g.:*

- A subject suddenly remembered that the Queen greeted him/her when he/she was a child because she recognized him/her as a member of the royal family.
- A female patient suddenly remembered that she had been attacked and raped by her brother and his friend in the midst of a family gathering. This conviction emerged de novo. The lady could not point to anything that suggested such an event. On the contrary, she was constantly surprised that everything and everybody around her were so normal and apparently unaware of the terrible happening, even those she believed to be involved.

Delusional ideas—the false belief arrives in the patient's mind suddenly, fully elaborated, and unheralded by any related thoughts—e.g., a schizophrenic patient may be suddenly and completely convinced that he/she is changing sex, without ever having thought of it before and without any preceding ideas or events that could have led in any understandable way to this conclusion. The examiner would find it difficult to account for the arrival of the false ideas when asked to explain it, and to understand how the person had come to believe his/her delusion.

Delusional awareness is an experience that is not sensory in nature, in which ideas or events take on an extreme vividness as if they had additional reality. Delusional significance is the second stage of the occurrence of delusional perception. Objects and persons are perceived normally, but take on a special significance that cannot be rationally explained by the patient.

Mood Congruent vs. Mood Incongruent

This distinction is based on whether delusions are going with the patient mood or not. The weight of delusion in diagnosis of psychosis was heavily weighted in old literatures and classifications. Mood-congruent delusions are understandable in terms of mood disorders, e.g., in manic patients the content of delusions is usually consistent with the themes of inflated worth, power, knowledge, or identity (e.g., the patient believes that he/she is a multimillionaire and is irresistibly attractive to all women). In depressed patients the content of delusions is usually consistent with the themes of personal inadequacy, guilt, disease, nihilism, or deserved punishment. Mood-incongruent delusions (e.g., thought broadcasting) in a depressed patient necessitate careful evaluation; that is, does the patient truly have a mood disorder, or is a schizophrenia spectrum disorder more likely?

Monothematic or Polythematic

Monothematic (also called circumscribed or unelaborated) delusions are restricted to one particular topic and occur in the absence of other gross psychopathology such as hallucinations. Classically they are of somatic symptoms, such as of something foreign under the skin. A patient may be convinced of having fleas, scratch him/herself, and use the excoriated areas as evidence of infestation. They can be of other types; for example, isolated erotomanic or jealous delusions.

Monothematic can be contrasted with the polythematic and elaborated delusions or delusional systems in which some delusions were interwoven and some of which stood apart. Although psychiatric patients often have poly-thematic and elaborated delusional systems, they sometimes have delusions that are monothematic and at most only somewhat elaborated. Stone and Young (1997) noted that monothematic delusions that result from brain injury are often also circumscribed or unelaborated.

Organization (Systematized vs. Non-systematized Delusions)

The organization of the delusions is difficult to elucidate, and its content may not be interrelated. Delusions vary in the degree that they are organized or systematized. Delusions may be fragmentary, i.e., not organized into a consistent theme, e.g., the subject thinks the room is bugged, believes people doubt his sexual potency, and suspects he may be the son of God. *The organization of the delusions is difficult to elucidate, and its content is not interrelated.*

Sometimes delusions form a coherent system that appears superficially logical, composed of a central single false belief with multiple ramifications or a cluster of false beliefs that the patient relates to a single event or theme.

Although there is overlap, poorly systematized delusions tend to be more common in transient organic states (especially delirium) or at the time of onset of a psychotic condition, whereas chronic psychotic patients usually integrate their new symptoms to the matrix of old ones to form a stable set of delusions in which various psychotic features tend to interrelate, and the patient is able to discuss most things in terms of his or her delusional system. Such delusions are appropriately labeled systematized.

Bizarre vs. Non-bizarre

The term bizarre delusion is used to describe certain delusions as totally implausible that cannot occur in real life, e.g., a patient may believe that he/she was born on Venus, divided into pieces, transported to Earth 30 years ago, before he/she was reassembled in the current shape. On the other hand, because it may happen in reality that the CIA, KGB, or Mafia might follow people, a delusion of being trailed by one of these organizations cannot be described as bizarre. The presence of bizarre delusions was considered a sufficient criterion of schizophrenia till the *Diagnostic and Statistical Manual of Mental Disorder*, fifth edition (APA, 2013), so long as dysfunction/suffering and length of illness criteria were satisfied, a matter that illustrates the importance of its distinction.

Though diagnosis of delusions in general has an acceptable reliability, this is not the case with bizarre delusion, either with structured interviews or other instruments. The problem of finding a reliable and valid consensual definition of bizarre delusion remains unresolved, and has led to loss of its privilege as a useful sole diagnostic feature of schizophrenia. Current approaches apply several distinct (if somewhat overlapping) criteria to bizarre delusions; *these emphasize several notions:*

1. apparent physical or logical impossibility (implying extreme implausibility);
2. presence of a belief that is not consensually shared in a given social or cultural context;
3. absence of historical or what Jaspers called "genetic understanding": this refers to an inability to understand how a given state of mind could emerge from relevant biographical antecedents;
4. incomprehensibility, in the sense of a lack of what Jaspers called "static understanding": this refers to the capacity to empathize with, to imaginatively identify with, a given state of mind;
5. notion of "not being derived from ordinary life situations."

Content of Delusions

The content of delusions is variable, but certain general topics commonly occur. It is usually determined by the patient's emotional, intellectual, social, and cultural background. Common general themes include persecution, jealousy, love, and grandiose, religious, nihilistic, and hypochondriacal feelings, and several others.

DELUSION OF PERSECUTION

Delusion of persecution is the most frequent content of delusion in general psychiatric practice. The affected person has false beliefs that he/she is stalked, spied upon, poisoned, followed, deceived, or that one's mail is being opened, the telephone tapped, one's room or office bugged, or that the police, government officials, neighbors, or fellow workers are annoying the patient and trying to inflect harm on him/her, damage his/her reputation, or drive him/her insane. Sometimes the patient experiences persecution as a vague influence without knowing who is responsible. The patient may take legal action because of imagined mistreatment. Delusions of persecution are of little help in diagnosis, as they can occur in organic states, schizophrenia, and severe affective disorders. However, the patient's attitude to the delusion may point to the diagnosis: in a severe depressive disorder he/she characteristically accepts the supposed activities of the persecutors as justified by his/her own guilt and wickedness, but in schizophrenia he/she resents them, often angrily.

PARANOID DELUSIONS

The word paranoid is taken to mean "self-referent" and is not limited to persecutory delusions. The term paranoid originally was synonymous with delusional insanity. Kraepelin (1905) used the term more specifically to describe the condition in which there are delusions but no hallucinations. Thus, the term paranoid delusion is redundant and should be replaced in the psychiatric vocabulary by more precise phrases such as persecutory delusions, delusions of reference, or delusions of jealousy.

DELUSIONS OF INFIDELITY (MORBID JEALOUSY, OTHELLO DELUSION)

The subject believes that his mate or lover is unfaithful. The person makes much effort to prove the existence of the affair, searching for hair in the bedclothes, the odor of shaving lotion or smoke on clothing, or receipts or checks indicating a gift has been bought for the lover. Elaborate plans are made to trap the two together. It is common among men. Not all jealous ideas are delusions; less intense jealous preoccupations are common, and some obsessional thoughts are concerned with doubts about the spouse's fidelity. However, when the beliefs are delusional they have particular importance because they may lead to dangerously aggressive behavior toward the person thought to be unfaithful.

DELUSIONS OF LOVE (EROTOMANIA—AMOROUS DELUSIONS)

Erotomania was described by Sir Alexander Morrison (1848). It is a delusional belief that someone is deeply in love with them. Erotomanic delusions often occur in patients with schizophrenia and other psychotic disorders, but can also occur during a manic episode. The patient believes that a secret admirer is declaring his or her affection for the patient, often by special glances, signals, telepathy, or messages through the media. Usually the patient then returns the perceived affection by means of letters, phone calls, gifts, and visits to the recipient. Even though these advances are unexpected and often unwanted, any denial of affection by the object of this delusional love is dismissed by the patient. De Clerambault syndrome is a variation of erotomania, that was described by de Clerambault and retained his name (1942); it refers to a woman who believes that a man, who is typically older and of higher social status, is in love with her (Sims, 1995).

GRANDIOSE DELUSIONS

The subject believes that he/she has special importance, power, abilities, or identity. He/She may believe him/herself to be a famous celebrity or to have supernatural powers. Expansive or grandiose delusional beliefs may extend to objects, leading to a delusion of developing some wonderful new invention, he/she is writing some definitive book, or composing a great piece of music. The subject is often suspicious that someone is trying to steal his/her ideas, and may become irritated if his/her abilities are doubted. Such delusions occur in mania and schizophrenia, especially the paranoid type.

RELIGIOUS DELUSIONS

The subject is preoccupied with false beliefs of a religious nature. Sometimes these exist within the context of a conventional religious system, such as beliefs about the Second Coming Anti-Christ. At other times, they may involve an entirely new religious system or a mixture of beliefs from a variety of religions, particularly eastern religions, such as ideas about reincarnation or nirvana. Religious delusions may be combined with grandiose delusions (if the subject considers him/herself a religious leader), delusion of guilt, or delusions of being controlled.

   Religious delusions must be outside the range considered normal for the subject's cultural and religious background. The form of the delusion is interpreted in the face of cultural and religous background; i.e., religious delusions are not caused by excessive religious belief, or by the wrongdoing that the patient attributes as cause. Although common, they formed a higher proportion in the nineteenth century than in the twentieth century and are still prevalent in developing countries.

DELUSIONS OF GUILT AND UNWORTHINESS

Delusions of self-reproach (unworthiness, guilt, or sin) are where the patient feels that he/she is wicked, full of sin, unfit to live or mix with other people, or that he/she has committed an unpardonable sin and insists that he/she will rot in hell for this. Sometimes the subject is excessively or inappropriately preoccupied with things he/she did wrong as a child, such as masturbating.

Sometimes the patient feels responsible for causing some disastrous event, such as a fire or accident, with which he/she in fact has no connection. They are found most often in depressive disorders, and are therefore sometimes called depressive delusions.

DELUSIONS OF NEGATION/NIHILISTIC DELUSIONS

The false belief that one's body, or parts of it, is disintegrating, or that one is deprived of all resources, or that one has no money. It also includes pessimistic ideas that the patient's career is finished, he/she has lost all possessions, has lost internal organs, that one is dead and is in need of burial, the outside world does not exist, one's family has been destroyed, and so forth. Comparable ideas concerning failures of bodily function (e.g., that the bowels are blocked with putrefying matter) often accompany nihilistic delusions. Nihilistic delusions are associated with extreme degrees of depressed mood. Such delusions are also sometimes labeled delusions of negation or Cotard's syndrome. It is reported in depressive disorders, schizophrenia, and lesions of the non-dominant hemisphere.

DELUSION OF REFERENCE

The patient believes that insignificant remarks, events, statements, objects or other people in the immediate environment refer to him/her or have special meaning for him/her, e.g., a patient may believe an article in a newspaper or a remark heard on television to be directed specifically to him/her; thus it is sometimes productive to ask the patient whether he or she has noted anything about him/herself in any of these media: "Have you been getting any special messages from TV or radio?" Although most delusions of reference have persecutory or negative associations, they may also relate to grandiose or reassuring themes.

DELUSION OF POVERTY

The patient believes that he/she lost or will be deprived of all his/her money, property, or will be bereft of all material possessions. A rich person may refuse to get a psychiatric appointment, because he/she thinks he/she does not have enough money, or thinks that his/her children will not find food to survive. It is a common accompaniment of psychotic depression.

HYPOCHONDRIACAL DELUSIONS

The patient is convinced that he/she has a physical disease in the absence of any evidence of physical illness. Such delusions are common in the elderly, reflecting the increasing concern with health among mentally normal people at this time of life. It is to be differentiated from **hypochondriasis**, which is characterized by persisting overwhelming concern about having a serious disease in spite of lack of evidence on physical examination or laboratory investigations, and appropriate medical assurance. It is less firmly held than hypochondriacal delusions.

DELUSION OF INFESTATION

The patient believes that he/she is infested with small but macroscopic organisms, e.g., parasites, spiders, and lice. It occurs in schizophrenia, and organic and toxic states.

SEXUAL DELUSIONS

They are simply delusions with a strong relation to erotic feelings and activities. In some cases, these delusions may modify an individual's perception of his or her own sexual identity; a schizophrenic patient may have delusions of being of the opposite biological gender, or may reimagine their sexual preferences and histories. Other sorts of sexual delusions involve the belief in erotic relationships where none are present or perhaps even possible.

SOMATIC DELUSIONS

A delusion that there is some alteration in a bodily organ or its function; the subject believes that somehow his/her body is diseased, abnormal, or changed, e.g., a post-menopausal woman may believe she is pregnant, or one person may believe that his hands have become enlarged. Sometimes somatic delusions are accompanied by tactile or other hallucinations, e.g., the subject believes that he/she has ball bearings rolling about in his/her head, placed there by a dentist who filled his/her teeth, and can actually hear them clanking against one another, or that he/she is bothered by the movements of hormones synthesized in the pituitary gland down to its targets outside the brain.

DELUSION OF CONTROL (INFLUENCE)

The patient believes that his/her actions, impulses, will, feelings, or thoughts are controlled by an external force (e.g., electricity, wireless, or other persons). The central requirement for this type of delusion is an actual strong subjective experience of being controlled. The subject must describe, for example, that messages are sent to his/her brain by radio waves, causing him/her to experience particular feelings that he/she recognizes are not his/her own. Delusions of control do not include simple beliefs or ideas that friends or parents are trying to coerce him/her into something. It is not to be confused with the experience of hearing commanding auditory hallucination that the patient obeys voluntarily. Also, care must be taken that the patient has not mistaken the question for one about religious beliefs concerning the divine control of human actions.

Delusional Misidentification

REDUPLICATIVE PARAMNESIA

This can involve place, other persons, or self (including body parts). In reduplicative paramnesia for places, those with this delusional theme believe that a specific place or location has been replicated and exists in multiple locations simultaneously. Sometimes an individual with this delusional theme may believe that a place has been relocated or transferred to another place. *Commonly described reduplicative paramnesia include:.*

1. **Capgras syndrome**: a delusional belief that someone important to the patient (often a spouse) has been replaced by an identically physically appearing double, e.g., my husband is replaced by Mr. X. Thus, Capgras syndrome is a fixed delusional belief in the existence of a presumed double; this differentiates it from an illusion, hallucination, misperception, cognitive deficits, or amnesia. It may be selective to certain persons, while most people in the environment are correctly identified.
2. **Fregoli syndrome**: patients believe a stranger has taken on the appearance of a familiar person. The patient perceives both as physically different, but psychologically identical: "I am being followed around by people who are known to me but who are unrecognizable because they are in disguise."
3. **Syndrome of intermetamorphosis**: the patient believes a stranger has taken on the appearance of a familiar person, both the familiar person (usually regarded as persecutor) and the misidentified stranger share physical as well as psychological similarities.
4. **The syndrome of subjective doubles**: the patient believes that another person has been physically transformed into his/her own self, e.g., my neighbor acquired the physical characteristics and identity of my own.
5. **Self-misidentification**: the self as perceived in the mirror is not regarded as one's self.
6. **Reduplication of time**: the subject exists in the present and in duplicate time.
7. **Reduplication of body parts**: the subject believes there are more than the usual number of body parts, e.g., having two hearts.

Delusions Concerning the Possession of Thought

1. **Thought insertion**: the patient has the experience that his/her thoughts are under the control of an outside agency, he/she believes that

thoughts that are not his/her own have been implanted into his/her mind by other people or forces, e.g., the subject may believe that his/her neighbor is practicing voodoo and implanting alien sexual thoughts in his/her mind.

2. **Thought withdrawal**: delusions that thoughts or ideas are taken away from his/her mind by other people or forces. The patient describes a subjective experience of beginning a thought that is suddenly removed by an outside force. This delusion usually accompanies thought blocking, so that the patient experiences a break in the flow of thoughts through his/her mind and believes that the "missing" thoughts have been taken away by some outside agency, often his/her supposed persecutors.

3. **Thought-reading (mindreading)**: the patient believes that other persons can read his/her mind or know his/her thoughts. It is not merely that they know their secret thoughts from their words, actions, or facial expression, but that the thoughts are directly available and can be, in a real sense, read by others. There is a sense of having become transparent, making one's innermost thoughts open to direct observation. It is different from thought broadcasting in that the patient subjectively experiences and recognizes that others know his/her thoughts, but he/she does not think that they can be out loud. If the patient believes that he/she can read other people's thoughts, it should be scored under grandiose delusions (as it entails having a special power or ability).

4. **Thought broadcasting (audible thoughts)**: delusion that one's thoughts (unspoken thoughts) leave one (broadcast) and are being diffused widely out of a subject's control so that, he/she or others can hear them. Sometimes the subject experiences his/her thoughts as a voice outside his/her head; this is an auditory hallucination as well as a delusion. Sometimes the subject feels his/her thoughts are being broadcast, although he/she cannot hear them him/herself. Sometimes he/she believes that his/her thoughts are picked up by a microphone and broadcast on the radio or TV.

Communicated Insanity (La Folie à Deux)

Occasionally, a delusion is transferred from a psychotic person (usually dominant) to one or more closely related normal persons, who are usually deprived and disadvantaged, so that those persons share the false belief of the psychotic patient (Sims, 1995). *Folie à deux is divided into four possible relationships between the principal (mentally ill person) and the associate:*

1. **Folie imposée**: a dominant psychotic person (e.g., a mother and her son) imposes his/her delusions into a normal person (e.g., you should not speak to our neighbors because they plot to harm us). Separation of the pair is often followed by remission of symptoms in the associate.

2. **Folie communiquée**: a normal person suffers the same delusion as that of another person who is emotionally closely related (e.g., friend or spouse), after resisting it for long periods. It is not due to imposition of the ideas, but continuous sharing and communication of it. Once acquired, these beliefs become maintained even after their separation.
3. **Folie induite**: a psychotic person adds to his/her delusions that of another patient (e.g., patients in the same ward).
4. **Folies simultanée**: a delusional system emerges concurrently and independently in two closely related persons; the separation of the two would not be beneficial in the resolution of the delusions.

Case Example of Delusions

AZ is a 21-year-old man who presented to casualty having got into a fight, as he thought he was being watched and felt threatened. He looks suspicious and is reluctant to be examined or undergo an X-ray, though he appears to have fractured his thumb. Though he cannot explain why, AZ is absolutely convinced that the government is after him; he states that over the last few months he has been carefully monitored by government agencies. AZ is afraid to face the X-ray because he is convinced that any machine enables the government to get inside his head.

What Are the Main Symptoms in This Case?

Delusion of persecution is the main symptom in this case: this man believes that he is watched and followed by the government, and that the government uses machines to get inside his head. The latter statement needs explanation; if AZ is under the influence of any of these machines, it will denote delusion of influence or control. Delusion of persecution ushers to a psychotic process, but is not specific to a certain disorder. It may be drug-related, or due to schizophrenia, delusional disorder, schizoaffective disorder, bipolar disorder, or psychotic depression. The specific diagnosis will depend on associated features, e.g., evidence of drug intoxication or withdrawal, presence of manic or depressive symptoms, or presence of other psychotic symptoms in the absence of mood symptoms.

Is It Possible to Give a Conclusive Diagnosis Based on These Data?

It is not possible to give a conclusive diagnosis based on this history; additional signs and symptoms are needed as stated above. Social and occupational functioning is important in differential diagnosis, course of the illness, and mental state examination will be critical in conclusion of differential diagnosis of such a case.

IV. Obsessions and Compulsions

Obsessive-Compulsive Disorder (OCD) is a common, chronic disorder in which a person has uncontrollable, reoccurring thoughts (obsessions) and/or behaviors (compulsions) that he or she feels the urge to repeat over and over. Obsessive-compulsive disorder usually includes both obsessions and compulsions, but it is also possible to have only obsessive symptoms or only compulsive symptoms.

Obsession

Diagnostic and Statistical Manual of Mental Disorder, fifth edition (APA, 2013) defines obsessions as recurrent and persistent thoughts, urges, or images that are experienced, at some time during the disturbance, as intrusive and unwanted and that in most individuals cause marked anxiety or distress. The patient tries to ignore or suppress such thoughts, urges, or images, or to neutralize them with some other thoughts or actions. The patient's doubt regarding their obsessions makes them apprehensive and drives them to behave as if the content of their obsessions might come true. Thus, in spite of being fully aware about the excessiveness and unreasonableness of their doubt, obsessions push them to perform rituals, e.g., obsessions of contamination lead to compulsive hand-washing, and obsessions of doubt lead to compulsive checking rituals (Oulis et al., 2013).

TYPES (FORMS) OF OBSESSIONS

Obsessions are not restricted to thoughts, but extend to include urges, or images:

1. **Obsessional thoughts**: repeated and intrusive words or phrases that are usually upsetting to the patient. The intrusive thoughts are repetitive and not voluntarily produced; they cause the sufferer extreme distress. Obsessive persons are not likely to act on their obsessive thoughts as they find them unpleasant on one hand, and unaccepted, and try to avoid and prevent them happening on the other hand. The theme of obsessional thoughts can cover any subject, but the more common areas revolve around relationships, sexual thoughts, magical thinking, religious thoughts, and violent thoughts.

    *   **Relationship intrusive thoughts**: the main focus of this category of obsessional thoughts is on thoughts questioning the suitability of a relationship, and one's partner or one's own sexuality. It may also include constantly scrutinizing the depth of feelings for one's partner, placing the partner and the relationship under a microscope, a matter that places immense strain on the relationship. Sometimes there are obsessive doubts that one's partner is being faithful, or the reverse:

doubts that one may cheat on one's partner. The patient does not believe in the reality of these thoughts; this distinguishes it from delusions of infidelity. However, the patient may think about ending the relationship to rid him/herself of the doubt and anxiety that are frequent.

- **Sexual intrusive thoughts**: this category of obsessional thoughts revolves around causing inappropriate sexual harm to another person, e.g., thoughts of being a pedophile, being sexually attracted to members of one's own family, or thoughts of inappropriately touching a child. This category of obsessional thoughts may also involve thoughts of being attracted to members of the same sex in a heterosexual subject, or for those who are gay, fear of being attracted to members of the opposite sex, or the constant questioning of one's own sexuality; these are the main focuses of these obsessional doubts. In an attempt to avoid sexually intrusive thoughts, the patient may avoid public places such as shopping centers, and may avoid spending time with children of the family, in an attempt to avoid coming into close contact with children. Similarly, parents with this form of thoughts may avoid bathing and hugging their own children; a matter that can lead to emotional suffering for both children and parents. Sexually intrusive thoughts usually cause marked distress and disturbance to patients and make them shameful and fearful of being labeled; this can lead to their reluctance to seek professional help.

- **Religious intrusive thoughts**: religious thoughts are a frequent obsessive theme, sometimes called scrupulosity. It includes offensive thoughts about God, saints, or religious figures, constant questioning of a person's faith, unwarranted concern about committing a sin, intrusive bad thoughts during prayer that will ruin or cancel out its value. Religious obsessive thoughts are very distressing to the sufferers and may lead them to avoid religious practices that trigger these thoughts, and prevent the person deriving peace from their religion.

- **Violent intrusive thoughts**: intrusive thoughts of executing violent acts against people in general and loved ones in particular, e.g., thoughts of hitting or stabbing one's children or beloved persons. Most sufferers with these types of fears falsely believe that having the thoughts means they are capable of acting upon them. Some patients may hide these thoughts, so as not to be labeled as bad persons. A person with these types of intrusive thoughts will avoid public places such as shopping centers, where social interaction may be required, to avoid coming into close contact with people that may trigger the obsessive thoughts.

- **Magical intrusive thoughts**: the patient is overwhelmed by intrusive ideas, that thinking about bad things will make them more likely to happen, e.g., having thoughts that one's child will catch a serious infection will result in actual infection. It is sometimes called thought–action fusion. In a trial to overcome these magical thoughts, the patient may perform rituals (called magic rituals), that are usually bizarre and time-consuming, e.g., the patient may frequently repeat the word health thrice in a trial to overcome the thinking that his/her child will catch an infection in the previous example.

- **Thoughts about dirt and contamination**: fear of contamination is one of the most prevalent obsessions. Typically the contamination worry is based on a fear of some sort of disease or illness, e.g., the person is worried about getting a sickness or disease by touching a public door handle, using a public restroom, or handling money. Exaggerated fear from serious effects of household bleaches and cleaning supplies, or environmental contaminants like radiation, asbestos, pesticides, toxic waste, radon, mold, lead paint, etc. may be experienced. The fear of catching a disease is not always the cause of dirt and contamination obsessions, e.g., a person may be worried by gluey or oily substances (e.g., glue, butter, cooking oil, etc.) on one's hand leading to distress and frequent hand washing.
- **Obsessions of doubt**: these are repeated themes expressing uncertainty about previous actions, e.g., whether or not the person has locked the door, turned off an electrical appliance or turned off the stove which might cause a fire, counted their money properly, or answered all questions in an exam test.
- **Obsessional ruminations**: rumination refers to excessive questioning or thinking about themes that are undirected and unproductive. It never leads to a solution or satisfactory conclusion, but those persons run over in their minds various considerations and arguments of what superficially appeared to them to be compelling evidence. In distinction from obsessive thoughts, ruminating persons do not resist the thoughts but indulge in them. The themes of ruminations usually involve religious, philosophical, or metaphysical topics, e.g., one may endlessly question who created God?

2. **Obsessional urges (impulses)**: repeated impulses to carry out actions that are aggressive, dangerous, or socially embarrassing, e.g., the urge to jump in front of a train or fast-moving bus; acting on unwanted impulses, e.g., stabbing someone; urges to shout obscenities or act inappropriately; or thoughts about accidentally touching someone inappropriately, with the aim of hurting them. In spite of the great distress and fear caused by these impulses, sufferers do not act upon them.

3. **Images**: sufferers have reoccurring images in their minds that are disturbing or horrific, e.g., images showing personally annoying and unacceptable violent or sexual scenes such as stabbing or abusing someone, or being unfaithful.

Compulsions

Compulsions are repetitive behaviors or mental acts that an individual feels driven to perform in response to an obsession or according to rules that must be applied rigidly. Compulsions are usually "but not always" actions that parallel obsessions and may be the motoric product of similar obsessive thoughts and urges such as obsessions. Like obsessions, they are unwanted and ego dystonic. They are often recognized by the patient as unreasonable and he/she unsuccessfully attempts to voluntarily stop or suppress them. During trials to suppress compulsions, the patient grows anxious, and the anxiety is relieved by yielding to performance of the compulsive act. The compulsive act is stereotyped (i.e., it is the same act over and over), often ritualistic (i.e., it is performed in the same manner each time; hence naming it ritual), and often quite trivial.

There are many habitual behaviors that have at times been labeled compulsions; frequently these are named with suffixes -mania or -philia (kleptomania (stealing), pyromania (fire-setting), trichotillomania (hair pulling), necrophilia (sexual attraction to corpses), pedophilia (sexual attraction to children), nymphomania (a female's compulsion to engage in sexual intercourse), and satyriasis (a male's compulsion to engage in sexual intercourse)).

Most people who engage in habitual behaviors are not truly compulsive; the term compulsion should be used only if the impulse is repetitive, ritualistic, and essentially irresistible. The content of obsessions and compulsions varies among individuals; *the following kinds are particularly common*:

1. CORRECTING OBSESSIONAL THOUGHTS (MENTAL RITUALS)

As a way of getting rid of unpleasant thoughts or bothering images, the obsessive person may repeat alternative thoughts that do not disturb him/her; this is called neutralizing thoughts, e.g., repeatedly counting, praying, or saying certain words.

2. RITUALS

Rituals are behaviors that patients feel driven to act out again and again, usually in an attempt to make obsessions go away. However not all rituals or habits are compulsions. *Everyone double checks things sometimes, but a person with obsessive rituals generally*:

- can't control his or her thoughts or behaviors, even when those thoughts or behaviors are recognized as excessive;
- doesn't get pleasure when performing the behaviors or rituals, but may feel brief relief from the anxiety the thoughts cause;
- experiences significant problems in his/her daily life due to these thoughts or behaviors.

Common rituals include:

- Checking rituals: often concerned with safety (e.g., checking over and over again door locks, window locks, or that gas or electric stove knobs, water taps have been turned off). The checking is repeatedly executed, sometimes for hours, resulting in the person being late in his/her daily duties and appointments—a matter that may have serious implications on his/her job and relationships.
- Cleaning rituals: often take the form of repeated handwashing or household cleaning, until the person "feels" it is clean, rather than "seeing" it is clean. Excessive cleaning can have a physical health impact due to constant scrubbing and cleaning on the skin, especially the hands. Sometimes, an obsessive person may avoid entire places at which they experience contamination fears.
- Counting rituals: usually associated with doubting thoughts that necessitate the person to repeat counting to make sure it was carried out adequately; it may be spoken aloud or rehearsed silently. Sometimes counting must be done in a special way, e.g., in threes.
- Dressing rituals: the person has to lay out his/her clothes in a particular way, or put them in a special order. The rituals are usually associated with doubting thoughts that lead to seemingly endless repetition.

3. OBSESSIVE PERFECTIONISM

Perfectionists are persons with high personal standards of performance who give attention to details that are appreciated by others. Those persons are intelligent, hard-working, and passionate about schedule deadlines. In contrast, the obsessive perfectionists typically miss deadlines and fail to carry out outstanding work, or may fail to do any work at all. They have difficulty finishing projects; though, they usually spend excess time and effort working, as they usually get stuck in repeating and rechecking tasks. Because of their lack of tangible output, others may consider them lazy or irresponsible.

4. SYMMETRY AND ORDERLINESS

Symmetry refers to a characteristic feature of an object where one half appears to mirror the other half. The body of most multicellular organisms exhibits some form of symmetry, e.g., facial symmetry generally is one of a number of traits associated with health and beauty. However, excessive or irrational concern with or preference for symmetry may also be indicative of psychopathology. Examples include: perfectly lining up books in a row on a bookshelf, putting canned food items all facing the same way on a cupboard shelf, or perfectly hanging clothes on the rail all facing the same way.

Symmetry and orderliness compulsions exhaust their sufferers, both mentally and physically. Those persons spend a considerable amount of time trying to get precise symmetry. This results in being late for work and appointments, and may have a negative impact on social relationships because of avoiding social contact at home to prevent disturbance of symmetry and order.

5. AVOIDANCE

Avoidance is a common compulsive behavior; a person with OCD will avoid touching particular objects, and avoid objects, places or person/people who trigger their OCD. Avoidance conserves time and alleviates distress and suffering resulting from performing the intrusive thoughts or rituals, e.g., the person who has an obsessional thought of sexually harassing children avoids contact with children.

6. REASSURANCE SEEKING

Obsessive persons commonly ask for assurance as a way to support themselves against their distressing intrusive thoughts, e.g., "Are you sure there is no dirt on my clothes?" "Are you sure nobody got or will get hurt due to my thoughts?" etc.

People with obsessive-compulsive disorder will make every effort to alleviate their distress. If they cannot assure themselves, they may ask for help from the nearest person who they think can assure them. Also, they may even tirelessly spend excessive time searching the Internet for an alleviating answer.

Case Example of OCD

XY is a 33-year-old male, suffering from excessive preoccupation with ideas of getting dirty and fear of catching HIV or hepatitis C infection. Thus, he is particularly concerned with urine, feces, saliva, and semen. The obsessive ideas push XY to do repeated meticulous cleaning and washing rituals, spending a lot of time in handwashing, showers, and lengthy wiping and cleaning rituals after using the toilet. However, XY is sure that his ideas and rituals are excessive and unjustifiable.

The patient declared that during his past school years, he spent a lot of time on his homework because of his marked attention to being perfect with no erasures, and spent hours arranging his room. Because of time spent in rechecking work assignments, he usually failed to complete assignments and did not participate in many extracurricular activities. Because of fear of being labeled as crazy, XY was hesitant to go to a therapist.

After about 6 weeks on sertraline 100 mg per day, XY reported a significant improvement in his ability to control his troubling ideas and being able to delay or stop his rituals. however, he continued to obsess about 3 hours per day about contaminants and to wash unduly. The patient accepted adding exposure and response prevention sessions to the SSRI. XY participated in

18 sessions, where he confronted feared contaminants in sessions and at home without ritualizing. By the end, XY improved markedly with improvement in his work and social functioning, and optimistic views about his future.

This case scenario illustrates that:

1. OCD may start in childhood (20 percent of all affected persons in the USA suffer from manifestations of the disorder at age 10 or even earlier).
2. Unlike delusions, OCD patients are distressed by their obsessions, recognizing their absurdity, though they may act on them.
3. OCD symptoms change over time; the theme of OCD is not important in diagnosis, but it may be relevant to the degree of distress and suffering of the patient as in the case of religious obsessions.
4. OCD waxes and wanes over time even without medication.
5. In mild-to-moderate cases patients are able to tolerate cognitive behavior therapy, but in severe cases pharmacotherapy is a good start.

Differential Diagnosis of Obsessions and Compulsion

Obsessive thoughts should be differentiated from:

1. **Preoccupations of healthy people**: normal individuals have varying degrees of preoccupations, and these tend to be exaggerated under stress. Such behaviors can be adaptive and help in adjustment and reaching solutions.
2. **Preoccupations of anxious and depressed patients**: anxious and depressed persons may have a variety of preoccupations that are congruent with their emotional state. They are usually focused on physical health and life stresses but, contrary to normal preoccupations, they are excessive, non-adaptive, and lead to more suffering.
3. **Recurring ideas and urges encountered in sexual deviations or drug dependence**: the person experiences insistent ideas and images restricted only to their sexual practices or drug taking habits, but these ideas are usually welcomed rather than resisted.
4. **Delusions**: the definition of delusions implies that, at least at the peak of a psychotic episode, patients consider their delusions as totally justified true beliefs and they invariably hold firm conviction about their accuracy. Thus, psychotic patients see no reason to doubt the validity of their delusions, to oppose or resist them. By contrast, obsessive patients realize that their obsessive thoughts, images, or impulses are excessive, unreasonable, and rationally unwarranted and thus distressful; features that jointly constitute the "ego-dystonic" nature of obsessions (Oulis et al., 2013).

Delusional beliefs are usually incorporated into patients' total belief system. This incorporation may drive the patient to review some of their beliefs in order to keep their systemic coherence. Similarly, patients' attitudes and possibly their manifest behavior may reflect their delusions, e.g., patients who are persecuted by certain persons may try to avoid or challenge them. By contrast, obsessive patients experience great distress and anxiety due to their "ego-dystonic" nature, and the failed efforts to repress them. The primarily internal origin of anxiety and distress in obsessions contrasts with the external source of anxiety and distress that may result from delusions. This identification of internal or external origin of anxiety can help in differentiating both obsessions and delusions (Oulis et al., 2013).

Compulsions should be differentiated from:

1. **Repetitive delusional behaviors**: delusions may lead to the performance of repetitive acts, e.g., a bizarre delusion that the world will end soon unless the patient repeatedly says some verses or make certain arrangements at home, may push the patient to repeatedly doing such behaviors. Similarly, a patient may check repeatedly whether persecutors are after him/her if the patient has delusions of persecution. Thus, repetitive behaviors in patients with schizophrenia may originate from their delusional beliefs and are congruent with them, and hence these repetitive behaviors do not increase distress or anxiety of the patient, and may even alleviate it (Oulis et al., 2013).

2. **Hoarding**: the inability to discard useless or worn out possessions. The expressed cognitions of individuals who hoard can be understood as an obsessive fear of losing things and compulsions to acquire and save objects, and hence, hoarding symptoms were often classified as an aspect of OCD until DSM-5. A number of factors suggest that hoarding may be a unique variation or even entirely distinct from OCD. Unlike obsessions, hoarding thoughts are not generally experienced as troubling or intrusive; instead they feel like a normal stream of thought. More than 80 percent of individuals with hoarding symptoms do not show any of the core symptoms of OCD, while hoarding symptoms are more often comorbid with major depression, social phobia, and generalized anxiety disorder than with OCD (Bloch et al., 2014).

3. **Body dysmorphic disorder**: characterized by preoccupation with one or more perceived defects or flaws in physical appearance that are not observable or appear only slight to others, and by repetitive behaviors (e.g., mirror checking, excessive grooming, skin picking, or reassurance seeking), or mental acts (e.g., comparing one's appearance flaws with those of other people) in response to the appearance concerns.

4. **Trichotillomania (hair-pulling disorder)**: characterized by recurrent pulling out of one's hair resulting in hair loss, and repeated attempts to decrease or stop hair pulling.

5. **Excoriation (skin picking)**: disorder characterized by recurrent picking of one's skin resulting in skin lesions and repeated attempts to decrease or stop skin picking.

The body-focused repetitive behaviors that characterize trichotillomania and excoriation are not triggered by obsessions or preoccupations; however, they may be preceded or accompanied by various emotional states, such as feelings of anxiety or boredom. They may also be preceded by an increasing sense of tension or may lead to gratification, pleasure, or a sense of relief when the hair is pulled out or the skin is picked. Individuals with these disorders may have varying degrees of conscious awareness of the behavior while engaging in it, with some individuals displaying more focused attention on the behavior (with preceding tension and subsequent relief) and other individuals displaying more automatic behavior (with the behaviors seeming to occur without full awareness).

Obsessive-Compulsive Disorder (OCD) in Children

Children's OCD symptoms are essentially similar to adults'. Unlike adults who can tell about the rationale of their compulsive act, e.g., I wash my hands repeatedly as I feel they are dirty, children may not be able to explain their underlying worries, and consequently may not ask for help, though they may try to minimize their compulsions in front of others to avoid any blame. Therefore, caregivers should make every effort to identify these symptoms and seek treatment.

It may be difficult for parents, teachers, and peers to understand thoughts and behaviors associated with obsessive-compulsive disorder. Variation of these symptoms over time and change in the way they appear can further complicate its understanding and diagnosis. The symptoms may also fluctuate, with more symptoms displayed at stressful periods and fewer symptoms at other times. Thus, recognizing the obsessive-compulsive disorder symptoms may be challenging, as the symptoms can easily be misinterpreted as willful disregard, opposition, or meaningless worry.

Children are usually resistant to stopping the obsessions or compulsions and show extreme distress if others interrupt a ritual. At school, students may be successful in suppressing symptoms, while they may be unable to do so at home. Families often seek treatment once symptoms affect school performance, which may stem from difficulty concentrating (due to persistent, repetitive thoughts), social isolation, low self-esteem, and problem behaviors, such as fights or arguments, resulting from misunderstandings between the child and peers or staff.

Insight and Obsession

Although a main feature of OCD is that the person recognizes that the obsessional thoughts, impulses, or images are the product of his or her own mind, in some cases there is poor or even a lack of insight into their symptoms, where an individual does not recognize that the obsessions or compulsions are excessive or unreasonable. The presence of overvalued ideation denotes poor insight while a degree of delusional intensity corresponds to a lack of insight. The general view is that there is a continuum from an obsession, with full or good insight at one end of the continuum, to a poorer insight with overvalued ideation in the middle, and a delusional intensity of belief at the other extreme; a matter that was included in DSM-5 specifiers of OCD (good or fair insight, poor insight, and absent insight/delusional beliefs).

Clinicians experienced with OCD recognize that insight into the senselessness of obsessive-compulsive fears is often situation-bound: an individual is more likely to demonstrate insight under non-threat conditions, i.e., when there is no impending contact with the feared situation, than when facing such a situation. Thus, when patients are asked during a clinical interview how they assess danger "objectively," they are more likely to show insight than when they are afraid.

Observations of lack of insight by some patients about their obsessive beliefs raise questions about the distinction between obsessions and delusion, and the relation between OCD and schizophrenia or psychosis in general.

Obsessions and Psychosis

A major distinguishing feature of psychosis is impaired reality testing, and the presence of delusions constitutes an indicator of such impairment. If delusions entail psychosis, can obsessive-compulsives who perceive their obsessions as sensible and do not resist them be considered delusional, and therefore psychotic?

There is robust interest in the relationship between obsession and schizophrenia; obsessive-compulsive syndrome was considered at a time as a prodrome or as a form of schizophrenia. *Research in this area is full of limitations and flaws, and led to the following conclusions:*

1. Some obsessive patients may lack insight about their obsessions (become delusional).
2. Some schizophrenic patients have obsessive symptoms either during prodrome or active illness.
3. Some individuals meet criteria for both OCD and schizophrenia. However, the rates of schizophrenia among those with OCD do not indicate a special association between the two disorders. Comorbidity of OCD with other anxiety disorders and with depression is considerably higher than that with schizophrenia.

PERCEPTUAL DISORDERS

In order to survive and function well in the world, an animal needs to know what is in its environment. The main processes involved in our exploration of the world are sensation and perception.

Sensation is the process through which the senses detect visual, auditory, and other sensory stimuli and transmit them to the brain.

Perception is the process by which sensory information is actively organized and interpreted by the brain, i.e., it is the process of giving meaning to a sensation. Perceptual disorders include sensory distortion, sensory deception, or disorders in the experience of time.

Distortion of Perception

A real perceptual object is perceived in a distorted way:

1. **Change in intensity of perception:**

   - **Hyperesthesia**: lowering of physiological threshold leading to increased intensity of stimuli:

     – for sounds, e.g., in anxiety, the person cannot tolerate noises;
     – for colors, e.g., some people under the effect of LSD see colors brighter than they are.

   - **Hypothesia**: in depression, surroundings look dim and lifeless, colors look dull and pale, and everything is tasteless. In delirium, patients have hypoacusis (hearing threshold is high), which is accentuated by defective attention. So it is important to speak to those patients loudly and slowly, to enable them to hear and attend properly.

2. **Change in quality of perception**: perceptions may be abnormally heightened, dulled, or take on a different quality, e.g.:

   - **Mania**: everything looks perfect and beautiful.
   - **Depression**: things appear unreal and strange.
   - **Toxic substances may color perception**: colorings of yellow, green, and red have been named xanthopsia, chloropsia, and erythropsia respectiely.

3. **Change in form of perception (Dysmegalopsia):**

   - **Micropsia, Macropsia**: stimuli look smaller or bigger respectively. This is usually met with in organic mental disorders (particularly related to temporal lobe) and delirium (particularly alcoholic withdrawal delirium).

- **Metamorphopsia**: stimuli are perceived as mutilated or irregular in shape, occurring in dreams, edema or scars of the retina, but most commonly in depression where the disfigurement of mutilation is related to the patient attitude toward the world.
- **Split perception**: the patient is unable to form the usual link between two or more perceptions. The patient sees a bird and hears its sound but is unable to feel the connection between the bird and the song. The sound of the TV is split from the picture as if the patient is listening to a radio and simultaneously watching a silent film. The words of a speaking person may sound like they are coming from a far source while the person is perceived independently. This occurs in organic mental disorders and in the case of schizophrenia.
- **Trailing phenomenon**: moving objects are perceived as a series of discrete and discontinuous items or images. This serial disconnection may be related to disconnection of time sense. This phenomenon is usually associated with the use of hallucinogenic drugs.

Deception of Perception (False Perception)

A new perception exists that may or may not be in response to external stimuli; this includes illusions or hallucinations (respectively).

Hallucinations

Hallucinations are false perceptions without an external stimulus. *Proper hallucinations have the following characteristics:*

- They are actual false perceptions, not distortions of real perceptions.
- They are experienced as being out there in the world and as inhabiting objective space.
- They are experienced as having the qualities and force of the corresponding normal perceptions. Hallucinations do not yield to arguments, but the experienced reality of hallucinations can vary. So, we may find a patient who tries to explain how the voices or visions differ from actual perceptions.
- They are usually experienced alongside and simultaneously with normal perceptions (complex visions may be an exception). However, patients usually find no difficulty in discriminating between their hallucinations and true perceptions, so a telephone operator who is continually troubled by auditory hallucinations may continue his work efficiently.
- They are as independent of our will as are any normal perceptions, i.e., they cannot be called or dismissed. The hallucination may show a greater independence from will and action than a normal perception, e.g., though I can turn away from looking at a page in front of me or cease attending to the voice of a lecturer, my hallucinations will continue to

force themselves on my attention. Thus, hallucinated voices will continue even after destruction of the ear drums, thus producing deafness and silence of the rest of the world. Similarly, a blind person can experience visual hallucinations.

Classification of Hallucinations

Hallucinations can be classified according to different perspectives; *these include*:

ACCORDING TO SENSORY MODALITY

1. **Auditory hallucination**: the most frequently encountered type of hallucination, and particularly important in primary psychotic illnesses. Some patients perceive hallucinated voices as originating within their heads, whereas others perceive them as coming from outside, like normal conversation. Although some consider the former to be relatively healthier and/or more insightful, this has not been established. *Auditory hallucination may take the form of*:

   • Vague voices, indistinct sounds, or a buzzing or ringing in the ears. These less distinct hallucinations are less valuable to establishing a diagnosis of schizophrenia. Hallucinations of buzzing or elemental sounds are more suggestive of a neurologic problem (e.g., ear, acoustic nerve, or central auditory system pathology). Ringing in the ears, or tinnitus, occurs with ototoxic drugs. Formed musical hallucinations can occur in psychotic illnesses, and occasionally in patients with right temporal lobe epileptiform discharges.

   • Clearly articulated voices are most frequently reported by psychotic patients. If the voices give directives or instructions, they are termed command auditory hallucinations. These voices give commands to patients: e.g., "Hit him." Auditory hallucinations are often insulting, or critical of the patient. Some voices may give commands to patients, e.g., hit him. Certain types of auditory hallucinations are classified among the first rank symptoms (Schneiderian). *These include*:

     – auditory hallucinations of one or more voice in a running commentary that remark on the patient's thoughts and behavior;
     – hearing more than one voice conversing with each other referring to the patient as he or she (e.g., he is a homosexual);
     – hearing thoughts spoken aloud—patients hear their own thoughts as a voice at the same time as they think of them, not afterwards.

   Auditory hallucinations usually occurs in one's own language but could occur in a foreign or even a new language. In themselves they do not point to a particular diagnosis, but their content and especially the patient's reaction may do so, e.g., voices with derogatory content suggest severe depressive disorder, especially when the patient accepts them as justified, e.g., "you are wicked"; in schizophrenia the patient more often resents such comments.

2. **Visual hallucination**: false perception involving vision, consisting of both formed (complex) images, e.g., people, and ill-defined (elementary) images and colors, e.g., flashes of light. They may appear normal or abnormal in size; if the latter, they are more often smaller than the corresponding real percept (sometimes called Lilliputian). Visual hallucinations occur in many mental disorders, often in conjunction with auditory hallucinations. However, visual and tactile hallucinations are usually linked to organic conditions (Tombini et al., 2012); i.e., they occur more in cases of dementia, delirium, recently developed blindness, drug withdrawal states, drug intoxications (e.g., hallucinogenic, anticholinergic, or dopaminergic substances), temporal lobe epilepsy, migraine, and other organic mental disorders. Ill-defined visual experiences occur in ocular and neurologic diseases, e.g., flashing lights occur with retinal detachment, whereas scintillating lights, a series of undulating jagged lines, blurred areas, or dark spots occur in migraine (scotomas). Seeing a curtain of darkness over the lower visual field is a sign of transient ischemic attack. Small dark specks, called floaters, that drift across the visual field are a common and benign result of senescent changes in the eye.

3. **Olfactory hallucination**: false perception of smell usually experienced as an unpleasant smell. It may occur in schizophrenia or severe depressive disorders, but it should also suggest temporal lobe epilepsy or irritation of the olfactory bulb or pathways by a tumor.

4. **Gustatory hallucination**: false perception of taste such as an experience of unpleasant taste may be caused by an uncinate seizure.

5. **Tactile (haptic) hallucination**: false perception of touch or surface sensation. This may be experienced as sensations of being touched, held, hit, pricked, or strangled. It may also be felt as movements just below the skin, which the patient may attribute to insects, worms, or other small creatures burrowing through the tissues (formication). In cocaine psychosis this type of hallucination usually occurs together with delusions of persecution and is known as "cocaine bugs." Some patients may feel cool winds blowing on them, a sensation of heat, or electrical sensations. Tactile hallucination may also take sexual coloring to form what is called sexual hallucination, e.g., orgasm or erection forced on males, and rape or sexual abuse with females. It usually suggests schizophrenia especially if interpreted in an unusual way, e.g., resulting from intercourse with a series of persecutors.

6. **Proprioceptive hallucination**: it affects deep sensation or sense of position. Thus, hallucinations are related to muscle and joint sense, e.g., the

patient feels that their limbs are being bent or twisted, or their muscles squeezed.

7. **Kinesthetic hallucinations**: perceptions of the movements of body parts that are not actually moving.
8. **Vestibular hallucination**: a sense of flying through the air, or sinking into the bed. It occurs in acute organic states and delirium.
9. **Somatic hallucinations** (visceral hallucinations, cenesthetic hallucination): peculiar bodily sensations that are not perceived under appropriate physiological conditions in or to the body organs, most often visceral in origin, e.g., feeling of electricity running through one's body, burning sensation in the brain, or flowing of blood inside blood vessels. Sometimes, somatic hallucinations merge with tactile hallucinations or delusional beliefs about bodily change, making difficulties in distinguishing them. One patient may describe his semen drawn out of him by an evil presence. Clearly connected with this bizarre delusional belief is tactile hallucination involving the perceptions of being pricked with pins and tingling sensations around the base of the spine, but also somatic hallucinations involving the experience of the testicles and penis shrinking into the abdomen and the spine feeling as if it is hollow and cracking. Somatic hallucinations may accompany epileptic activity. A common autonomic aura is the so-called epigastric aura, a rising feeling originating in the abdomen and climbing to the chest, throat, and/or mouth; this reflects a partial seizure involving the mesial temporal region.
10. **Multimodal or scenic hallucinations**: complex visual and auditory hallucinations are experienced.

ACCORDING TO RELATION TO EMOTIONAL STATE

This depends on whether the contents of hallucinations match the patient's mood (mood congruent) or not (mood incongruent); e.g., in depression the patient may hear voices that disregard and humiliate him/her.

ACCORDING TO COMPLEXITY

1. **Elementary hallucinations**: ill-formed stimuli such as flashes of light, tinnitus, or buzzing. Olfactory and gustatory hallucinations are predominantly elementary.
2. **Complex and elaborate hallucinations**: more sophisticated and relatively meaningful stimuli such as hearing voices or seeing persons.

ACCORDING TO EGO-QUALITY

1. **Ego syntonic**: hallucinations go in harmony with the ego, so the patient does not complain about it unless they are uncovered by chance or become disturbing and handicapping (ego dystonic).

2. **Ego alien**: hallucinations are perceived as a strange, foreign body apart from the self. They are further classified into ego syntonic (in harmony and accepted by the patient), or ego dystonic (noxious and boring).

ACCORDING TO OTHER ASSOCIATES

1. **Functional hallucination** (conditioned hallucination): an external stimulus is necessary to provoke hallucination, but the normal perception of the stimulus and the hallucination in the same modality are experienced simultaneously. For example, "each time the patient hears a dog barking he hears a voice calling his name." Both hallucination and provoking stimulus are perceived at the same time.
2. **Reflex hallucination**: stimulation of one sense evokes hallucination in another sense, e.g., the sound of music may provoke visual hallucination, or pain is felt in the head when the patient hears other patients sneeze and he/she is convinced that the sneezing caused the pain, or "a man hears insulting voices when he is driving only when the traffic light is amber, and it ceases with the red and green lights." It may occur after taking drugs such as LSD or rarely in schizophrenia.

A similar phenomenon called synesthesia is described in some people where one of the five senses simultaneously stimulates another sense. A person with such a condition may not only see alphabets but also associate them with particular scents. This happens when the different parts of the brain that are responsible for identifying color, sound, taste, and smell somehow get interlinked and thus one sense triggers another sense. In literature, synesthesia refers to a technique adopted by writers to present ideas, characters, or places in such a manner that they appeal to more than one sense, such as hearing, seeing, smell etc., at a given time.

SPECIAL TYPES OF HALLUCINATIONS

1. **Thought echo** (*echo de la pensée*): hearing one's own thought being spoken aloud.
2. **Extracampine**: hallucinations out of the field of perception, e.g., a person sees someone standing behind him/her.
3. **Autoscopy**: the experience of seeing all or part of one's own body projected into external space, usually in front of oneself, for short periods. This experience may convince the person that he/she has a double. It occurs in a small minority of patients with temporal lobe epilepsy or other organic brain disorders.
4. **Negative autoscopy**: projected self-nihilism; on looking at a mirror the patient sees the mirror blank, not reflecting his/her figure as he/she does not exist.

5. **Negative hallucination**: failure to perceive things that are present. This occurs in dissociative states.
6. **Lilliputian hallucination**: false perception in which objects are seen as reduced in size (also termed micropsia).
7. **Trailing phenomenon**: perceptual abnormality associated with hallucinogenic drugs in which moving objects are seen as a series of discrete and discontinuous images.

Reaction to Hallucinations

This varies in different patients:

1. **Astonishment**: it usually occurs with genuine hallucinations and in early psychosis where insight is still preserved and critical attitude to the starting experience is coloring the picture.
2. **Anger**: when the patient views the hallucinatory voices or figures as enemies.
3. **Terror**: may be a reaction to a hallucinatory threat or a reaction to the experience of change in self in early psychosis.
4. **Discourse (conversation)**: more with visual than auditory hallucinations.
5. **Habituation**: as the hallucination persists, it becomes a part of the patient's life.
6. **Welcome**: in chronic cases of schizophrenia, hallucinations form part of the personality and become indispensable.
7. **Obedience**: this is associated with passivity phenomenon.
8. **Resistance**: this is another form of resentment that is less strong than anger; however, it could denote some sort of insight into the hallucinatory experience.

Causes of Hallucinations

1. **Normal hallucination** may be met in the following conditions:

   - **Hypnagogic and hypnopompic hallucinations**: false perception occurring while falling asleep and while awakening from sleep, respectively. Although frightening, these perceptual disturbances are naturally occurring phenomena (Cheyne & Girard, 2007), and are generally considered non-pathological. They occur during drowsiness, are discontinuous, appear to force themselves on the subject, and do not form part of a dream. They may take the form of geometrical designs, faces, and figures or scenes from nature. Auditory hallucination may take the form of animal noises, musical sounds, hearing one's name being called, and sometimes the voice says a sentence or phrase that has no meaning. In a subject deprived of sleep, a hypnagogic state

may occur, in which case there are hallucinatory voices, visual hallucinations, ideas of persecution, and no insight into the morbid
phenomenon. This condition usually disappears after the subject has
had a good sleep.

- **After physical stimulation of sense organs**: e.g., flashes after pressing
  the eyeball.

2. **Psychological disorders**:

   - **Psychotic disorders**: e.g., schizophrenia, and mood disorders with
     psychotic features.
   - **Sensory deprivation**: blocking or reduction of all incoming stimuli
     to a minimum in normal subjects usually results in hallucination in
     those subjects. These hallucinations are usually in the form of visual
     hallucination and repetitive words and phrases.
   - **Situations of extreme stress**: whether physical or mental, where
     high levels of general arousal are present, fleeting perceptual disturb-
     ances may be present.
   - **Grief**: hallucinations and pseudo-hallucinations of the lost one are
     common and are normal phenomena.

3. **Toxic state**: e.g., anticholinergic toxicity, hallucinogenic drugs.
4. **Psychomotor epilepsy.**
5. **CNS lesions**: either due to focal lesion, e.g., tumors, encephalitis, or due
   to systemic disease.

DIAGNOSTIC GUIDELINE

Hallucinations carry no specific diagnostic significance to a particular disorder.
However, some characteristics may be of value in prioritized certain disorders:

1. **Organic hallucinations**: always occur in clouded consciousness, are mostly
   visual, accompanied by fear and have an acute onset and rapid course.
   They could be understood to arise from diminished awareness and
   apprehension.
2. **Schizophrenia**: hallucinations always occur in clear consciousness, are
   mostly auditory, typically discussing the patient in the third person, commenting on his/her acts, repeating his/her thoughts or calling his/her
   name. They have an insidious onset and prolonged course. They cannot
   be understood as arising from other mental mechanisms.
3. **Depressive disorders**: hallucinations occur in clear consciousness and
   may be accusatory voices, scenes of deaths, or somatic or bodily changes.
   The patient accepts them because they relieve his/her sense of guilt. The
   contents of depressive hallucinations are understandable as arising from
   the depressive mood or the sense of guilt.

Case Example of Hallucinations

AW is a 20-year-old man who presented to outpatient clinic with his mother. The mother stated that her son had been socially withdrawn along the past few months; he stayed alone most of the time, sometimes speaking and laughing with himself. AW affirmed that he heard voices whose source he could not determine. The voices heard by AW may negatively comment on his action, and occasionally they spy. Sometimes he heard derogatory conversations by more than one voice. Occasionally the voices joked with AW.

What Are the Main Symptoms in This Case?

Auditory hallucination is the main symptom in this case: sometimes AW heard one voice only, but occasionally he heard more than one voice talking to him (third voice auditory hallucination). The voices negatively comment on AW's actions, but also occasionally joke with him.

Is It Possible to Give a Conclusive Diagnosis Based on These Data?

Auditory hallucination clearly refers to the presence of a psychotic disorder; however, its type needs more additional data. Though commenting and third voice auditory hallucination were at once diagnostic of schizophrenia (Schneiderian first rank symptoms), current classifications do not give them this advantage.

So, it is not possible to give a conclusive diagnosis based on this case scenario; there is a need to investigate the presence of depressive symptoms that may explain the presence of voices making negative comments, spying on him, and making derogatory conversation (mood congruent).

Symptoms that may refer to schizophrenia in this case scenario include voices joking with the patient, though it needs more clarification. Social withdrawal may be present in depression and schizophrenia. Others symptoms (e.g., sleep, eating), past psychiatric history, other items of mental state examinations, and course of symptoms will help in reaching final diagnosis.

Differential Diagnosis of Hallucinations

1. **Illusions**: see below.
2. **Misinterpretation**: the person perceives normal percepts, but he/she wrongly interprets its value or meaning. Thus, a shiny metal may be mistaken by the weary prospector for gold.
3. **Pareidolia**: a state in which real and unreal percepts exist side by side, the latter being recognized as unreal. The perceptions can be called up by ill-defined sense impressions such as those that occur when staring into the dying embers of an open fire, or seeing different shapes on staring at

cracks on a wall. Pareidolia can occur in a considerable portion of normal people and can be induced deliberately; causes include use of psycho-mimetic drugs and acute organic disorders caused by fever.

4. **Mental imagery**: the simulation or re-creation of perceptual experience across sensory modalities in the absence of appropriate external stimuli, which can be called up and terminated by voluntary effort. Imagery experiences are understood by experiencing persons as echoes, copies, or reconstructions of actual perceptual experiences from their past; at other times they may seem to anticipate possible, often desired or feared, future experiences. Such imagery has been shown to play a key role in various psychological disorders, including posttraumatic stress disorder (PTSD), social phobia, prospective imagery in schizophrenia, and depression.

5. **Pseudo-hallucinations**: a perceptual experience that is recognized by the subject as having no external correlate, it may have a definite outline and vivid details, it may be retained for some time, but it cannot be deliberately evoked. It is sometimes described as an "as if experience." Pseudo-hallucinations are not pathognomonic of any particular mental illness, and may occur in people without mental illness at times of life crisis, e.g., during bereavement. Therefore, the significance of pseudo-hallucination lies only in its differential diagnosis from hallucination, as pseudo-hallucination is not necessarily psychopathological.

Illusions

Illusions are misperception or misinterpretation of a real external stimulus, such as hearing the rustling of leaves as the sound of voices, or seeing a rope as a snake. The perceptual stimulus arises from an actual object and the illusion is formed by the perception's transformation. Other characteristics of illusions are identical to those of hallucinations. However, illusions have a more transient nature than hallucinations and often vanish when attention is drawn to the misperception. *Illusions are most likely to occur in the following conditions*:

1. **A reduced general level of stimulation**; thus they are more common at dusk and in dim light.
2. **A reduced level of consciousness**: a delirious patient may mistake in-animate objects for people even with good illumination.
3. **Reduced focusing** on the sensory modality.
4. **The presence of a strong affective state**: a frightened person in a dark lane is more likely to misperceive the outline of a bush as that of an attacker.
5. **Epilepsy**, especially temporal lobe epilepsy.

The following are special kinds of illusions:

- **Déjà vu (illusion of familiarity)**: a new situation is incorrectly perceived as duplication of a previous one, i.e., the sense of having previously seen or lived the current setting or situation.
- **Jamais vu (illusion of unfamiliarity)**: a familiar situation is incorrectly perceived as a new, unfamiliar one.
- **Déjà entendu**: illusion that you have already heard something similar before, e.g., a new song.
- **Déjà pensé**: a totally new thought looks familiar to the person who feels that he/she has had the same thought before.

These symptoms have been associated with complex partial epilepsy, but can occur in a variety of psychiatric and neurologic disorders, and, if of moderate or less degree, can be experienced by otherwise healthy persons.

Disorders of the Experience of Time

These disorders can be looked on as distortions of perception and logically should be discussed in the section of sensory distortions. From the psychopathological point of view there are two varieties of time, physical and personal. The first is determined by physical events, while the second is a personal judgment of the passage of time. The influence of mood on the experience is well known; when we are happy the time flies, but it drags when we are sad. Some investigators found that psychotic patients show differences of time judgment. Patients with organic brain syndrome without gross disorientation may overestimate the passage of time.

Depersonalization and Derealization

Depersonalization is a feeling that one's self or one's body is unreal or unfamiliar. This includes a sense of being outside of one's self, that one's goals or mores are wrongheaded or meaningless; it is generally accompanied by anxiety or dysphoria. **Derealization** refers to the feeling that the world is unreal or has abruptly taken on unreal characteristics. Except in the most extreme cases, patients with depersonalization or derealization have the feelings of unreality, yet intellectually recognize what is or is not real. Thus, depersonalization and derealization are usually not delusional. Depersonalization and derealization are most commonly encountered in borderline personality disorder, partial complex seizure disorders, conversion or hysterical disorders, early or mild psychotic states, and normal adolescence. These experiences are usually transient, lasting minutes to hours, but may recur. Some patients experience both derealization and depersonalization.

DISTURBANCE OF ORIENTATION

Orientation is the ability to locate oneself accurately in one's environment with reference to time, place, and people at the present moment. Various perceptual cues and correct sense of time and place enable the person to come to appropriate conclusions from his/her context. Orientation to person, place, and time is a basic cognitive function. Essentially, this means that patients should know who they are, where they are, and what the time and date are. Disorientation makes it difficult for the patient to understand the context of his/her present situation or to connect outside objects and events with him/herself. *Orientation is assessed by asking the person about*:

1. **Time**: this is tested by asking the time of day, day of the week, month, day of the month, year, and season.
2. **Place**: this is tested by determining whether the patient knows the name of the hospital or clinic and the floor of the building; the city and state in which the interview is taking place.
3. **Person**: orientation to person is the ability of the person to identify those around him/her, including to one's family and friends, and those in contact with the patient in the hospital or clinic. Impairment usually begins with those least well known to the patient: the nurses, doctors, therapists. Their names or functions may be forgotten, and, more commonly, they may be misidentified as hotel staff, as an old friend, or as torturers. Next, more familiar persons, such as neighbors or family members, may be misidentified. And finally, the patient may no longer know his or her own identity.

It is not unusual that a patient who has spent a lengthy time convalescing may not be sure about the exact time or date. However, a cognitively intact person can usually give an approximate date, and it is unusual for them not to know the day, month, or year they are in. Similarly, orientation to persons usually remains intact except in patients with severe cognitive disorders. Thus, one could presume that a patient who is disoriented to persons, but otherwise cognitively intact, is most likely suffering from another disorder (e.g., a dissociative disorder), or possibly malingering, rather than having a cognitive disorder.

Orientation for time is worth testing in all patients, as it is usually the first to suffer in the course of mild impairment of consciousness or intellectual impairment, followed by place and, lastly, person. Milder degrees of disorientation are shown by inaccuracy of more than half an hour for the time of day or duration of interview, while more advanced states are demonstrated with incorrect day of the week, year, or period of day. With further disturbance the season of the year is not known correctly.

Orientation in place is disturbed later in the disease process than time. A patient may be unable to find his/her way, especially in an area that is relatively new to him/her. Disorientation in time and place are, when clearly established, evidence of an organic mental state. In disorientation for person, the patient fails to remember names of his/her own relatives.

Disordered orientation is caused by all causes of organic brain diseases, either acute or chronic. However, it is to be noted that disorientation can occur without organic brain disease; it may be present in situations where the patient has no access to the sensory cues that are required for orientation, e.g., hospitalized patients commonly lose track of the exact day of the month, but should remain clear on the month, season, and year, and should be close on the day of the week and whether it is the beginning, middle, or end of the month.

Delusions that mimic disorientation: a delusion may result in misinterpretation of place, of a situation or of person (delusions of misorientation), e.g., a person on the ward may believe him/herself to be in prison and a visiting relative may be considered to be an interrogator from the Gestapo. Both consciousness and memory are not disturbed with delusions of misorientation.

Dissociation and disorientation: a patient with dissociative disorders may mimic disorientation. However, careful examination of mental state is likely to reveal discrepancies, e.g., disorientation for a person may be much more marked than for time, or may be bizarre to an excessive extent.

Although disorientation is most commonly observed in confused states and severe amnestic syndromes, extensive damage to the prefrontal cortex (usually bilateral) may result in disorientation. Damage to the frontal lobes from trauma or surgery can also impair orientation. An unusual condition, called transient global amnesia, also involves temporary disorientation and memory deficits, possibly related to temporal lobe dysfunction. Moderately to severely demented persons can become disoriented. Sedation from medications can also interfere with orientation. Psychotic patients usually retain reasonably good orientation, unless impaired by marked disorganization of thought processes or marked preoccupation with delusions or hallucinations.

DISTURBANCE OF ATTENTION AND CONCENTRATION

Attention is an umbrella term for a number of processes and abilities. These include the ability to focus consciousness on a single aspect of the environment or activity (voluntary attentional vigilance) on one hand, and automatic, uncontrollable responses to unusual or unexpected events (involuntary attentional capture) on the other hand. This division of attentional processing into automatic and controlled processes has led to the development of what are called two-process theories. Automatic processes require fewer of our precious mental "resources" to operate, as they are automatic. This, in itself, would make them very valuable as we can get some things done while directing our limited resources elsewhere. Concentration is the ability to sustain attention over a period of time. It could be affected by various variables including motivation, emotional state, preoccupation with other stimuli, and a lot of medical causes.

Three systems are involved in the physiology of attention: Ascending Reticular Activating system (ARAS), intralaminar thalamic nuclei, and cerebral cortex. The ascending RAS projects to the intralaminar nuclei of the thalamus that projects widely throughout the cortex. A small lesion in the ARAS results in coma. However bilateral extensive lesion of the cortex is needed to disturb arousal, but does not result in coma. It is to be noted that attention is a different function from consciousness, but dependent on it. Thus, variable degrees of attention are possible with full consciousness, but complete attention and concentration is impossible with diminished consciousness.

Disturbances of Attention

Sohlberg and Mateer (1989) described five different kinds of attentional activities of increasing difficulty; they are useful for the evaluation of attention in patients with different neurologic pathologies.

Focused attention refers to the most basic level of attention; the ability to respond discretely to specific visual, auditory, or tactile stimuli. Focused attention impairments are seen most commonly in people with a decreased level of consciousness, such as those emerging from coma. When individuals emerge from coma, they gradually progress from responding only to internal states (such as pain) to noticing events in the external environment. **Trance** is a state of focused attention and altered consciousness; it is usually seen in hypnosis, dissociative disorders, and ecstatic religious experiences. **Narrowing of attention** refers to restriction of attention to a limited set of critical scenes in stressful situations. It results in a person processing a narrow band of information, and neglecting other information, e.g., when driving to the hospital for a medical emergency, the driver focuses attention on the road ahead and neglects events at the side of the road. It should be noted that hallucinations and delusions may also direct involuntary attention elsewhere, causing narrowing of attention.

Sustained attention refers to the ability to stick with an activity over time; the ability to maintain a consistent behavioral response during continuous and repetitive activity. After a brain injury, individuals often have difficulty maintaining their attention or concentration on any one task. They may become easily tired or fatigued. Tasks that they carried out prior to the injury, automatically, or without much effort (such as holding a conversation, writing a sentence, driving a car), may now require a greater amount of energy and concentration to complete. Problems with sustained attention may also show up as inconsistent performance on an activity or task. There may be periods of very accurate performance, and periods where the person makes lots of mistakes—or cannot do the task at all.

Selective attention is the ability to ignore distractions in the environment and pay attention to the important information, i.e., to maintain a behavioral or cognitive set in the face of distracting or competing stimuli. Impairments in this area are evident when individuals are easily distracted by surrounding noise in their environment, e.g., after brain injury a person may have difficulty paying attention to a conversation or task if traffic is going by the window, children are playing nearby, or other people are talking in the background. People with impairments in selective attention may become easily irritated and frustrated by such extraneous noise.

Alternating attention is the ability to switch attention easily from task to task, i.e., the mental flexibility that allows individuals to shift their focus of attention and move between tasks having different cognitive requirements. People with this impairment may continue to perform aspects of the original task after they have moved on to a new activity.

Divided attention is the highest level of attention and refers to the ability to respond simultaneously to multiple tasks or multiple task demands at the same time. Normally our brains are able to take in information from several sources simultaneously, e.g., we can drive our cars while listening to the radio or talking with a companion. After a brain injury, a person may have difficulty paying attention to more than one thing at a time.

The degree to which attention deficits occur can vary greatly among individuals. Following a brain injury, a person may experience one specific type of attention difficulty (such as not being able to handle distracting noise), or have a more generalized attention problem, with difficulty across all types of attention. The severity of attention problems may cover a broad range of experience. One person may encounter severe impairments in focused attention, while another may be challenged by subtle problems with alternating or divided attention. Fortunately, the severity of attention impairment often lessens over time as the person recovers from the injury.

Causes of Impaired Attention and Concentration

Attention is reduced in normal people during sleep and sleep-deprived hypnotic states, fatigue, and boredom. Attention is reduced pathologically in organic states, metabolic disorders, intoxication, withdrawal syndromes, head injury, epilepsy, cerebrovascular stroke, and increased intracranial pressure. These conditions are associated with lowering of consciousness.

Psychological conditions that can interfere with concentration include attention deficit hyperactivity disorder, anxiety, depression, bipolar disorder, emotional trauma, and stress.

Therefore, abnormalities of attention and concentration do not refer to specific diagnosis. Nevertheless, these abnormalities are important in a management plan; the safety of patients should be considered and decision making in this condition needs careful consideration and revision from caregivers.

Assessment of Attention and Concentration

Marked difficulties with attention and concentration will usually become apparent in the course of history taking and examination. Note deficiencies on the way in which attention is aroused or sustained, whether the patient is readily distracted by external or internal stimuli, and whether attention fluctuates from one moment to another. There may be difficulties in shifting attention from one topic to another, or attention may be diffuse so that it cannot be directed to a particular purpose.

There are a number of traditional means of testing concentration:

1. **Digit span test**: repeating a series of numbers in the order in which they are presented and then backward. Some claim that a normal person should be able to sequence 6 ($\pm$1) numbers forward, and 5 ($\pm$1) numbers backward. The digits must be delivered in an even tone and at a rate of one per second if accurate comparisons are to be made. Begin with a two-digit series, then proceed to a three-digit series, four, five, and so on, until the patient cannot perform correctly. Once the digit span, that is, the maximum number of digits done correctly on two consecutive trials, is established, then the patient should be asked to repeat some series backward.

2. **Repeating in reverse order test**: e.g., the days of the week or the months of the year in a reverse order.

3. **Serial subtraction test**: using, for example, serial seven- or serial three-subtraction tests: ask the patient to subtract 7 from 100 and repeat the subtraction from each remainder ($100 - 7 = 93 - 7 = 86 - 7 = 79$, etc.). In serial three-subtraction test: ask the patient to subtract 3 from 100 and repeat the subtraction from each remainder ($100 - 3 = 97 - 3 = 94 - 3 = 91$, etc.). Generally, the patient should be asked to perform five subtractions. In patients with an IQ below 80, subtract 3 serially from 30. Some claim that a normal person should be able to subtract serial 7s without mistakes within 90 seconds. Patients who have difficulty concentrating might try to think out loud or they might try to use their fingers (discourage this). Or they might lose track of the task, or have long pauses

between numbers. These are all indicative of some degree of difficulty in concentrating, even if the calculations are correct.

4. **Counting backward test**: a simple test is to ask the patient to count backward starting at 65 and stopping at 49. The task should be stated only once and not repeated after the counting has begun. Inattentive persons will continue counting beyond 49, or will lose track of the task during the counting. This is a good test for the elderly, in whom serial sevens may be too sensitive to the effects of normal aging.

5. **Spelling backward test**: spelling various simple words backward, e.g. spelling the word WORLD or EARTH backward.

6. **Standardized tests**: tests that assess attention and concentration include the Trail Making Tests, Symbol Digit Test, Mesulam's Cancellation Tests, and Stroop Color-Word Test.

MEMORY DISTURBANCE

Memory is a very broad function that includes several distinct abilities. Memory could be defined as the capacity to retain information over time and to retrieve that information later. It involves the encoding, storage, and retrieval of information. Some memories are temporary, whereas others become more permanent. *Human memory behaves as if organized in three kinds of "stores"*:

1. **Sensory stores**: have limited capacity to receive information from the sense organs and to retain it for a brief period (about 0.5 second).

2. **Short-term memory**: allows a person to recall something after a short period of time without practicing or rehearsing. It precedes the consolidation of long-term memories and occurs successfully only if attention to and registration of information precede it. Short-term memory is temporary, lasting from seconds to a few minutes; this information can be used immediately in decision making and/or passes into long-term memory. Short-term memory, in contrast, is limited in capacity and can be saturated. There are two short-term stores, one for verbal and the other for visual information, located respectively in the left and right hemispheres.

3. **Working memory**: refers to memory as it is used to plan and carry out behavior. Holds transitory information and processes that allow this information to be manipulated. A common example of working memory is asking for a phone number and "holding" the number long enough to go to the phone and press in the numbers. Both short-term memory and long-term memory hold information available for working memory usage.

4. **Long-term memory**: it receives information that has been selected for more permanent storage. It has large capacity and holds information

for a long time. There are two types of long-term memory: procedural and declarative. Procedural memory involves remembering how to perform a set of skills, such as driving, skiing, swimming, or riding a bicycle. After initial practice and mastery of these perceptual-motor skills, procedural memories become implicit; that is, not in conscious awareness. Procedural memory remains intact in most amnestic patients, both for previously learned skills and for learning new skills. Declarative memory includes **episodic memory** (memory for specific events), and **semantic memory** (concerned with language, knowledge, and facts).

Disorders of Memory

Patients may acknowledge memory problems in the absence of evidence of memory impairment; i.e., subjective memory complaints (Kurt et al., 2011; Table 2.3). Depressed patients may exaggerate the extent to which their cognitive skills have diminished, complaining to great lengths that something is wrong with their brain (Othmer & Othmer, 2002). In other occasions, patients with evident memory impairment deny memory problems and try to cover them up through confabulation; this is more likely to occur with brain pathology.

Memory is liable to quantitative lowering (amnesia) or qualitative distortion of its contents (dysmnesia). Hypermnesia means enhanced memory; it cannot be considered a disorder.

Table 2.3 Summary of Memory Disorders

Disorders of Memory	Type	Characteristics
Distortion of memory (dysmnesia)	Distortion of recall (paramnesia)	Confabulation Retrospective falsification Delusional memory Retrospective delusions
	Distortion of recognition	*Déjà vu* *Jamais vu* Misidentification
Amnesia	Anterograde amnesia	Loss of memory following certain point
	Retrograde amnesia	Loss of memory prior to certain point
	Total amnesia	Loss of memory following and prior to certain point
	Circumscribed amnesia	Loss of memory for a limited period

Distortion of Memory (Dysmnesia)

1. Distortion of recall (paramnesia): *it may take the form of*:

    - **Confabulation**: a spontaneous and sometimes repetitive fabrication or distortion of memories (Gilboa & Verfaellie, 2010). The patient gives imaginary accounts of his/her own activities or an event that may be influenced by suggestion. The intent of confabulation is supposed to be "covering up" for a putative memory deficit. It occurs usually in organic brain syndromes (e.g., frontal lobe damage, Korsakoff's syndrome), and occurs unconsciously. Historical analysis shows that "confabulation" entered psychopathology at the turn of the century as a member of a set of concepts (that included delusion, fixed idea, obsessions, overvalued idea, etc.) concerning narratives of doubtful content. This means that confabulation is not an autonomous concept but part of a "discourse formation," i.e., it only has meaning within a given context. If so, it can be predicted that it will become unstable when used as if it were an independent piece of behavior. Confabulations need to be recalibrated together with current understanding of the set of concepts to which they belong, before they can play a useful role in current psychiatric diagnosis, treatment, and research.
    - **Retrospective falsification**: unintentional distortion of memory to conform to present psychological needs. Events and experiences are remembered somewhat inaccurately, selectively biased, and some irrelevancies and distortions are added. Recall tends to take shape in ways focused upon "making sense" of "the now": reinforcing current beliefs, with the past interpreted through the lens of conclusions reached in the present. The new details have been invented without any care about whether they are correct or not. People who retrospectively falsify a story also tend to embellish the positive and delete the negative aspects of the situation. We all falsify the past to some degree; it is generally an unconscious process. The depressed patient looks back over the past and see only his/her failures, insisting that he/she was a useless or worthless person. Histrionic and borderline personalities may produce a falsified set of memories about an event or a relationship.
    - **Delusional memory**: primary delusional experiences may take the form of memories (see before).
    - **Retrospective delusion**: a delusion in which a psychotic patient has interwoven fragments of true memories with delusional beliefs.

2. **Distortion of recognition**:

    - *Déjà vu*: a new situation is incorrectly regarded as a repetition of a previous memory.

- *Jamais vu*: false feeling of unfamiliarity with a real situation one has experienced.
- **Misidentification:**
    - **Positive**: to recognize strangers as friends or relatives occurs in acute confusional state and in schizophrenia.
    - **Negative**: to recognize friends and relatives as strangers. Capgras syndrome is a form of a negative misidentification.

Amnesia

Amnesia means loss of memory, which may be partial or complete. Variable types of amnesia could occur. Almost everyone has a lapse of memory from time to time. But when memory loss interferes with work, social activities, and daily tasks, it may need medical assessment and care. Amnesia may take one of the following forms:

1. **Anterograde amnesia**: refers to a loss of memory for events subsequent to an incident (e.g., car accident or cerebrovascular stroke); that is, the inability to learn, store, and retrieve information about the accident and from a period after the trauma that usually lasts for hours or days. In some cases anterograde amnesia extends indefinitely, that is, it becomes an amnestic syndrome.
2. **Retrograde amnesia**: refers to loss of memories that were consolidated just prior to the insult or event that produced the amnesia, e.g., inability to recall events before an incident of head trauma, usually for hours or days prior to the accident.
3. **Total amnesia**: refers to loss of memory for recent and remote events.
4. **Circumscribed amnesia**: refers to loss of memory for a limited period (amnesic gap).

Causes of Amnesia

1. **Normal forgetfulness**: healthy people can experience memory loss or memory distortion, but they are not extreme, persistent, or impairing. *Examples of these circumstances include:*
    (a) **Tendency to forget facts or events over time**: it is normal to forget things from time to time, and it is normal to become somewhat more forgetful as you age.
    (b) **Forgetting when you don't pay close enough attention**: e.g., forgetting where you put your book or keys, because you didn't focus on where you put it in the first place.
    (c) **Memory blocks**: failure to answer a question and the answer is right on the tip of your tongue.

(d) **Bias**: even the sharpest memory isn't a flawless snapshot of reality. It is filtered by personal biases including experiences, beliefs, prior knowledge, and mood at the moment.

(e) **Suggestibility**: information that was learned about an incident becomes incorporated into memory of the incident, even though those details were not experienced.

2. **Brain pathology**: a variety of brain pathologies can give rise to severe memory impairment, *the most common causes include the following*:

(a) Degenerative disorders (particularly Alzheimer's disease and Huntington's disease).

(b) Chronic alcohol abuse giving rise to Korsakoff syndrome.

(c) Traumatic head injury.

(d) Temporal lobe surgery.

(e) Encephalitis.

(f) Cerebral vascular disorders (including subarachnoid hemorrhage resulting from ruptured aneurysms).

(g) Anoxic brain damage (following, for example, myocardial infarction, carbon monoxide poisoning, or respiratory arrest).

(h) Cerebral tumors.

3. **Amnestic syndromes** are defined as a memory disturbance associated with significant decline in previous social or occupational functioning. New learning or recall of previously learned information is impaired. The disturbance does not occur exclusively during a delirium or dementia, and persists beyond the usual duration of states of intoxication or withdrawal.

4. **Electroconvulsive therapy**: during a course of ECT about half of patients experience temporary anterograde amnesia that resolves in 2–6 weeks following the last treatment.

5. **Psychiatric causes**: dissociative disorders are marked by a disruption of and/or discontinuity in the normal integration of consciousness, memory, identity, emotion, perception, body representation, motor control, and behavior. Dissociative amnesia is characterized by an inability to recall autobiographical information that is inconsistent with normal forgetting. This amnesia may be localized (i.e., an event or period of time), selective (i.e., a specific aspect of an event), or generalized (i.e., identity and life history).

6. **Fugue** is now a specifier of dissociative amnesia; people with dissociative fugue temporarily are confused about their sense of personal identity and might even create new identities and impulsively wander or travel away from their homes or places of work. The person's outward behavior of people with this disorder appears normal. Dissociative fugue has been

linked to severe stress, which might be the result of traumatic events, such as war, abuse, accidents, disasters, or extreme violence that the person has experienced or witnessed. The use or abuse of alcohol and certain drugs also can cause fugue-like states, such as alcohol-induced "blackouts."

7. **Dissociative identity disorder** is characterized by the presence of two or more distinct personality states or an experience of possession, associated with recurrent episodes of amnesia. Individuals may experience discontinuities in identity and memory that may not be immediately evident to others or are obscured by attempts to hide dysfunction.

8. **Mood disorders** may be associated with memory complaints. In depressive disorders, sometimes, there is differential recall of unhappy memories; also, memory impairment may be so severe that it accounts for what is called "depressive pseudodementia." Pseudodementia is a term used in describing patients whose memory deficits are presumably due to a psychiatric disorder, rather than to structural brain damage. Pseudo-demented patients show a pattern of spotty deficits and inconsistent performance on most memory testing, related to their attentional deficits and inconsistent motivation. Truly demented patients have more difficulty with recent than with remote information, until later in the disease when both are impaired.

9. **Severe anxiety disorders** can interfere with memory functions due to a lack of attention.

10. **Schizophrenia**: in addition to memory distortion experienced by some individuals diagnosed with schizophrenia, memory deficits may be another problem for some individuals, especially those who are disorganized.

Assessment of Memory

Memory is not a single process that is easily assessed by one screening test. During the psychiatric interview some information about memory will be available from the history and conversation of the patient. The ability of patients to give a clear account of their life from the remote to the recent past is an indicator of good memory. When memory function is of primary concern to the family, the patient may not be able to remember why she or he is present or may offer poor memory as the reason for the presentation. Full details of any claimed memory loss and the associated affect displayed at that time are investigated and recorded. It may be necessary to distinguish loss of memory from loss of insight.

Assessment of memory depends on the aim of assessment; evaluation of memory capacity, establishing of etiology of memory change, or localization of anatomical brain pathology. Evaluation of memory capacity includes assessment of different subdivisions of the memory system.

REGISTRATION

The examiner should assess registration via immediate recall of the material presented to the patient, e.g.:

1. The examiner says, "I am going to tell you four digits—2, 9, 1, and 5—which I want you to repeat. Please repeat them now so I shall know you heard them."
2. The examiner says, "I am going to tell you words which I want you to repeat, the words are brown, honesty, tulip, and eyedropper. Please repeat them now so I shall know you heard them."

If the patient can repeat previous items, registration is apparently adequate. If not, the examiner should repeat them and ask the patient to recite them until they are registered. The number of trials required for registration should be noted; more than two trials suggest inadequate registration. It is particularly important to notice that recall is closely related to attentional ability, degree of motivation, and current mood.

WORKING MEMORY

Working memory is assessed by digit span and similar tests. A normal person of average intelligence is usually able to repeat seven digits correctly. Working memory is always assessed before proceeding with other memory assessments, all of which are dependent on adequate attention and working memory. After ensuring the registration is adequate, the examiner notifies the patient that he/she will ask him/her to repeat the digits or words already registered after 5 minutes, then proceeds with other tasks of examination. After 5 minutes, the patient is asked to state the digits or words that were requested. One point is scored for each correctly remembered word in this short-term recall test (e.g., recall is 2/3 digits/words after 5 minutes). Then, to assess further the severity of any recent memory deficit, the patient is cued for any missing digits/words using a category, or the patient is given several possible digits/words, including the correct one, from which the patient can choose. The examiner should not score any points for a word recalled by category cueing, but record that cuing was helpful.

The ability to recite digits in a reverse order is sometimes used to assess memory. However, there is no agreement on how many digits the normal individual is able to reverse, and it appears to depend more strongly than the forward digit test on the ability to concentrate. This is why it is not usually recommended as a test of memory.

Another test of short-term memory is to read a story aloud. The examiner should preface it by explaining to the patient that he/she will be expected to retell the story from memory. When the patient retells the story, the examiner counts the number of important words or phrases remembered. An example might be: Mary / is a TV / news reporter. / She was covering an earthquake / in London. / She interviewed / a woman / named Carol / whose car / was parked on a street / which caved in / during the earthquake. / The car / disappeared / into the earth.

In each sentence, the different notable phrases to be recalled are separated by slashes to illustrate the 15 different ideas expressed. Remembering at least eight of them would be a normal performance; the recall does not need to be verbatim, but should include the important words.

Visual short-term memory can be tested by showing patients a picture of six simple designs for five seconds and then they are asked to draw (affected also by a visual or visuospatial deficit) what they remember, to name them, or to recognize a larger number of similar designs.

DECLARATIVE MEMORY

Both the episodic and semantic subtypes of declarative long-term memory can be assessed.

1. **Episodic memory** is time-specific, personalized, and experiential knowledge. The patient is asked to describe important personal events, such as a wedding, entering college, past medical history, and so on. The examiner should verify from other sources the data gathered from episodic memory testing; family, neighbors, or old medical charts can help. One can informally gather episodic information while eliciting the patient's past medical and psychiatric history during the interview. The examiner should be wary of confabulation; patients with memory deficits may go on and on with interesting stories that have no basis in fact. Unbelievable stories may indicate spontaneous confabulation.

2. **Semantic memory** involves recall of general information that a person could reasonably be expected to have learned, the names of states or governorates in his/her country, naming the world's continents, the current football team winner of the World Cup, ten capital cities, the name of five presidents of European countries. Semantic memory can also be tested by asking the patient to list orally as many things as possible in one minute that can be purchased in a grocery store; normal persons can list at least 18 different things.

Neuropsychological Testing of Memory

A lot of neuropsychological tests are available; each examines a distinct set of memory abilities. Each test has its own validity and reliability, which have to be known before using them. Among neuropsychological tests of memory, *Wechsler Memory Scale* is the most widely used test battery for adults. It is composed of eight brief subtests for short-term learning and memory (involving paragraphs, paired associates, digit span, mental control, design reproduction, and figural recognition) and four subtests of long-term retention of verbal and figural material. Two major composite scores are derived, yielding a general memory index and an attention concentration index. The general memory index can be partitioned to provide composite scores for verbal and visual memory. The memory for paragraphs and mental control subtests were found to be among the most efficient neuropsychological measures differentiating patients with mild senile dementia of Alzheimer's type from normal subjects.

EVALUATION OF KNOWLEDGE BASE

Assessment of the extent of the patient's general information about the environment is often a critical factor in determining how successfully they interact with the environment and are in touch with their surroundings or are living in a world of their own. This knowledge can be tested by simply asking patients about recent items of interest in the news; whether political, sporting, or otherwise in accordance with the patient's known interests and activities. Patients are also examined by asking about the name of the current president and then to list in the order of their service as many previous presidents as they can. Sometimes, inquiries are made about the names of other political figures or other well-known historical figures. Geographical knowledge can also be tested, e.g., naming state capitals, rivers, or distances between various localities, if conforming to their interests and abilities.

ABSTRACTION ABNORMALITIES

Abstract thinking is the capacity to conceptualize meanings of words beyond the most literal (concrete) interpretation. This includes the ability to form concepts, to analyze information according to themes, to generalize from a single incident, applying procedural rules and general principles, to categorize information, to appreciate double meanings, to make comparisons, to hypothesize, to keep in mind various aspects of a situation, to grasp the essentials of a whole, and use metaphors, and to reason using deductive and inductive thinking. It corresponds to Piaget's formal operations period of cognitive development. Abstracting ability may be affected by developmental level in children, intelligence, level of education, and by cultural factors. *Concrete thinking* means difficulties in understanding the metaphoric meaning of a phrase, joke, or a proverb and interpreting it in a concrete literal way. It is also called literal thinking.

Abstraction is a function of the frontal lobe. Impaired abstraction is present in frontal lobe lesions, dementia, and schizophrenia.

Goldstein (1944) suggested that in schizophrenia and organic brain diseases there is loss of the abstract attitude, so that thinking becomes concrete; i.e., "the patient is unable to free him/herself from the superficial concrete aspects of thinking."

Patients with impaired higher cognitive function usually demonstrate a kind of thinking that is referred to as concrete. They seem to be stimulus bound and have difficulty in changing their responses and pulling their attention away from their focus at a given moment. In the interview, loss of abstraction may manifest in the inability to relate events to one another during history taking, to assess the importance and meaning, or to conceptualize aspects of one's interaction with the environment in the earlier phases of one's disturbance.

Concreteness may be indirectly evident during the MSE interview. If the examiner asks; "what brought you to the hospital?" An abstract answer might be, "I have been feeling depressed." A concrete answer might be, "the ambulance." Because concrete answers are not expected, they might at first seem humorous or lead the examiner to think the patient is trying to be facetious.

Common approaches to testing abstraction are to detect similarities and differences between various objects, and to interpret proverbs:

1. **Similarities**: the patient is asked to conceptualize the category to which two items belong. The patient is asked about commonalities or similarities between the following items: an orange and an apple. An answer that they are both fruits is abstract, that they are round is concrete; that they can both be eaten is somewhat less concrete. Other similarities that are commonly used include a bicycle and an airplane or a car and a boat (both are modes of transportation), a typewriter and a pencil (both are a tool for writing), symphony and painting (both arts), a dog and a tree (both are living things), a shirt and a coat (both are clothing).

2. **Proverb interpretation**: this is another way to test abstraction. It also measures divergent reasoning. Proverbs are intrinsically significant when generalized or abstracted, rather than in literal interpretation. Proverbs vary in their level of complexity; some persons may be able to interpret only the simpler ones. One should begin by explaining to the patient what is meant by a proverb; it is a saying with a broader meaning. An example should be found that the patient may already have heard. Easier proverbs include the following: don't count your chickens before they hatch, and a stitch in time saves nine. Abstract interpretations of these are, respectively, don't be prematurely expecting something that might not happen, and take action today to avoid consequences or complications tomorrow. Possible concrete interpretations are, respectively, you won't know how many chicks will be born by counting the eggs, and sewing prevents more rips. If the patient gives appropriate responses to these simple proverbs, more difficult proverbs are given, e.g., Rome wasn't built

in a day, people who live in glass houses shouldn't throw stones, loose lips sink ships, every cloud has a silver lining, and a rolling stone gathers no moss. Proverb interpretation is dependent on the patient's cultural, intellectual, and educational background. Many well-educated young adults are unfamiliar with proverbs, so responses must be interpreted with care. The ability to provide an abstract response requires an intact fund of general information and the ability to apply generalities to new information. A drawback of the proverb test is that the patient who has experienced many psychiatric evaluations may learn the correct answer. Furthermore, proverb interpretation is not standardized and normative data are lacking. There are several possible explanations for an inability to interpret proverbs abstractly: inadequate education (less than eight years), acute psychosis, dementia, delirium, head injury, frontal lobe damage, low IQ (including intellectual disability), and lack of cultural applicability of the proverb. Sometimes because interpretations of easier proverbs have been learned, patients can recite them from memory; still they cannot reason out unfamiliar ones. The main value of the proverbs test in schizophrenia lies not in the degree of concreteness of responses (which may be due to low intelligence and social restriction) but in the patient's tendency to give bizarre and idiosyncratic responses.

3. **Completion test**: another aspect of conceptualization is the ability to switch mental sets quickly, e.g., between letters and numbers (as in Trail making B Test), or between symbols and numbers. Ask the patient to complete several conceptual series, e.g., 1, 3, 5 or A, 2, B, 4, C, 6.

INTELLIGENCE

Evaluation of intellectual functioning is a controversial subject, perhaps especially so when evaluation takes place during a brief clinical interview (Mackintosh, 2011). Despite this controversy, general statements about intellectual functioning are usually made following a mental status examination. There is no standard definition of what exactly constitutes "intelligence." Some researchers have suggested that intelligence is a single, general ability; while others believe that intelligence encompasses a range of aptitudes, skills, and talents. Intelligence could be defined as a combination of the ability to learn, and to explore and solve problems.

In most clinical interviews, intelligence is inferred rather than tested specifically. *The most common ways to do this are*:

1. Intelligence is inferred from a patient's self-help, academic, social, and working functional level.
2. The patient's ability to give a clear coherent history of his/her complaints and history.

3. Assessing the patient's vocabularies, complexity of concepts he/she uses and progressively more difficult questions about current events. Although they are heavily culture-bound, questions about popular TV shows or sports events, as well as names of the governor or vice president can provide an adequate estimation of intelligence. Intellectual functioning may be overestimated if a patient's vocabulary or educational background is particularly strong. Therefore, a formal examination of the several areas of intellectual competence is often needed.

4. Calculation:
    -   serial sevens: e.g. $7 + 7$, $14 + 7$, $21 + 7$, etc.;
    -   doubling three: used if the patient had difficulty with serial sevens test (note how the patient is able to go and how long it takes);
    -   performing increasingly difficult mental arithmetic: e.g., $2 + 3$, $7 + 12$, $21 - 9$, $36 \div 9$, 4×9; etc.

5. The ability to interpret a proverb. The capacity to abstract general meaning from the literal understanding of a proverb draws upon intelligence, which does not require schooling. Poor or concrete interpretation of a proverb suggests either a cultural block or low intelligence. Contrary to earlier beliefs, concrete proverb interpretation is not indicative of any disorder.

6. The Rapid Approximation Intelligence Test (RAIT): this consists of a multiplication task: 2 3 3, 2 3 6, 2 3 12, 2 3 24, 2 3 48, etc. The non-retarded patient should be able to multiply 2 3 24. Patients who cannot multiply 2 3 24 have an 85 percent probability of having a Wechsler Adult Intelligence Scale (WAIS) IQ score of less than 84.

7. Formal intelligence testing: this is usually carried out when there is a need to get a thorough formal assessment. This is accomplished either through Wechsler Intelligence Scale (for adults or children), or Stanford-Binet Intelligence test.

ABNORMAL INSIGHT AND JUDGMENT

The concept of insight is a topic of interest in philosophy "which is out of the scope of this discussion" and psychiatry. Till recent times, good insight was a cardinal differentiating point between neurosis and psychosis, a matter that was not so accurate, as some of the so-called neurotic disorders may be associated with lack of insight, and only 50–80 percent of patients with schizophrenia do not believe they have a disorder. This lack of association with psychotic disorders did not refute that lack of insight is a cardinal feature of impaired reality testing.

In psychiatry, insight can be defined as "the patient's awareness and understanding of their attitudes, feelings, behavior, disturbing symptoms; and understanding how the illness affects individuals' interactions with the world." So, the term "insight" should not be considered as an isolated symptom that is present or absent. Instead, it may be more appropriate to think of insight as a continuum of thinking and feeling, affected by numerous internal and external variables.

Most authors and researchers follow the multidimensional concept of insight given by Amador and Gorman (1998) that includes:

- awareness of mental disorder;
- understanding of the social consequences of disorder;
- awareness of the need of treatment;
- awareness of specific signs and symptoms of the disorder;
- the attribution of symptoms to disorder.

Gelder, Gath, and Mayou (1983) graded insight into:

1. **Complete denial of illness**: the patient does not consider him/herself abnormal by any means.
2. **Slight awareness of being sick or needing help**: the patient denies it at the same time.
3. **Awareness of being sick**: the patient blames others, external events, medical or unknown organic factors as causative factors.
4. **Intellectual insight**: a deceptive understanding and intellectual interpretation of a perspective or a situation that is not reflected in the person's ability to apply that understanding in any useful way to master his/her symptoms or disease.
5. **True emotional insight**: emotional recognition of the motives and feelings within the person, awareness of the underlying meaning of symptoms, and of how this recognition leads to changes in personality and future behavior, openness to new ideas and concepts about self.

So, poor insight or lack of insight is not an all or one phenomenon but is a continuum; its significance is a matter of clinical judgment.

Factors that May Influence Insight

1. Cultural models of illness.
2. General intelligence and knowledge.
3. Doctor–patient relationship.
4. Symptomatology (delusions/depression).
5. Denial: motivation, preservation of self-esteem, avoidance of stigma.
6. Personality: compliance non-conformity as a trait.

Textbooks contain a lot of terminology that refers to insight that is impaired in some way. It will be listed here so as not to be confused with true insight.

These terms include:

1. **Pseudo-insight**: the patient repeats overheard explanations arising out of different theoretical perspectives.
2. **Partial insight**: this may take one of several different forms:

    *   **Admitting but not convinced**: the patient admits verbally that he/she is ill, but he/she is not appreciating the degree of seriousness of the situation nor is convinced of being ill. This may be just to satisfy the parents or to end an interview.
    *   **Admitting but giving undiscussable rationalization**: the patient admits that he/she is ill, but shows an exaggerated degree of rationalization.
    *   **Admitting but placing blame elsewhere**: the patient admits that he/she is ill but blames other, external factors, or attributes his/her mental illness to medical rather than psychological factors.
    *   **Admitting but not cooperating in therapy**: the patient declares that he/she is ill, but this does not mean that he/she should be treated or that others are different.
    *   **Admitting but not persistent**: the patient admits that he/she is ill, starts treatment apparently cooperatively, but soon stops taking medicines or discontinues attending treatment.

3. **Sectorial insight**: insight is intact in a restricted area of behavior or symptomatology, e.g., a patient may have or develop insight that his/her thoughts are delusional or that the area related to his/her family life is a pathological area. Simultaneously, all other aspects of the illness situation may be denied or disguised.
4. **Intellectual insight**: an apparent understanding and intellectual interpretation of the objective reality of a set of circumstances without the ability to apply the understanding in any useful way to master the situation.
5. **Double bluffing insight**: the patient admits that he/she has certain symptoms or illness to hide some other more serious symptoms. It is not necessarily that the covering complaints are of a different nature from the covered genuine illness.
6. **Psychotic insight**: some sort of autochthonous delusional misinterpretation which is absolutely psychotic, described early in the genesis of schizophrenia, where the patient after a period of overwhelming perplexity, all of a sudden finds an explanation for his/her condition that is able to solve completely his/her perplexity.
7. **Paradoxical denial insight**: the patient has some critical attitude in the genuineness of his/her symptoms. He/she may comment on his/her complaints, saying "do not believe me, I may be pretending" or "it is strange to have such feelings, possibly they are simply imagined, let us forget them."

8. **Hyperawareness insight**: some patients early in the development of the psychotic process feel changes inside themselves, which they cannot describe or describe them in a way that may be considered by some psychiatrists as falsification, pseudophilosophical, or delusional. Soon after developing such awareness, this genuine insight is liable to be intellectualized and the psychotic process could proceed to overshadow it.

Judgment

Judgment is the ability to assess a situation correctly and to act appropriately within that situation, i.e., it is in one's capacity to evaluate information and use this knowledge to plan for and deal with life situations. It is frequently assessed retrospectively on the basis of the person's behavior. It is related to the ability of the individual to grasp current information, to assess realistic situations, and to have a logical attitude and performance that is compatible with the situation as a whole.

Critical judgment refers to the ability to assess, to discern, and to choose among various options in a situation. **Impaired judgment** refers to diminished ability to understand a situation correctly and to act appropriately.

Tests of judgment in psychiatry focus on one's capacity for prospective planning. The traditional tests of judgment are: "What would you do if you smelled smoke in your apartment?" "What would you do if you had severe "chest pain while you were alone at home?" or "What would you do if you saw a 2-year-old child playing at the end of a pier?" However, these questions can detect only gross impairments in judgment, and may not be impaired in a grossly impaired psychotic patient. This type of inquiry may be beneficial in forensic situations.

In clinical psychiatric practice, judgment is best assessed by the patient's attitude regarding the question of need for treatment, hospitalization, and discharge.

CORTICAL FUNCTIONS

Agnosia

Agnosia is a failure of recognition through a sensory modality of a previously known stimulus, although there is no perceptual disorder of the sensory modality and the patient is alert and cooperative (Table 2.4).

Varieties of Agnosia

1. **Visual agnosia**: in extreme forms, patients are unable to recognize seen objects, although they could recognize them from their sounds or through palpation.

Table 2.4 Summary of Varieties of Agnosia

Type	Domain of Impairment
Visual agnosia	Seen objects
Prosopagnosia	Sight of familiar faces
Simultanagnosia	The meaning of a picture as a whole
Visuospatialagnosia	Visual recognition of familiar themes
Auditory agnosia	Auditory recognition of meaning of sounds
Amusia	Perception of tones, pitch, timbre, chords, and melodies is specially impaired
Astereognosis	Inability to recognize objects placed in the patient's hand with his/her eyes his closed
Tactile agnosia	Inability to recognize objects by manipulation in the absence of perceptual somatosensory defects
Agraphaesthesia	Inability to recognize numbers and letters written on the patient's hand with his/her eyes closed
Asomatognosia	Body awareness
Anosognosia	Patient is unaware of weakness of affected side

2. **Prosopagnosia**: the patient's inability to recognize familiar faces of relatives and friends by sight, though they could recognize them from their sounds. The disorder usually extends to recognition of familiar buildings and landscape (called loss of topographic memory).

3. **Simultanagnosia**: there is failure to grasp the meaning of a picture as a whole, although parts of it are recognized.

4. **Visuospatialagnosia**: some patients cannot visually recognize their familiar surroundings, famous monuments, or the plans of similar cities or countries.

5. **Auditory agnosia**: patients can hear sounds but cannot recognize their meaning; familiar voices and tunes for instance go unrecognized, though the patient could recognize the pictures of subjects producing these v oices.

6. **Amusia**: a special type of auditory agnosia in which the perception of tones, pitch, timbre, chords, and melodies is specially impaired. Right-sided temporal lesions play a significant causal role.

7. **Astereognosis**: inability to recognize objects placed in the patient's hand with his/her eyes closed, although there is no or minor impairment in the elementary sensations of touch, pain, and temperature.

8. **Tactile agnosia**: inability to recognize, with either hand, objects by manipulation in the absence of perceptual somatosensory defects. Such patients can tell the shape, the texture, and the nature (e.g., rubber, wood etc.) of the manipulated object, but cannot recognize it.

9. **Agraphaesthesia**: inability to recognize numbers and letters written on the patient's hand with his/her eyes closed.
10. **Asomatognosia**: a disorder of body awareness characterized by partial or complete forgetting, ignoring, denying, or misperceiving the body. It is caused by neurological damage.
11. **Anosognosia**: patient is unaware of weakness of affected side (usually left) and will often move the right side when asked to move the left.

NB: Anton's syndrome: a syndrome of cortical blindness in which the patient denies being blind and confabulates responses when confronted with their errors, making excuses. They may have simple or complex visual hallucinations. It is usually associated with bilateral infarction in the territory of posterior cerebral arteries that involve primary visual areas and association areas.

Apraxia

Apraxia is the inability of the patient to perform everyday motor behavior or a skilled act in the absence of sensory or motor or coordination deficits.

Types of Apraxia

1. **Ideomotor apraxia**: patients cannot perform on command acts that can be performed spontaneously. This results from lesions in the supramarginal gyrus presumably involving the fibers of the left arcuate fasciculus or in the left premotor cortex. *Commands should include those for*:
   - *orofacial* (e.g., drink through a straw, lick lips, blow out a match);
   - *limb* (e.g., hammer a nail, a military salute, waving goodbye);
   - *whole body movements* (trunk apraxia): there is inadequate positioning of the body in bed or chair (e.g., stand like a boxer).

2. **Ideational apraxia**: the inability to perform an organized motor sequence, although the individual components can be performed separately. It is possibly due to fear about how to carry out a movement, but once the patient has been cued he/she produces the correct response. It could be tested by asking the patient to show how he/she folds a letter, places it in an envelope, and then seals and stamps the envelope; lighting a candle with matches; or making a cup of coffee. To the observer, the patient gives the appearance of being naïve or unfamiliar with the sequence of activities that should occur. These patients fail to use everyday objects correctly. Ideational apraxia affects the limbs on both sides. It results from lesions in the region of the left angular gyrus.

3. **Motor apraxia**: a breakdown in the smooth execution of a movement despite preservation of the intended motor pattern. The performance is not affected by the modality of request (e.g., spoken or written). The disturbance is purely one of output. Movements such as quickly opposing each fingertip to the thumb, flipping, or passing a coin from the palm to the thumb and index are clumsy, but the plan of action is not disturbed.

NB: The term apraxia is traditionally applied to the following disorders although their mechanisms are different from that of apraxia:

- **Gait apraxia (frontal gait)**: there is no significant weakness, loss of sensation, or cerebellar incoordination, hence the controversial term of "gait apraxia." Although the patient is unable to walk properly, he/she can make walking movements when lying or sitting. When standing, the feet are wide apart, and walking starts after a long delay. The feet look as if they are frozen to the ground, and then small shuffling steps are obtained. They come to a halt or are followed by a few better long steps, ending also in a halt. In advanced cases patients are unable to walk and sit. When standing, the patient generally falls backward. Grasping, groping, sucking, and pouting reflexes are often associated. On moving the limbs passively the patient shows resistance (Gegenhalten). Cognitive impairment is often associated. Normal pressure hydrocephalus, tumors, and diffuse lesions are the main causes.

- **Ocular or oculomotor apraxia**: some alert and cooperative patients cannot initiate saccades on command to a novel target entering the visual field. Vestibular induced saccades and optopkinetic nystagmus are less severely disturbed. The condition may be congenital or result from bilateral frontoparietal lesions.

- **Dressing apraxia**: an inability to dress. It is not a true apraxia. It is often associated with left visual field deficits and topographic disorientation. Left sensory or motor neglect can be the basic disorder.

- **Constructional apraxia**: there is defect in the ability to use two- or three-dimensional space. The patient is asked to draw on command or copy with a pencil and paper, matches, or block design constructions such as a square or a diamond (two dimensions) or a cube or a house (three dimensions). In the latter, the lines indicating perspectives are likely to be the most inadequate. It results from parietal lobe lesion on either side. Right parietal lobe lesions are probably apt to cause specific disorders. It is generally held that it results from disorders of visual processing with defects in spatial organization. *Other tests of constructional apraxia include:*

    –   *Clock face*: ask the patient to draw a clock face and to fill in the numbers. Ask him/her then to draw the hands at a given time, e.g., ten to four: if unable to do so, it may indicate constructional apraxia. If there is half a clock missing it may indicate visual inattention.

    –   *Map test*: ask the patient to indicate the site of cities on a map outline.

    –   *five-pointed star*: ask the patient to copy a five-pointed star. If unable to do so it may indicate constructional apraxia.

In summary, testing apraxia can be achieved through:

1. Observing the actions of the patient as he/she engages in such tasks as dressing, washing, shaving, and using eating utensils;
2. Asking the patient to wave goodbye, shake his/her fist as though angry, salute, and blow a kiss: symbolic acts;
3. If he/she fails, asking him/her to imitate the examiner, who performs these acts;
4. Asking him/her to show how he/she would hammer a nail, brush his/her teeth, comb his/her hair, and so forth, or to execute a complex series of acts, such as lighting and smoking a cigarette or opening and drinking a bottle of cola.

Parietal Lobe Functioning

The dominant parietal lobe generally influences verbal and symbolic abilities, and the non-dominant parietal lobe influences non-verbal motor-perceptual abilities.

    Impairment in parietal lobe functioning is more likely to present as a neurological rather than a psychiatric problem, but sometimes the impairment or the patient's response to impairment is quite similar to the symptomatology seen in certain psychiatric syndromes. *Patients with parietal lobe dysfunction may manifest by:*

In Patients with Non-dominant Parietal Lobe Lesions

- There may be ideomotor and/or ideational apraxia.
- There is difficulty copying simple figures such as a square or cross without removing their pencil from the paper.
- Diminished capacity to recognize certain aspects of the environment or of one's own body (usually on the left side). There may be denial of the illness, a denial of the existence of body parts, and uncertain recognition of familiar people.

In Patients with Dominant Parietal Lobe Lesions

- Spatial categorization problems.
- Right–left disorientation: can be tested by asking the patient to touch one part of the body with a contralateral part: "touch your right ear with your left hand."
- Difficulty in naming his/her own fingers correctly (finger agnosia).
- Difficulty in performing mathematical calculations (dyscalculia), difficulty in writing (dysgraphia), or difficulty in reading (dyslexia). These functions can be tested by asking the patient to do simple calculations, to write a sentence, or to read aloud.

GENDER IDENTITY

Normal human sexual development requires the compatibility between genetic sex (sex chromosomes), gonads (testes or ovaries), genitalia (external and internal sex organs), other secondary sexual characteristics, and the congruent subjective experience of the gender. Sexual identity is the biological sexual characteristics: chromosomes, external genitalia, internal genitalia, hormonal composition, gonads, and secondary sex characteristics. Sexual orientation describes the object of a person's sexual impulses; heterosexual, homosexual, or bisexual.

Gender identity is the person's sense of maleness or femaleness that identifies the person as being male, female, or ambivalent. Differentiation of gender identity usually takes place in infancy or early childhood. Gender identity is modestly shaped by family and cultural influences, such as rearing practices, peer gender-specific behaviors, and individual traits. It is reinforced by the hormonal changes of puberty. Gender non-conformity refers to the extent to which a person's gender identity, role, or expression differs from the cultural norms prescribed for people of a particular sex. Gender dysphoria (also known as gender identity disorder, gender incongruence, transgenderism) refers to discomfort or distress that is caused by a discrepancy between a person's gender identity and that person's sex assigned at birth (and the associated gender role and/or primary and secondary sex characteristics). Parents of boys with gender identity disorders report that at a very young age the boys insist on being treated as girls and being dressed as girls. Only some gender-nonconforming people experience gender dysphoria at some point in their lives.

Gender dysphoria includes cross gender identification (characterized by strong and persistent identification of the opposite sex) or discomfort with one's assigned sex (characterized by desire to be of the opposite sex, insistence that one is the other gender; a strong preference for cross-dressing, cross-gender roles, and playmates of the other gender; and dislike of sexual anatomy and their primary and/or secondary sex characteristics) (American Psychiatric Association, 2013).

Intersex: persons identified as "intersex" have ambiguous external sexual characteristics. The condition is defined as a "congenital anomaly of the reproductive and sexual system." Intersex persons are born with external genitalia, internal reproductive organs, and endocrine systems that are deviant. There is no single intersex condition, and the term includes a wide variety of degrees of abnormality. Intersex is not an identity condition and intersex persons are biologically male or female and have a male or female identity.

Assessment of Gender Dysphoria

Clinical assessment may require several sessions, carried out a number of months apart, to confirm diagnosis and to determine a management plan. *Assessment includes discussion of the following topics:*

1. Gender mismatch between your biological sex and gender identity.
2. Desire to change physical characteristics as a result of any mismatch.
3. Coping with any difficulties of a possible mismatch.
4. Feelings and behaviors that have developed over time.
5. Life after gender transition and surgical reassignment.
6. Potential difficulties and obstacles encountered following transition.
7. Any previous or current mental health concerns or diagnoses.
8. Available supports, such as friends, family, and in the workplace.

DISTURBANCE OF SELF

Our body is unique in that it is experienced with both subjective experience and as an object with the same materiality as any other physical object in the world, i.e., a person is subjectively aware that his/her own body is different from how he/she experiences a block of wood, but at the same time he/she is aware that his/her body is an object in the world, to be viewed and even acted on by others.

We become aware of our body in extraordinary conditions (distress or pain), e.g., an anxious patient feels a pounding heart or shaking hand. We have an awareness of our self and an awareness of our bodies; both overlap, but are slightly different. Though distinction made between self-awareness and awareness of the body is artificial, it is useful to fully discuss both topics. Many different terms are used to describe the way a person conceptualizes him/herself. Neurologists, neuropsychiatrists, psychoanalysts and psychologists have used variously the terms self-concept, body image body schema, body concept, body cathexis, and perceived body. They describe approximately the same thing but with different expressions.

Self-concept

The term self-concept refers to how people think about, evaluate, or perceive themselves. *Lewis (1990) suggested that self-concept has two aspects:*

1. **The Existential Self**: the sense of being separate and distinct from others and the awareness of the constancy of the self. This is the most basic part of the self-scheme or self-concept. According to Lewis, awareness of the existential self begins as young as 2–3 months old and partly arises from the interaction of the child with the world, e.g., the child smiles and someone smiles back or the child touches a movable object and sees it move. Finally, the child realizes that they exist as a separate entity from others and that they continue to exist over time and space.
2. **The Categorical Self**: the child becomes aware that he or she is an object in the world that can be experienced and characterized by some properties, such as age, gender, size, or skills. Age and gender are the first categories to be applied (I am 3 and I am a girl). In early childhood, children apply very concrete categories to themselves (e.g., hair color, height, and favorite things). Later, self-description begins to include reference to internal psychological traits, comparative evaluations, and to how others see them (Lewis, 1990).

Carl Rogers suggested that the self-concept has three different components: self-image, self-esteem or self-worth, and ideal (Rogers, 1959).

Self-image

This refers to the way we see ourselves, when we look in a mirror or when we picture ourselves in our mind. *It encompasses the following components:*

1. **Perceptual component**: this refers to how persons see themselves. It is not always a correct representation of what one actually looks like, e.g., a girl may perceive herself to be fat when in reality she is slim.
2. **Affective component**: this refers to the feelings one has regarding one's own body, e.g., people may be satisfied or dissatisfied regarding their appearance, weight, shape, and body parts.
3. **Cognitive component**: this refers to the way you think about your body, e.g., beliefs about your own appearance. Some people think that they

would feel better about themselves if they were thinner, while others think that they would look better if they developed more muscle.

4. **Behavioral component**: this refers to behaviors that a person does because of the way he/she sees body image. When a person is dissatisfied with the way he/she looks, he/she may develop destructive behaviors such as excessive exercise or an eating disorder as a means to change appearance. People who feel bad about the way they look may avoid others and isolate themselves.

Self-image can affect the way a person thinks, feels, and behaves in the world. One may perceive oneself as a good or bad person, beautiful or ugly; a matter that may not reflect reality. Indeed a person with anorexia nervosa who is thin may have a self-image in which the person believes they are fat.

Positive body image usually correlates with a higher level of physical and psychological health, and superior personal development. A positive body image will affect self-esteem levels and self-acceptance. Factors that affect self-image include influences of parents, friends, teachers, other people, media, etc.

The media: repeated exposure to popular media such as movies, TV, the Internet, and magazines can shape our view of what is ideal and desirable. Comparing oneself with promoted good models may leave the person disappointed at not being good enough.

Other people: culture tends to judge people based on their looks, sometimes even the smallest comment of your friends, peers, or parents about how you look can feel very hurtful. This may have positive or negative impact on the individual, depending on how they feel about themselves or how they relate to others. Clothes and image play a critical role in individual expression, which is usually about being unique (establishing identity) or belonging (fitting in and being accepted) to a certain group or culture. Others' comments and behaviors can range from direct critical comments and questions about how you look to their beliefs about their own body image (you need to eat more (or less), that dress makes you look fat, you look so nice when you take off that make-up). If one does not have a real sense of being good, others' comments and behaviors can have long-term emotional effects.

Self-esteem (Self-worth)

This means the extent to which a person accepts, values, likes, or approves him/herself. It involves a degree of evaluation that may be either positive (high self-esteem) or negative (low self-esteem). High self-esteem tends to lead persons to have confidence in their own abilities, self-acceptance, not worrying about what others think, and optimism. Low self-esteem tends to lead persons to lack of confidence, desire to be someone else, worry about what others might think, and pessimism. *Factors that may influence self-esteem include*:

1. **Reaction of others**: the ways in which others (particularly significant others) react to us. People tend to develop a positive self-image when others admire them, seek out their company, listen attentively, and agree with their opinions. By contrast, people tend to develop a negative self-image when others avoid or neglect them, or when others have bad opinions about them.
2. **Comparison with others**: comparing oneself with someone who is less successful than the person's own image will enhance positive self-image, while comparison with someone who is more successful, happier, richer, or better looking tends to develop a negative self-image.
3. **Social roles**: this depends on categorization of our social role being prestigious or stigmatizing. Prestigious social roles, e.g., judges, doctors, and airline pilots promote self-esteem. Stigmatizing social roles, e.g., prisoner or unemployed person, do not promote self-esteem.
4. **Identification**: people usually identify with the positions they occupy, the roles they play, and the groups they belong to; that is, roles become part of our personality. However, people differ in their degree of identification with assumed roles.

Ideal Self

This is the person one would like to be. It consists of our favored goals and ambitions. The ideal self is continually changing, thus it differs in childhood from in our teens or late twenties etc. The degree of similarity between actual self-image and ideal self is likely to affect how much one values him/herself. All people experience a certain amount of incongruence between actual and ideal self. The development of congruence is dependent on unconditional positive regard. Rogers (1959) suggested that self-actualization is accomplished when one has a state of congruence. Therefore, there is an intimate relationship between self-image, self-ideal, and self-esteem.

Positive Body Image

This refers to a realistic perception of one's shape; where the person sees various parts of his/her body as they really are. Those persons accept and respect their natural body shape and understand that a person's physical appearance has little effect on their character and value as a person. Thus, those persons are comfortable and confident in their body, as they accept their unique body and refuse to spend time worrying about their weight, and controlling food and calories.

Negative Body Image

This refers to a distorted perception of one's shape, where parts of the body are perceived in an undesirable way, and may be considered as a sign of personal failure. Conversely, those persons perceive other people as being attractive. This leads those persons to feel ashamed and anxious about body shape, and feeling uncomfortable in their bodies.

What's the Difference between Healthy and Unhealthy Body Image?

A healthy body image refers to being comfortable in your own skin, being happy most of the time with the way you look, and feeling good about yourself.

An unhealthy body image is thinking your body is disgusting, unsightly, or not good enough, e.g., thinking that you look too fat even though others tell you this is not true, thinking that you're not pretty enough or muscular enough. It can also mean believing what you look like determines your value as a person. Someone with negative body image can become fixated on trying to change their actual body shape.

Disorders Characterized by Disturbance of the Awareness of the Body (Body Image)

- Undue concern with illness: *hypochondriasis*.
- Dislike of body: body dysmorphic disorder, gender identity disorder, *transsexualism*.
- Undue concern with appearance: *narcissism*.
- Distortion of body image: *anorexia nervosa*.

Body Image and Eating Disorders

Negative body image is frequently associated with eating disorders and feelings of depression, isolation, low self-esteem, and obsessions with weight loss.

The Experience of Self

Jaspers ([1962] 1997) pointed out that there are four aspects of self-experience:

1. The awareness of existence and activity of the self.
2. The awareness of being a unity (singleness) at any given point of time.

3.   The awareness of continuity of identity over a period of time.
4.   The awareness of being separate from the environment (awareness of ego boundaries).

Disturbances of Self-experience May Affect One or More of These Aspects

Disturbance of Awareness of Self-activity

A sense of personal possession is achieved when events can be brought into consciousness; though this is not usually in the forefront of consciousness. The sense of existence and the awareness of the performance of one's actions are the two main aspects of the sense of self-activity. *Disturbance of awareness of self-activity include:*

1. DEPERSONALIZATION

The patient feels that he/she is no longer his/her natural self. This is usually associated with a sense of unreality, so that the environment is experienced as flat, dull, and unreal. This aspect of the symptom is called derealization. It may be present in short episodes or as a continuous state. It can be found in dissociation, anxiety, depression, schizophrenia, and epilepsy.

Depersonalization (as if feeling) is not a delusion (experience of unreality that occurs in psychosis). Depersonalization should be distinguished from nihilistic delusions in which patients deny that they exist or they are alive or that the world or other people exist.

2. LOSS OF EMOTIONAL RESONANCE

In depression, there is a general lowering of the mood, in addition to loss of normal emotional resonance, and the patient has the feeling that he/she cannot experience emotion.

3. ABNORMALITIES OF EXPERIENCE OF ONE'S OWN ACTIVITIES

It usually results from mood changes; so, it is not unusual to see a depressed patient who believes that he/she is unable to do anything.

4. ABNORMALITIES IN WILLPOWER

It refers to difficulties or inability to initiate activity, and lacking power in the face of life's fluctuations. In schizophrenia, the patient may even feel that his/her will is no longer his/her own.

Disturbance of Immediate Awareness of Self-unity

In depersonalization, the patient feels that he/she is talking and acting in an automatic way, this may lead him/her to say that he/she feels as if he/she is two persons. The subject with demoniac possession may feel that he/she is two people: him/herself and the devil. Some schizophrenics may also feel that they are two or more persons.

Disturbance of the Continuity of Self

A fundamental assumption of life is that competent behavior cannot take place without a feeling of continuity between oneself and one's role. Thus the same person is the same as he/she was last week or month, or many years ago, will be the same next week, next month and in years to come.

Accepting that changes in one's total state at present are due to illness (insight) is a part of the continuity of self. Thus, the complete alteration in the sense of identity is characteristic of psychotic patients. In schizophrenia, a patient may feel that they are not the person that they were before the illness. This may be expressed as a sense of change, but another patient may claim that he/she died under their old name and has come to life as a new person. However, the sense of complete change of the personality may occur also in religious conversion.

A less intense degree of disturbance of the continuity of self may be experienced in health, and in some neurotic patients and personality disorders is the feeling of loss of continuity without an element of passivity. The person recognizes him/herself, both before and after, as truly him/herself, but he/she feels being overly altered from what he/she was. This is particularly liable to occur following unduly significant life situations.

Disturbance of the Boundaries of Self (Ego Boundaries)

One of the most fundamental of experiences is the distinction between one's body and the rest of the world. Disturbance in ego boundaries occur if there is impairment to knowing where I ends and not I begins.

Most schizophrenic symptoms result from breakdown of the boundary between self and environment. In the early stages of schizophrenia patients may experience this breakdown of the limits themselves as a change in their awareness of their own activity which is becoming alienated from them. This is in contrast to depersonalization in which patients feel that they are like machines; their actions are carried out automatically. In the alienation of personal action that occurs in schizophrenia, the patient has the experience that his/her actions, thoughts, and feelings are under the control of an external power.

First rank symptoms of schizophrenia have in common permeability of the barrier between the individual and their environment, loss of ego boundaries (falsely attributing actions to influence from outside, their actions are not their own, hearing one's own thoughts spoken aloud, and thought broadcasting).

3   The Psychiatric Interview

The psychiatric interview includes psychiatric history, mental status examination, physical examination, diagnosis, and management plan.

The psychiatric history is usually classified into: identification data, chief complaint, history of the present illness, personal history, and family history.

The purpose of the psychiatric history is to provide the psychiatrist with an understanding of the patient's current condition. This is accomplished with an understanding of personal development, the environment in which it occurred, the significance of the principal figures in that environment, and the patient's adaptive techniques, such as defense mechanisms. In short, the history attempts to answer the question "How did the patient reach the current condition?"

OUTLINE OF PSYCHIATRIC HISTORY

1. Identification data
2. Chief complaints
3. History of present illness
4. Past illnesses

   - Psychiatric
   - Medical
   - Alcohol and other substance history

5. Personal history (anamnesis)
6. Family history.

IDENTIFICATION DATA

Identification data include the patient's name, age, sex, address, occupation, marital status, religion, ethnic background, type of consultation, source of referral, cause of referral, and an idea about the informant if available.

The main aim of obtaining personal data is to provide an introductory identification and to get a smooth start with the patient, though, many inferences could be elicited from these data. *Some of these possible inferences are summarized below.*

1. **Name**: *giving the name of the patient may help in:*
    - Identification of the patient: this facilitates communications and gives a sense of familiarity.
    - Registration: this helps in the follow up of the patient and in future researches.
    - Giving the name may reflect suspiciousness of the patient, e.g., a patient hides his or her name.
    - Some patients may be traumatized by their names.
    - The name may reflect the patient's culture (certain names are common in certain cultures, also, certain names are used to prevent death of children "prevent the eye").
    - The name may reflect delusions of the patient, e.g., a patient who believes that he is Napoleon.

2. **Age**:
    - Knowing the age of the patient helps in prioritizing possible differential diagnosis; certain diseases are most common at certain ages, e.g., anorexia nervosa, somatization disorder, and schizophrenia are seen more often in young patients. Degenerative dementia is common in the elderly.
    - A patient who appears older than his/her stated age may have a history of substance abuse, cognitive disorders, depression, or physical illness.
    - Prognosis may differ according to age, e.g., prognosis of schizophrenia is better in cases with onset after puberty.
    - Selecting type of drugs and treatment modality is partly dependent on the patient's age. Side effects of a drug may be dangerous and better avoided at certain ages (e.g., anticholinergic drugs in old age).
    - Adjusting doses of drugs, the golden rule in children and old people is to start low and go slow.

3. **Gender**:
    - Incidence of different disorders may differ in both males and females, e.g., in males, antisocial personality and alcohol and drug abuse are more common. In females anorexia and bulimia nervosa, somatization disorder, and depression are more common.
    - Age of onset, course, and prognosis of different disorders may differ in both males and females, e.g., schizophrenia occurs earlier in males, and females have better prognosis.

- Sexual identity may be the presenting complaint in gender identity disorder.

4. **Address:**

- Registration: it is important in the follow up and retrospective studies.
- It may give knowledge about the patient's culture and socioeconomic state. *Knowledge about culture and socioeconomic state may:*
    - shape the patient's symptoms, e.g., a depressed patient may not mention that he/she is depressed as he/she thinks that this is an objection to the will of the God;
    - reflect awareness and knowledge about psychiatric illness;
    - reflect degree of social support system and hence expected compliance on treatment;
    - affect the prognosis of the illness, e.g., in schizophrenia, deterioration of personality and social roles become more marked in urban than in rural areas because of multiple responsibilities and duties of persons living in urban areas.

Case Example

FA is a young woman from the Gulf area; she was studying engineering at graduate level in the United States. She had an unfortunate interaction with a male graduate student. After this interaction, she went to the student counseling service for short-term counseling because she was quite upset and could not study effectively. The male counselor met her in the waiting room, introduced himself, and offered to shake hands. The Arabian student shrank away. The counselor noted this, and concluded that she was either shy or had issues with men. He believed his hypothesis was correct as the student shared her story about the rude male student at the graduate social gathering.

This way of thinking ignored the cultural differences of that female; the therapist did not realize that for a Muslim woman, it's not proper to touch a male, even to shake hands. Her behavior was complying with her religious practice and nothing to do with the incident she came to talk about.

5. **Current living situation:**

- Lives alone, lives with one or both parents, lives with a relative, unknown.
- Private residence, rooming hours, group residence, homeless, shelter, other/unknown.

6. **Highest level of education completed.**

7. **Occupation**: current employment state, e.g., unemployed; on bench; homemaker; student; skilled or unskilled manual worker, clerical, sales, technician, or farmer; owner of small business, minor professional, or administrative personnel; major professional and high executive. Detailed occupational history is assessed later on.

8. **Marital state (civil status)**: includes identifying the patient as married, separated, divorced, widowed, or single, and number of living children.

9. **Religiosity**: religious beliefs add meanings to life and enable patients to deal with daily stress, tragedy, and the existential issue of death. They also play an important role in the development of one's conscience and value system. Religious faith may be recorded here in identification data, while thorough religious history is dealt with later on.

10. **Race and ethnic group**:
    - Race and ethnic background can be a source of stress and adjustment reactions, and can influence the onset and prevalence of mental disorders.
    - Some cultures ascribe different meanings to behavior; the person with psychotic delusions may be seen as possessed by spirits, e.g., for some Asian American cultures, problems are to be dealt with in the family, and bringing a problem to a therapist is a deeply shaming experience. Individuals with this cultural background may wait a long period before they consult mental health professionals and may show greater signs of deterioration in psychological functioning.
    - Discrepancy between the psychiatrist and patient's race, ethnicity, or nationality can influence their interaction, the patient usually reacts with caution and distrust.
    - Some ethnic background is associated with certain psychiatric disorders, e.g., drinking is more common among Irish, some native-American tribes, French, and Italian than Asian Americans.

11. **Type of consultation**: it could be either voluntary or compulsory. This may denote the degree of patient's insight.

12. **Source of referral**: source of referral indicates anyone who is responsible for the patient coming to the clinic (with their full, partial, or no agreement). The patient may come to a psychiatric clinic by his/her own will or referred from another authority for assessment. Those may be:
    - a member of the family;
    - a work authority;
    - legal (or police) authorities;
    - other medical specialties.

13. **Cause of referral**: the patient may come into clinical contact for a variety of causes:

- Personal suffering, e.g., depressed mood, obsession, compulsion, insomnia, sexual dysfunction.
- Threats of dangerousness: the patient may be suicidal or homicidal.
- Relief of the family; due to difficulties in dealing with the patient because of his/her illness, e.g., ADHD, delusional patient, or personality disorder.
- Assessment of legal responsibility; when referred from court.
- Marital or premarital counseling.

14. **Other sources of information**: sometimes, other sources of information are essential to ascertain a diagnosis and to assess the impact of the disorder on the patient in different situations (academic, family, social, or work). These include relatives, friends, and school or work reports. It is important to make an impression about the informant's reliability and their level of cooperation.

15. **Type of admission**: in cases of inpatients, the patient may be admitted to the hospital voluntarily or by compulsory admission. This may denote the degree of the patient's insight. Both types of admission are different from the administrative and legal points of view.

CHIEF COMPLAINTS

Chief complaints should always be stated in the patient's own words. Although the patient's family may describe the problem quite differently, the manner in which the patient perceives events is of great importance to the psychiatrist. Precise recording of the chief complaint permits the psychiatrist to review it periodically with the patient, in an attempt to detect improvement or worsening of the illness, and early signs of relapse. *The patients differ in the way they give an account about their problems*:

1. Some patients give direct and explicit responses to questions such as "What is bothering you?" or "What can I help you with?": e.g., "I cannot sleep," "I drink too much," "I am depressed," "I am too nervous at work."
2. A group of patients give vague complaints: e.g., "I feel that I am not OK," "I do not think other people like me," "I am just not happy."
3. Some patients come with medical complaints, even though they know they are coming for psychiatric evaluation: e.g., "I suffer from backache," ". . . difficulty in breathing," etc.
4. Some patients may make inappropriate complaints that suggest severe psychopathology: e.g., "The CIA is following me," "They put a computer in my stomach."
5. Some patients deny having any symptom.

Whatever the complaint that brings the patient for psychiatric evaluation, every patient should be screened for all possible symptoms. These include: cognitive impairment (e.g., consciousness, memory impairment, etc.), substance abuse, mood changes, thought disorders, perceptual disturbances, behavioral disorders, physical complaints or anxiety about illness, sexual problems, eating problems, sleeping problems, problems with impulse control, and adjustment problems.

HISTORY OF PRESENT ILLNESS

History of the present illness represents the chief part of an interview. When properly taken, it allows the clinician to collect the essential information and symptoms needed to reach proper diagnosis and allow appropriate treatment. The essential skill in history taking of the present illness is careful listening. However, this should be done in a structured format that is not too rigid in administering to restrict proper evaluation or too loose to miss its goal.

History of the present illness clarifies the manner in which the patient's symptoms develop. It is desirable to start by determining when the symptoms began. When this is difficult, the patients are urged to come back to a time when they were symptom free and describe what has happened to them since then.

In evaluating history of the present illness, type of onset should be defined: was it sudden, gradual, or insidious; was there any precipitating factor, if so what was its role in the causation of the disorder; how have the symptoms been influenced by the environment from the time they first began? It is important to determine whether the patient's symptoms are progressing, static, or remitting, intermittent or continuous (course of symptoms). Also, the effect of the illness on the patient's social, occupational, or academic functioning is determined, and results of previous treatment trials (type, dosage, and duration) should be documented.

The patient should know that, no matter what he/she has to report, the psychiatrist, in contrast to his/her family or friends, will listen uncritically and will not argue or attempt to deny the perceptions of events, or ridicule the patient for reporting strange ideas.

The patient is usually repetitious in discussing his/her illness, rarely speaking in a chronological order but he/she usually give emphasis to those aspects that most trouble him/her. The psychiatrist should listen patiently, permitting the patient to tell his/her story, and carefully observe the patient's behavior, changes in posture, intonations, facial expressions, and emotional reactions to the various subjects discussed.

Evaluation of the Presence of Stressors

Stress is subjective and personal. It begins when we perceive a situation, a person, an event or even an object as a stressor. This means that the brain does not respond blindly, but exercises a degree of subjective interpretation. How we perceive events depends on our concepts of self, ego strength, value system, and even heredity. So, the same situation can be perceived totally differently by two individuals; one may perceive it as an exciting challenge, while the other perceives it as life threatening.

Some patients directly relate their difficulties to psychosocial stresses: family, work, financial, legal, or health problems. Here the physician's task is to define the exact nature of the stress and how it has actually influenced the patient. Other patients do not believe that their symptoms are related to psychosocial stresses even when the relationships are obvious.

Whatever the case, the clinician should inquire about the presence of stresses or events that have precipitated the present episode. Also, the clinician should consider if the patient's perceptions of stress are correct, or on the contrary, the patient is incorrectly attributing symptoms to stress.

History of Substance Use

The psychoactive substance use history includes past and present use of both licit and illicit psychoactive substances, including but not limited to alcohol, nicotine, marijuana, cocaine, opiates, sedative-hypnotic agents, stimulants, solvents, and hallucinogens.

Relevant information includes the quantity and frequency of substance use and its duration, route of administration, the pattern of use (e.g., episodic versus continual; solitary versus social), drug effects, functional, interpersonal, or legal consequences of use, tolerance and withdrawal phenomena, any temporal association between substance use and present psychiatric illness, and any self-perceived benefits of use.

Obtaining an accurate substance use history often involves a gradual, non-confrontational approach to inquiry with multiple questions seeking the same information in different ways and/or the use of slang terms for drugs.

History of Medical Diseases

Individuals with psychiatric disorders can have medical conditions that influence their functioning, quality of life, and life span. Relative to the general population, mortality rates are increased for individuals with mental illness, particularly those with psychotic disorders, depressive disorders, alcohol/substance use disorders, personality disorders, and delirium (Chang et al., 2010; Fok et al., 2012; Markkula et al., 2012; Witlox et al., 2010). Information about current and past medical history may show how patients view their medical illness, how the illness interfered with their usual activities, how the illness influenced the environment, and how the illness may have influenced the patient's development. Current non-psychiatric illness may have either a direct or indirect relationship to the patient's psychiatric symptoms.

The general medical history includes available information on known medical and neurological illnesses (including hospitalizations, procedures, and medications), important physical injury or trauma, allergies and drug sensitivities, and undiagnosed health problems that have caused the patient pain and discomfort or functional impairment.

Case Example

A 37-year-old woman presents to her general practitioner complaining of feeling "tired all the time." The feeling of tiredness had been progressive along the past 6 months and she believes it is related to coping with rearing three children aged 12, 7, and 5 years. She says that her self-esteem has been low recently and this is made worse by having no work. It is also related to gradual weight gain. Her husband is supportive. She says she has found it increasingly difficult to concentrate. She has been weepy recently but has no thoughts of self-harm or harm to others. On systematic enquiry of her health, there is nothing of note except a history of constipation, which she puts down to lethargy and lack of exercise. She also has heavy periods. She is sleeping well, but sometimes she has unrefreshing sleep. She can enjoy herself, and says she enjoys her food, and indeed has put on a few pounds recently.

Is it a medical or psychiatric disorder? Feeling "tired all the time" is one of the commonest symptoms that a GP will see. What evidence should a GP gather to establish definite diagnosis? It is crucial to gather signs and symptoms that help in narrowing down the differential diagnosis. This means enquiry into both physical and mental health problems.

Early pregnancy, stress, poor sleep, and poor nutritional intake are the commonest causes of tiredness. A range of medications and recreational drugs can also cause tiredness and this should be enquired about, particularly if new medications have recently been introduced. Enquiry and examination about signs and symptoms of possible infections, endocrinal (diabetes, thyroid or pituitary disorders), cardiac, renal, hepatic, and gastrointestinal diseases will reveal the possibility of a general medical condition. Investigations would tend to depend on the full systematic enquiry but would certainly include thyroid function tests, full blood count, blood sugar, urea, and electrolytes and liver function tests in the first instance.

It is important to rule out more serious psychological or psychiatric problems. Depression and anxiety cause tiredness as do some somatization disorders. Enquiry should include questions about diagnostic features of these disorders. Past psychiatric and family history may be revealing. Mental state examination is a cornerstone in establishing diagnosis.

Case Example

MX is a 47-year-old-man with Stage 5 chronic kidney disease due to hypertension; he has been on hemodialysis for 6 months. He also is hepatitis C positive, but his liver function is within normal values. During the past few months he started to report feeling very tired, he says that his memory has been affected recently; he has also had a lack of interest in his hobbies and is finding it difficult to be able to enjoy everyday activities such as watching the television or sharing a meal with his family.

On examination: MX speaks in short sentences and rarely makes eye contact. Most of his replies are "yes" and "no" and he frequently needs direct questions to prompt answers. MX shows signs of poor hygiene and self-care.

In people with chronic diseases it can be hard to differentiate the symptoms caused by the chronic disease from depression. What questions could help to establish the presence of depression as a cause of these symptoms? *It is useful to ask the patient about*:

1. the presence of depressive symptoms during the last month ("Have you often been bothered by feeling down, depressed or hopeless?" or "Have you often been bothered by having little interest or pleasure in doing things?");
2. their previous history of depressive episodes and explore the biological symptoms of depression.

Past Psychiatric History

The past psychiatric history includes a chronological summary of all past episodes of mental illness and treatment, including psychiatric syndromes not formally diagnosed at the time, previously established diagnoses, prior suicide attempts or other self-destructive behavior, and otherwise unexplained episodes of social or occupational disability, treatments offered, and responses to treatment. The dose, duration of treatment, efficacy, side effects, and patient's adherence to previously prescribed medications, are part of the past psychiatric history.

PERSONAL HISTORY

The history of each period of the patient's life (infancy, childhood, adolescence, and adulthood) should be described separately. Writing the history in this chronological manner will show the behavior patterns that developed with maturity, and the environmental factors that facilitate its development.

In developing information about how the personal history is relevant to the present symptomatology, *it is useful for the clinician to make three general types of inquiries*:

1. How did certain characteristics of the past environment adversely influence the patient?

2. How did certain characteristics of the patient interfere with his or her capacity to meet environmental expectations?
3. How has the environment responded to the patient's deficiencies?

Assessment of Personal History Includes the Following Items

Early Development

Developmental history is of importance in children. In adults, it is useful in understanding developmental disorder extending into adulthood. *The following is assessed:*

1. Attitudes of the parents toward the child at the time of conception, whether the child was wanted or not, and the persistence and effect of these parental attitudes.
2. Diseases, medication use, or trauma during pregnancy.
3. Whether the mother was abusing drugs or alcohol.
4. Type of delivery and presence of complications during it, and any evidence of injury or birth defect at birth.
5. Major neonatal and early childhood disorders, and serious diseases especially any affecting the central nervous system.
6. Feeding habits: breast or bottle-feeding, eating problems.
7. Milestones of development (date of crawling, walking, talking, and sphincter control).
8. The stages of the patient's life, with special attention to patterns of response to normative life transitions and major life events.
9. Toilet training: age, attitude of parents, feelings about it.
10. Sleeping patterns: it is desirable to know what they were during infancy, and whether and when they subsequently altered. If an infant shared the intimacy of his/her mother's bedroom, but was displaced by the return of his/her father from travel or from military service, or by the birth of a sibling, the displacement could play a major role in subsequent emotional development and affect his/her relationship with his/her father or sibling.
11. Physical motility: infants display considerable variation in physical motility. Some are passive even if they are hungry; others display discomfort with loud noises, much crying, and thrashing about in the crib. There are indications that much of this variation is inborn. Parents may respond to it with attitudes ranging from guilt or displeasure to pride, depending on what they think their baby should display. When the infant's behavior does not meet the parent's expectations, a cycle may be established; disapproval from the parent, stemming from the infant's own anxiety, results in anxiety in the infant, which then causes more anxiety in the parent.

School Record

School represents the main environment that can show and enable a child's intellectual, social, motor, and many other abilities. This elucidates the importance of carefully recording school history. *The following items are important to ask about:*

1. **Age of beginning**: children start going to school at the age of 4–6 years. In extraordinary situations, and in some cases of autism or intellectual disability, parents may decide to postpone their children for an additional academic year.
2. **Type of school**: whether it is a regular school or special school for children with certain difficulties.
3. **Adjustment to school**:
    *   relationships with peers and teachers;
    *   favorite studies or interests, particular abilities or assets, extracurricular activities sports, and hobbies;
    *   abnormal behavior; e.g., bullying, school truancy.
4. **Academic achievements**:
    *   how far the patient progressed and his/her highest level of academic performance, and how far other members of the patient's family went in school and how this relates to the patient's progression;
    *   the patient's attitude toward academic achievement.

Causes of Difficulties of Academic Achievement

1. *Low intelligence*: this may result in low academic achievements.
2. *Social problems*: a child may be occupied in helping his/her family and has no time to study.
3. *Physical problems*: chronic or recurrent acute physical diseases.
4. *Mental disorders*: e.g., attention deficit hyperactivity disorder or major depression.

Occupational History

The work record is an indicator of both the patient's abilities and the stability of their personality. Work may be affected by mental disorder or substance use. However, loss or frequent changes of job may relate to external factors, e.g., social, national, economic, or political reasons.

It is useful to go through the patient's entire work history from first job to the current one. When time is limited, it may be more practical to ask what jobs the patient worked at for the longest period of time and to focus on the patient's current occupation. In either case the clinician should try to determine the status of the patient's jobs, the degree of success at work, and to assess whether the amount of energy needed in their work is static, decreasing, or increasing.

Even if there is no change in job performance it is useful to inquire whether it is getting more physically or intellectually taxing. Either upward or downward occupational mobility can be stressful. Reviewing the exact skills that are needed in the patient's current employment helps the physician to learn about various aspects of the patient's motor, social, and cognitive skills.

A high level of job satisfaction helps the patient to deal with mental illness. A low level of satisfaction may be a causative or complicating factor. Job satisfaction is determined by monetary rewards, the enjoyment of the work itself, and the quality of interpersonal experiences available on the job.

Stresses associated with the work environment may have deleterious effects on the patient's health (noise, chemicals).

Finally, it is to be noted that, even severely disturbed patients may be quite well at work, as they find work the only satisfying aspect of their lives or the most precious object that they should save. The presence of a positive work situation may be a critical factor in the clinician's decision to hospitalize the patient or not.

To summarize, it is good to ask about:

1. the sequence of jobs held, why taken on, how long held, payment received and reasons for change;
2. the patient's current or most recent employment, including whether current or recent jobs have involved unusual physical or psychological stress, toxic materials, a noxious environment, or shift work;
3. the patient's feelings about their current job, any work related conflicts, and the long-term ambitions and goals;
4. relation with his/her mates, subordinates, and his/her seniors;
5. discrepancy between individual's ability and either the nature of the job or payment.

Religious History

The most striking feature of religion is its universality. There are few societies in which religion plays no significant role. The involvement in certain religious groups may provide nurturance or conversely may be a source of additional stress. So, it is useful to inquire about the role of religion in the patient's upbringing and about the kinds of religious beliefs and experiences that the patient has had throughout their life.

Knowledge of the patient's religious belief may influence treatment planning. Patients who have strong fundamentalist beliefs may not respond well to psychotherapies that emphasize expression of feelings, particularly anger, or that encourage confrontation.

The key issue in taking a religious history is the physician's capacity to show respect for the patient's belief system. All patients should be asked about the nature and depth of their religious beliefs. Patients who deny religious beliefs can be asked, "are there other beliefs that provide meaning for you or help you cope with stress such as tragedy or death?" Most people have thoughts about these issues and are willing to discuss them.

At the level of clinical practice, it was found that the incidence of certain disorders is less common in certain religious groups. Knowledge of the patient's religious belief may also influence treatment planning. Religious institutions may help the patient to develop spiritual strength or subject him/her to brainwashing and coercion.

Lastly it is important to notice that religious experiences have some similarities with some psychiatric symptoms, a matter that needs careful assessment to delineate the pathological from the normal.

1. **Similarities between obsessive symptoms and religious experience**:

   - fixed stereotyped and rigid character of the behavior in each;
   - anxiety provoked when a specific action not performed or performed imprecisely;
   - some religious acts and thoughts are used to counter obsessive symptoms;
   - many obsessive thoughts are religious.

2. **Mystical trance** has been described frequently in some religious groups. It often resembles an episode of dissociation.

3. **Psychosis and religious experience and beliefs**: a religious belief may be bizarre and at variance with those held by the clinician; this does not make it abnormal, i.e., it is unwise to equate the surprising with the pathological. *Suggestive indicators for delineating religious experience from psychiatric morbidity are*:

   - In psychosis, the phenomenology of the experience conforms to psychiatric illness. There are recognizable symptoms of mental disorder; delusions, hallucination, disturbance of mood and behavior. Also, personality is disordered in a way consistent with the disturbance.
   - The religious experience conforms to the subject's recognizable religious traditions and peer group. The person understands, and allows the disbelief of others. Also, those persons usually consider that the experience implies some demands on him/her.
   - Religious experience provokes sustained meaningful goal-directed activity, while the behavior due to mental illness is often unreasonable in that it does not follow logically from the experience, is bizarre in disregarding and degrading popular customs, is concrete in making spiritual values physical.

- Religious experience is usually regarded by the believer as being metaphorical or spiritual, while with psychotics the experience is concrete and physical.
- Religious beliefs are held alongside the possibility of religious doubts, though the person shows some degree of reservation about discussing the experience with those he/she anticipates will be unsympathetic. Delusions and hallucinations in psychotic patients are accepted without doubt as "concrete reality," and the patient struggles to prove them in spite of lack of acceptance from others.

Sexual History

Although there has been significant change in attitude about sex in recent years, the physician should be aware of the risk of embarrassing the patient in the course of talking sexual history. Questions should be asked tactfully, and answers should be handled in the same way.

So, in the early phase of evaluation, a detailed assessment of sexual history is not needed unless the patient complains of sexual dysfunction or is involved in a type of sexual behavior that troubles him/her or others. In patients who report no sexual difficulties, the effort to take the history of past sexual experiences may not provide sufficient diagnostic or therapeutic information to justify the invasion of privacy and the possible loss of rapport that it may produce.

To summarize, it is good to ask about the following:

1. Early curiosity, infantile masturbation, sex play.
2. Acquisition of sexual knowledge: at what age, its source and content, how it has been modified or corrected later on. Attitude of parents toward sex. Sexual abuse.
3. Onset of puberty, feelings about it, kind of preparation, development of secondary sex character.
4. Gender identity, sexual identity, and sexual orientation.
5. Adolescent sexual activity: crushes, parties, dating, petting, masturbation, nocturnal emissions, and attitudes toward them.
6. Sexual practices: sexual problems, heterosexual or homosexual experiences, paraphilia, promiscuity, orientation preferences.
7. Attitudes toward the opposite sex: shy, timid, aggressive, seductive, need to impress, sexual conquests, anxiety.
8. Masturbation: its frequency, object, associated fantasy, level (mental, physical or both). Also mal-information about its hazards on physical health or being unforgivable sin, etc. This should be asked even in married individuals since it is sometimes practiced in married people. Females need tactful inquiry about this topic.

9. Circumcision: it could be associated with guilt, feelings of being crushed, devitalized, or castrated.

10. Unusual or abnormal sexual practice: as regards mode, object (homosexual), or stimulus (e.g., fetishism) should be reported especially if it represents a phase of development rather than a current presenting disorder.

11. The issue of patient's sexual preference may be obvious early in the interview. No matter how comfortable patients may be with their homosexual orientation at present, it is safe to assume it has caused them some painful moments in the past. Every homosexual must go through the process of realizing that his or her sexual preferences are different from those of his or her peers and is forced to deal with the many stresses that societies put on homosexuals. Adjustment to homosexual preferences influences other aspects of the patient's life and may be relevant to the current symptomatology.

12. In patients with sexual dysfunction, an elaborate past history is required. The clinician begins by determining whether the major problem is lack of interest in sexual activity with the available partner, or whether the patient has a sexual desire but is unable to perform sexual intercourse satisfactorily. In addition to taking history of physical illness and patterns of drug use, the clinician should inquire about when performance becomes a problem, what kinds of thoughts and feelings have compromised sexual enjoyment, and under what conditions sexual experience has been enjoyable.

13. Chronic lack of sexual interest may stem from abnormal physical conditions, personality problems, learned fear of sexuality, or it may develop gradually as a response to performance problems. In evaluating diminished sexual interest, the clinician should inquire about sexual feelings that may be manifested in fantasy or dreams. The clinician must ask also about non-sexual aspects of the relationships with partners.

Menstrual History

Menstruation is a unique part of a female's life. Unexpected onset of periods in an unprepared girl could give rise to anxiety. Dysphoric disorder may be related to menstruation in some girls. In a case of amenorrhea, pregnancy is suspected (with all precaution needed), though it may be a side effect of antipsychotic drug use. *The following items are important to ask about:*

1. Age of menarche, how the patient first learns about menstruation, attitude to periods, regularity, amount, dysmenorrhea, and premenstrual dysphoric disorder.

2. Date of last menstrual period.

3. Age at menopause and any symptoms at that time.

Marital History

Marital history provides a picture of the most important relationship of adult patients' lives. Thus it tells a great deal about a patient's personality traits and their stresses, their vulnerabilities, and their pattern of learning during adulthood. *There are certain areas that are especially important, including:*

Relationships with the Spouse

1. **Age of patient at marriage**: is there any age discrepancy with the other partner and effect of that discrepancy.
2. **Type of marriage**: marriage is not the same in all cultures:

    - *love marriage*: choice of the two partners after mutual attraction;
    - *arranged marriage*: the partners agree about the proposal suggested by a family member or a friend;
    - *forced marriage*: it is accomplished against the will of one or both partners;
    - *business marriage*: partners agree to marry to obtain certain benefits.

3. **Spouse occupation**: it may have implications on social and financial life.
4. **Spouse health**: it may have implication on social, financial, and sexual life.
5. **The quality of communication between partners**: marriage provides the opportunity to discuss feelings and problems with a loved empathic person. Ideally, marital partners can discuss freely with one another almost anything, particularly their feelings about one another. Patterns of communication could be revealed by asking the patient directly about them or by observing the patient's interaction with his or her spouse. As the patient reveals feelings such as anger, or fear, it is appropriate to ask, "Have you shared this with your spouse?" If the patient answers negatively, the physician should inquire, "Why not?" The answers to these questions are likely to clarify the limitation of communication that characterizes the marriage.
6. **The quality and frequency of sexual relationships**: changes in the quality or frequency of sexual activity may be associated with a mental or physical disorder, or with problems in the marriage such as conflicts or shifts in power within the relationship. Many men accept the idea of equality between sexes intellectually but still find it difficult to deal with the reality of a wife's being assertive or, perhaps, being the main breadwinner. This may have a negative impact on their sexual interest and performance. Women who feel that they are being committed to what they view as the low status role of homemaker may similarly resent their husbands' success in business, service, or academic career. Such resentment may be expressed as a loss of sexuality.

7. **Emotional relationship between partners**: some patients consider their spouses their best friend; both their non-sexual and sexual interactions are characterized by a great deal of affection and playfulness. Other patients seem to see their spouses primarily as sex partner, breadwinner, or homemaker; they show little indication of playfulness and tend to focus on their marital obligations or duties rather than their marital pleasures. Information about this aspect of marriage could be known by asking the patient, "What do you and your spouse like to do together?" or "Do you play together very much?" or "Do you laugh a lot when you are with each other?"

8. **The capacity of partners to retain separate identities**: it is not uncommon to see couples who show an excessive degree of mutual dependency; they cling to one another for support, and each may be unconvinced of his or her capacity to be free of despair without the other being constantly present and available. Information about this aspect of marriage could be known by asking the patient, "Do you have leisure interests that you pursue without your spouse?" or "How do you get along when you and your spouse are separated for several days?"

9. **Reaction of the spouse to the patient's illness**: some patients learn to receive more affection, compassion, and attention from their spouses as a result of their illness. This may lead to reinforcement of the symptoms of their couples, and being resistant to most treatments. This can only be ameliorated by education of the spouse, usually in the process of marital treatment.

10. **The existence of exploitation of one partner**: although most marriages eventually reach some type of equilibrium in which the two partners' dissatisfaction and gratification are approximately equal. However, there are some marriages in which one partner dominates and takes advantages of the other. It is still common to see marriages in which women are ignored, treated cruelly or harshly, or treated like property by their husbands. Because of personality difficulties, religious beliefs, or lack of alternatives, these women may continue to endure the marriages. Although women's physical abuse is the most common, it should not be surprising to find male patients who are physically abused by their spouses. When a patient describes her husband as domineering, it is useful to inquire, "Is your husband ever verbally abusive toward you?" or "Is this dominance associated with physical violence?" or "Does he get worse after drinking?"

11. **Patterns of arguments within the marriage**: some patients insist they never argue with their spouses, a matter that could be true. Sometimes, such a statement means that when they discuss conflicts with one another, the couple tries to mute their anger. When married people never argue, it is usually true that at least one partner is harboring strong resentment toward the other and would prefer a more open relationship. That person

may be more susceptible to psychiatric symptomatology. Arguments can induce acute episodes of anxiety or sadness in one of the participants and can exert a corrosive effect on the marriage. It is usually useful to inquire about the content of such disagreements; usually revolves around sex, money, and in-laws. The clinician should inquire about what starts the arguments, how long they last, what terminates them, whether they result in violence or compromise, and how they affect the participants afterwards.

12. **Previous relationships and engagements, and causes of failure**: frequent broken relationships before marriage may reflect abnormalities of personality; also, a previous relationship may determine the patient's attitude to the present marriage, e.g., when a first marriage has ended in divorce because of the husband's infidelity, or a woman may overreact to minor difficulties in her second marriage.

Relationships of Patients with their Children

The relationships of patients with their children may be a source of stress or gratification. Raising a sick or psychologically difficult child puts great stress on a marriage and increases the risk of psychiatric symptoms and divorce. On the other hand, children may provide hope for the future and for some patients, a reason to stay alive.

The clinician should inquire about number, age, and gender of all children, any difficulties they may have had or are currently having, and the nature of their relationship with their parents.

If the patient has no children, the clinician should ask tactfully about the causes, and note the patient's emotional reaction to this.

RESEARCHERS HAVE IDENTIFIED FOUR BASIC PARENTING STYLES

1. **Authoritarian parents** are strict, punishing, and unsympathetic. They value obedience from their children, do not encourage independence, and seldom praise their children. Children raised in this way tend to be unfriendly, distrustful, and withdrawn.

2. **Permissive parents** give their children complete freedom with little discipline. Children raised in this way tend to be immature, dependent, and unhappy.

3. **Authoritative parents** reason with their children, giving greater responsibilities with age. They set firm limits but also remain understanding and encourage independence. Their demands are reasonable, rational, and consistent. Children raised in this way tend to be friendly, cooperative, self-reliant, and socially responsible. They are also more successful in school and better tolerate divorce of their parents, if it should occur.

4. **Uninvolved parents** invest as little time, money, and effort in their children as possible, focusing more on their own needs over their children's.

Medical or Mental Disorders within the Family

In addition to being a source of stress within the family, genetic predisposition may be suspected in the presence of one of these disorders within the family.

Military History

Military service is a unique environment for most people; in some ways it is more stressful. Military service requires adjustment to a new geographical region while separated from the family and friends. It requires the capacity to live with very little privacy and in close proximity to members of the same sex, and the ability to adjust to a hierarchical culture in which one must submit to authority.

The military history may reveal something about the patient's personality traits. It is always useful to inquire about how successfully the patient accommodated to military life and to obtain information about various military experiences. The rapidity with which the patient advanced in rank provides a good index of the quality of their military adjustment. Inquiries about disciplinary problems or misconduct during this service may provide a clue about antisociality.

Special attention should be given to combat experiences and their subsequent impact on the patient. Also, it is useful to enquire about physical and mental problems that developed during the service and whether they have been dismissed as having service-connected disability.

Social History

The social history includes the patient's living arrangements and currently important relationships. Emphasis is given to relationships, both familial and non-familial, that are relevant to the present illness; act as stressors, or have the potential to serve as resources for the patient. Also included is a history of any formal involvement with social agencies or the courts, as well as details of any current litigation or criminal proceedings.

The current living circumstances include ascertaining with whom the patient is living: is it alone, or with one or both of his/her parents, with a mate or with one or more of his or her children? Knowledge about the type of dwelling in which the patient lives and the financial responsibility for the dwelling is important.

Habits

Habit is a fixed pattern of behavior. *It is divided into:*

1. Biological: e.g., sleeping, eating.
2. Psychological: e.g., smoking, alcohol drinking, drug abuse.

Premorbid Personality Assessment

Personality refers to the enduring qualities of an individual as shown in his/her ways of behaving in a wide variety of circumstances. Each person has his/her own pattern of perceiving, thinking about, or relating to themselves or to others. So, whether or not a formal personality disorder is diagnosed, all psychiatric patients have personality traits that influence the manner in which they deal with any mental illness they may develop.

Personality traits also influence the development and expression of physical illness, and response to treatment. Personality variables exert a direct influence on how an individual responds to stressful life events. Knowledge of personality traits helps the psychiatrist predict how patients are likely to respond to specific psychiatric disabilities and to specific treatment. *The clinician's task in evaluating personality traits is threefold*:

1. Description of the present personality traits.
2. Determination of the maladaptive traits.
3. Ascertaining how these traits influence the patient's response to any symptoms of mental disorders that may be present.

Studying the personality could help in:

1. **Diagnosis**: it supports the diagnosis since some psychiatric disorders are associated with specific premorbid features, e.g., patients with bipolar disorder may show cyclothymic traits, while patients with schizophrenia often show odd behavior and are socially isolated before the onset of the disorder.
2. **Determining** how the patient reacts to an illness.
3. **Prognosis**: setting the therapeutic goals beyond which treatment is less likely to produce improvement.
4. **Prevention**: by supporting the vulnerable personalities thus avoiding precipitating factors.

Evaluations of personality are made by obtaining a history of the patient's past pattern of perceiving, thinking about, or relating to themselves or to others. The maladaptive aspects of such traits can be inferred by inquiring about how the patient responded to a variety of past experiences and by noting when these responses have not served them well. Consequently, the physician notes whether any maladaptive patterns are detectable or expressed during interview. In determining the impact of personality traits on symptoms, the clinician must explore the manner in which patients perceive, think about, and deal with their disorders. *In evaluating personality, it is useful to evaluate the following*:

1. **Social relations**:

   - *To others (friendships)*: few or many (extroverted or introverted), superficial or close, leader or follower, e.g., relationships during a trip, with own or opposite sex. Relations with workmates and superiors. Difficulties in interpersonal relationships and their possible causes.
   - *To family*: dependent or independent (e.g., on choosing clothes).

2. **Intellectual activities and interests**: how a person spends leisure time (hobbies)? Leisure time is valued and spent in a variety of ways. The career-oriented patient may have little interest in leisure activity, but other persons may view work only as a means of facilitating their spare-time interests. Leisure may involve activities such as sports, shopping, watching television, reading, listening to music, working on crafts, home maintenance, or just spending time with friends and loved ones. Free or leisure time is a period of relaxation and joy, but for some persons it is a time of anxiety, boredom, or despair. One way to get this information is to inquire about how the person spends their evenings and weekends. Knowledge of how a person spends leisure time may help the physician to predict how the patient will respond to changes that may either compromise or expand leisure time. It may also provide clues to planning rehabilitative interventions.

3. **Mood**: normal mood varies according to situation, happy in good situations and sad in bad situations. However, some persons react excessively with undue readiness for environmental stimuli leading to apparent mood swings, others appear cold, optimistic, pessimistic, anxious (worrying, insecure, and self-doubtful), self-confident, or demonstrative in their reactions to situations. To obtain this information, it is useful to assess prevailing mood, mood reactivity, and stability or swinging of mood.

4. **Character**: the person as described by others (sensitive, reserved, timid, shy, suspicious, jealous, resentful, quarrelsome, irritable, impulsive, selfish, self-centered, self-conscious, lacking confidence, controlling, dramatizing, self-sacrificing, reclusive, impulsive, dependent, suggestible and good imitator, strict, fussy, rigid, meticulous, proud, aggressive, punctual, excessively tidy, idealistic and over careful, over-conscientious, religious and/or over concern about the body, health, and illness).

5. **Energy (behavior)**: describe the energy output in general (active vs. lazy), the pattern of the output of energy (sustainability, periodicity, etc.), and the domains of output. Field of energy output could be intellectual, business, work, social, sportive, or otherwise.

6. **Personal standards and attitudes**: this refers to a collection of moral, ideological, religious and political standards; the person would belong to some sufficient period.

Family History

Studies suggest that most major psychiatric disorders are familial, and the disposition to psychiatric disorders may be genetically transmitted, even though the mode of transmission is unknown. A history of psychiatric illness in biological relatives is a risk factor for most psychiatric illnesses. Information can be obtained from informants (family history) or by direct interview of each relative (family study).

Family history can be used to confirm a psychiatric diagnosis and to predict course and treatment response in young patients with their first encounter, especially when making the differential diagnosis of psychotic depression versus schizophrenia, or bipolar disorder versus schizophrenia.

Family history includes description of the parents and siblings in the patient's family of origin; their names, ages, occupations, economic and social status, marital records, and history of physical and mental illness.

1. **Parents**: current age (or at death if dead, give the cause of death), health, occupation, personality, was there divorce or marital separation and what was the emotional response of the patient, and quality of relation with patient (parenting style). A hint about step-parents is usually recommended if present.
2. **Siblings**: names, ages, marital status, occupation, personality, health, and quality of relation with patient.
3. **Socioeconomic state of family**: home atmosphere and family relationship currently and during the patient's childhood, number of rooms, and financial state.
4. **Family diseases**: mental illness (including suicide), psychiatric hospitalization, mental retardation, epilepsy, drug abuse, and relevant physical illness.

MENTAL STATE EXAMINATION

Mental State Examination (MSE) is the chief examination in psychiatry. For psychiatrists, the MSE is similar to the physical examination in general medicine (Siassi, 1984).This is why physician, psychotherapist, and counselor training all now include MSE skills. Talley and Littlefield (2009) reported devoting about five instructional hours per medical student to teach MSE.

Like internists who are experts in using physical examination techniques such as palpation, auscultation, etc., psychiatrists need to be expert observers of all significant positive and negative findings on metal state examinations. Such observations should take place throughout the patient interview, and not be limited to a particular point of examination. So, it is important to emphasize that the mental state examination is not a discrete aspect of the total examination. It does not begin at a distinct point in time, after the history has been taken, but most of the critical aspects of the patient's motor and verbal behavior and their experiences are revealed in the process of taking the history. However, the observations should be recorded in a specific structured format that is called the Mental State Examination (MSE). When properly done, MSE can give a detailed portrait of the patient's condition during the interview.

Though MSE deals mainly with the present, not the past, it is impossible to do such assessment without learning a little about the patient's past. Some symptoms, e.g., delusional beliefs or hallucinations, may not exist at the time of the assessment but may be a significant aspect of the patient's current functioning. Even though the account of these symptoms is derived from history taking, rather than direct observation, it would be confusing and inconvenient to report those as part of the history, rather than as an aspect of mental state examination, e.g., "a patient who hears voices only in the evening while the examination is performed in the morning," or "a patient who believes that he/she was followed by one person who left him/her during the examination."

Mental state examination is most useful when it is based on a phenomen-ological approach. This requires that psychopathology be observed and accurately described, and that an emphasis on explanation be postponed. Explanation of psychiatric findings may be useful in planning treatment, but explanatory systems should not be allowed to influence a phase of evaluation that requires objective observation.

Clinicians are advised not to trust their inferences and to test various aspects of mental state, as the performance of patients on formal testing may yield results that are different from what would be suspected from the observation during interview.

In summary, MSE should be recorded in a certain order and organized according to certain categories. However, the order of examination usually depends on the circumstances under which the patient and psychiatrist meet, the degree of cooperation that the patient displays, and the degree of intactness of his/her sensorium. In any particular situation, the examiner should use his/her judgment about which parts of the MSE are to be emphasized.

A comfortable transition from the history to examination must be made. Some possible transitional phrases are "before we end this interview, I am going to ask you some questions that will help in the evaluation of your thinking, mood, and cognitive functions." A typical MSE includes consideration of the following domains:

1. General appearance, attitude, and behavior
2. Mood and affect
3. Language and speech

4. Thought disorders
5. Perception
6. Cognition

    • orientation
    • attention and concentration
    • memory
    • abstraction and conceptualization
    • intelligence
    • fund of knowledge

 7. Insight and judgment
 8. Reliability
 9. Diagnosis and case formulation
10. Initial treatment plan.

General Appearance, Attitude, and Behavior

An MSE usually begins by describing the general appearance: a person's appearance can provide useful clues to their quality of self-care, lifestyle and daily living skills. *Observations on this topic include the following*:

• level of consciousness
• physical characteristics
• apparent age
• position and posture
• eye contact
• facial expressions
• dress and grooming
• attitude
• behavior.

Level of Consciousness

It is critical to assess level of consciousness at the start of examination. Disturbed consciousness will affect significantly other components of examination. Assessment of consciousness needs only observation of quantitative and qualitative disturbance of consciousness. Quantitative changes of consciousness are best assessed by the Glasgow Coma Scale, which depends on assessment of best motor response, best verbal response, eye opening. The highest score (15) means being fully conscious, while the lowest score (3) means deep coma. Qualitative changes of consciousness need observation of features of disorders described in the signs and symptoms section.

Attitude

Attitude toward the interviewer needs no specific inquiry, it just necessitates observation. Assessment of attitude provides an indication of the client's motivation for treatment. It includes degree and type of cooperativeness, and resistance. The examiner should note whether the patient appeared interested during the interview or, perhaps, if the patient appeared bored.

When appropriate, recording of the evaluator's attitude toward the patient ("countertransference") may be useful information. Doing so, the interviewer should be aware that the patient has a legal right to read the record. This necessitates recording attitudes in a diplomatic language that is devoid of strong emotions or reactions.

Common reported attitudes include the following:

- *Sensitivity*: easily hurt or damaged, delicate, susceptible.
- *Passive*: inactive submissive, no opposition.
- *Dependent*: requires assistance from others.
- *Dramatic*: vivid, emotional, with flair.
- *Entitlement*: exaggerated sense of importance.
- *Perfectionist*: demands higher quality of performance from self and others, more than what is required by the situation.
- *Anti-authority*: hostile to or opposes social establishments, legal authorities, etc.
- *Eccentric*: odd, deviation from established norms.
- *Manipulative*: self-serving, controlling for own advantage.
- *Suspicious*: distrustful, guarded.
- *Impulsive*: prone to act spontaneously.
- *Aggressive*: forceful, ready, pushy.

Apparent Age

The correspondence between the patient's age and his/her appearance is noted. The nature of any discord should be elucidated and possible explanation given.

Facial Expression

Facial expression displayed during interview is observed. Observations on facial expression are complementary to next coming item of affect and mood assessment. Appropriateness of the facial expression and its consistence with the subject under discussion should be observed. Patients with little or no facial expression (mask face) may have depression, a neurologic syndrome (e.g., Parkinson's disease, minor hemisphere stroke), or a drug-induced parkinsonian syndrome.

Eye Contact

The degree to which a patient makes eye contact with the examiner often indicates his or her level of comfort in the interview. The degree of avoidance of eye contact, and any evident explanation to that avoidance is noted and recorded. Possible comments about eye contact include: proper, poor, or exaggerated.

Position and Posture

Position and posture assumed by the patient are noted and recorded.

Physical Characteristics

Obvious physical stigmata and general state of physical health are to be noted. Striking physical characteristics such as shaved head, tattoos, needle marks, scars from prior suicide attempts or self-mutilation, skin lesions or discoloration, unusual facial markings, approximate height and weight (obesity or thinness), sweating, disabilities, and amputated limbs should be noted.

Apparent health condition should be noted and recorded, (e.g., wheezes, coughs, any odors emanating from the patient, including that of alcohol, feces, or urine).

Dress and Grooming

The manner of dress and grooming that is distinguishing to the patient is observed and recorded. Possible comments include: good, fair, poor. Explanation of these comments is valuable.

Behavior

The whole spectrum of abnormalities of behavior described before is to be noted and recorded, including motor, social, and sexual behavior.

Mood and Affect

Affect is assessed through observation of the following variables:

- **Affective content (type):** This involves identification of the patient's affective state during the interview: sadness, euphoria, irritability, anxiety, fear, shame, guilt, remorse, anger, or anything else. Indicators of affective content include facial expression, body posture, movement, and voice tone, e.g., sad affect may be inferred from seeing the patient tearing up with downcast gaze accompanied by psychomotor retardation. In contrast, clenching fists, gritted teeth, and strong language suggest an "angry" affect.

- **Intensity of affect**: observe the strength of emotional expression displayed by the patient. It is described as average (euthymic), blunted (reduced intensity of emotional expression), or flat (complete lack of emotional expression).
- **Range**: observe variations in emotional expression throughout the interview. Range of affect varies depending on the patient's current situation and the subject under discussion. Normal persons can show the whole range of affect, being anxious in scary situations, laughing when there are funny topics, and looking gloomy when sad or painful issues are discussed. In normal persons affect is of average intensity, stable, and congruent with the content of the conversation. In pathological cases, affective expression is also variable, e.g., persons with mania or histrionic traits may show an unduly wide range of emotions during the interview, from happiness to sadness.
- **Change pattern (lability)**: refers to the rate of change of emotional expression; it is usually described as stable (normal rate of change) or labile (rapid change in emotional expression, without external stimuli).
- **Appropriateness**: observe congruence of affect to thought content; it could be described as appropriate when congruent, or inappropriate when not. Caution is required when judging appropriateness of client affect, especially when interviewing clients with diverse cultural backgrounds.

Mood is best assessed by describing four variables: predominant mood, its duration, reactivity, and diurnal variation.

- **Predominant mood**: usually described as euthymic, anxious, apprehensive, depressed, dysphoric, euphoric, and irritable. Description of mood should be as specific as possible, and vague terms such as "upset" or "agitated" should be avoided.
- **Duration**: assess the persistence of the mood over time, measured in hours, days, weeks, months, or even years.
- **Reactivity**: assess whether or not mood changes in response to external events or circumstances.
- **Diurnal variation**: assess the consistency of the mood within the course of the day.

Some questions that may help in revealing mood include:

- "How are your spirits?"
- "How are you feeling?"
- "Have you been discouraged/depressed/low/blue lately?"
- "Have you been energized/elated/high/out of control lately?"
- "Have you been angry/irritable/edgy lately?"

If the patient is mute or communicates little, his/her mood is inferred on the basis of recent history, general appearance, or motor behavior. Associated symptoms may help in ascertaining mood, e.g., insomnia, anorexia, and withdrawal from activity in depression. Also the content of the patients' thoughts may help in understanding their feelings e.g., depressed patients report thoughts that revolve around guilt, loss, and hopelessness.

Language and Speech

Assessment of the amount and rate of speech is included by some authors in speech assessment; but this book is more apt to consider these abnormalities as part of formal thought disorders, described later.

The essential elements of language assessment are comprehension, repetition, fluency, naming, reading, and writing, all of which should be tested when assessing language. Speech is assessed for articulation, phonation, and fluency.

Assessment of spontaneous speech is the most important aspect of language examination. In particular, attention should be paid to fluency, grammar, any paraphasias (incorrect words), word finding, and articula-tion. Fluency refers to phrase length. This should not be confused with pauses due to word-finding difficulty. The nature of any paraphasias may also be illuminating. Phonemic paraphasias (e.g., SPORAGE for ORANGE) occur in damage to anterior language areas, as may neologisms (new words). Semantic paraphasias (e.g., FRUIT or ORANGE for APPLE) are indicative of semantic memory impairment.

Naming should comprise items of varying degrees of frequency (a mixture of common and uncommon objects), e.g., pen, watch, sleeve, buckle, nib, hand, stem, winder, band, belt, and watch. Low frequency words may be lost before high frequency words.

Comprehension needs to be assessed at different levels of complexity:

1. *Single words*: ask the patient to point to an object in the room, e.g., window, door, or chair.
2. *Complex instructions*: ask the patient to follow a complex order, e.g., "Open the box, withdraw the envelope, and give it to me."
3. *Conceptual*: ask the patient questions that reveal his/her understanding of a concept, e.g., "What is the name of an item in the kitchen used to drink?" "What is the name of an item in the kitchen that is used to eat?"

Repetition: the patient is asked to repeat a sentence after the examiner, allowing only one trial. Repetition should be tested for monosyllabic single words, then polysyllabic single words, and finally sentences. Phrases using small grammatical function words, such as "No ifs, ands, or buts," are particularly difficult for patients with conduction aphasia. Impaired repetition indicates perisylvian pathology.

Reading: the patient is asked to read and obey simple commands clearly written on a piece of paper, e.g., open your mouth, or close your eyes. While reading skills usually parallel spoken language abilities, this is not always the case. If a reading problem is identified, it is important to then establish what type of dyslexia is present. Analysis of performance on letter identification, reading exception words and non-words, and analysis of the type of reading errors allow determination of the type of dyslexia.

Writing: screening for the presence of dysgraphia may be achieved by asking the patient to spontaneously write some sentences; it is not a dictation, it is to be written spontaneously. The sentence should contain a subject and verb and be comprehensible. Correct grammar and punctuation are not necessary. If a deficit is detected, then the ability of the patient to write regular and exception words to dictation allows further subdivision of the dysgraphia. If the formation of letters suggests a motor problem in writing, then the subsequent finding of normal oral spelling can establish that this is a peripheral dysgraphia and not true language impairment.

Thought Disorders

Thought abnormalities should be recognized and documented including giving relevant examples using the patient's own words. Thus, in a patient who has "loosening of association" or "pressure of speech," it is good to document these findings, but it is more appropriate to include relevant quotes or to describe the behavior that led the examiner to arrive at them. Thinking is generally evaluated regarding their form, content, and the presence of suicidal and violent thoughts.

Formal Thought Disorders

Formal thought disorders are assessed through observation of the amount and form of speech during interview. During the interview, the clinician needs to observe the patient's response to questions regarding the patient's history and whether the patient answers the questions directly, follows side issues before giving the correct answer, follows side issues and does not give an appropriate answer, or any other abnormality of formal thought disorder. Possible descriptors of the patient response include goal-directed, circumstantial, tangential, loose associations, incoherent, evasive, racing, blocking, perseveration, and neologisms. Guiding the patient back to the topic at hand should follow any deviation of the patient from such topic, and the whole process should be documented.

Thought Content

Abnormal contents involve preoccupations, overvalued ideas, delusions, and obsessions. The skilled interviewer uses both careful listening and close questioning to assess the thought content. Details of the interview may give opportunities to understand better what is on patients' minds and to ask revealing questions to uncover delusions. Patients may be guarded and vigilant about describing their delusions.

Examination for Delusions

To determine whether a patient is having delusions, ask some general revealing questions: "What about your relationship with your friends, workmates, neighbors, and family members—is there any problem?" "Is there anyone who bothers you, follows you, or plans to hurt you?" Answers to these questions may reveal some irrational contents that could be clarified tactfully, e.g., "Do you have any special powers or abilities?" "Does the television or radio give you special messages?"

Examination for Obsessions

Like most signs and symptoms, the examiner uncovers obsessions through observation and questioning. "Are there any repetitive thoughts that bother you or that you can't stop?" "Are you afraid of dirt?" "Do you wash your hands often or count things over and over?" "Do you perform specific acts to reduce certain thoughts?" "Do you have any impulses that you want to stop but can't?" Signs of ritualistic type behaviors should be explored further to determine the severity of the obsession or compulsion.

If possible obsessions or preoccupations are uncovered questioning should focus on their content and frequency. It is very important to ascertain whether they are unwanted, whether the patient has tried to stop them, how they affect the patient's life, and whether they cause any actions or compulsions.

Evaluation of Suicidal Thoughts

A clear statement about the presence or absence of suicidal thoughts or intent should be included in mental status examination. Contrary to the belief that asking about suicide may inadvertently put the idea into the patient's head; exploring the possibility of suicide risk is very critical in taking appropriate preventive interventions. Though approaching suicidal risk can be difficult for the beginning clinician, a tactful way to inquire about suicidal ideas is to empathize with the patient's stresses and painful experiences and then ask whether he/she wishes to die to avoid such experiences. If the answer is affirmative, ask whether he/she has thought about ending his/her life. A *thorough evaluation of suicidal risk includes the following points:*

1. Presence of suicidal thinking: death wishes, or suicidal ideas. An intro-ductory exploration may begin by expressing an understanding of the patient's difficulties and explaining that some persons in similar situations may think about ending their life "Do you have similar thoughts?" If no, ask about previous suicidal attempts, and their motives; if yes, continue evaluation of suicide.
2. Define the time of onset and degree of intent of the patient to act on his/her thoughts.
3. Suicidal plan: is there a detailed plan for suicide? Are the planned means of suicide available to the patient? Are the means potentially lethal? Has the patient made any provision for being saved?
4. Availability of nearby help facilities or support.
5. Does the patient have another realistic alternative for suicide?
6. What are the causes that prevent or could prevent the patient from committing suicide?

Evaluation of Violent Thoughts

Even though the clinician cannot predict homicide or assaultive behavior, it is important to document the presence or absence of aggressive urges or plans in the MSE. The physician should inquire whether the patient has ever harmed anyone, ever seriously injured another person to an extent that medical treatment was necessary, or feels like hurting anyone currently or in the foreseeable future.

Commitment proceedings or police action may need to be initiated to deal with actively homicidal patients. Though laws and precedents vary regarding the duty to warn specific potential victims of homicidal ideas, a balance between the duties of patient confidentiality and protection of others is the rule of this issue; clinicians should educate themselves about laws and trends in their country or state.

Perception

Determine whether or not a patient is experiencing illusions or hallucinations. Illusions could be detected by asking about the occurrence of misinterpretations of perceived objects. The patient's attention and medical condition during illusion should be evaluated.

To assess the presence of auditory hallucinations, ask the patient "Do you hear voices when no one else is around?" When hallucinations are acknow-ledged by any patient, the examiner should attempt to clarify their content. In the case of auditory hallucinations, it should be established whether more than one voice is heard, whether the voice is of someone known to the patient, and whether it is derogatory or critical. It is extremely important to ascertain whether command hallucinations are present, especially those urging violent or dangerous behavior. If command hallucinations are present, it should be determined whether the patient has acted on them and how difficult they are to resist. For example, ask "When the voices tell you do something, do you obey their instructions or ignore them?"

To screen for non-auditory types of hallucinations, broad questions usually suffice, such as: "Have you had other unusual sensory experiences such as seeing things that aren't there, smelling things that aren't there, tasting something when there's nothing in your mouth, or feeling things that aren't real?" More detailed questioning is required if such symptoms are atypical, such as in patients with temporal lobe epilepsy.

Occasionally, hallucinations are covered up by patients who recognize that acknowledging presence of hallucinations can lead to hospitalization, increased medication, or some other undesired consequence. In such cases an indirect approach is indicated, such as observing behavioral evidence of their presence (e.g., talking to an unseen person). The physician should document the patient's denial and the examiner's reasons for suspecting their presence.

Cognition

Cognition refers to the ability to use the higher cortical functions including thinking, logic, reasoning, attention, and memory, though, a lot could be inferred about cognition from the whole examination. Assessment of cognition involves administration of specific tests of cognitive abilities. *Formal cognitive examination is usually divided into the following domains*:

1. Orientation
2. Attention and concentration
3. Memory
4. Abstraction and conceptualization
5. Intelligence
6. Fund of knowledge.

Orientation

The patient is asked about time, place, and person. Orientation for time is usually the first to suffer in the course of mild impairment of consciousness or intellectual impairment, followed by place and, lastly, person. *To assess orientation, ask the patient about*:

- Time of day, day of the week, month, day of the month, year, and season.
- Name of the hospital or clinic and the floor of the building; the city and state in which the interview is taking place.
- Name and function of nurses, doctors, therapists in the hospital or clinics. In the presence of family members, ask about their names and degree of relationships.

Attention and Concentration

When assessing attention, it is important to consider factors that can distort attention. These include the adequacy of sensory thresholds (auditory, visual, and tactile stimuli), and the effect of medications, fatigue, and environmental factors on attention. Assessment of attention starts with evaluation of simple tasks, and is completed with evaluation of more complex tasks of focused, sustained, divided, and rapid attentional alternation. A detailed discussion of tests that could be used to assess attention and concentration have been described on pp. 119–120. A bedside assessment of attention usually includes:

- Repeating the days of the week or the months of the year in a reverse order.
- Counting backward starting at 65 and stopping at 49.
- Serial seven-subtraction test or serial three-subtraction test (discussed on p. 119).
- Testing sustained attention by asking the patient to point to a series of objects in the room, e.g., pointing to ceiling, windows, or furniture in the room for 60–90 seconds. This can be also be tested by using letter or digit vigilance task; where the patient listen to a series of random numbers or letters and respond only to a target letter (e.g., "A") or number (e.g., "seven") by raising a finger or tapping a table.

More elaborate assessment of attentional capacities additionally test the ability to inhibit distraction or avoid unwanted attentional switching to automatic or overlearned processes (e.g., reading rather than color naming; stroop test). Specific psychometric tests can be used for elaborate assessment, e.g., Continuous Performance Test.

Memory

Assessment of memory include evaluation of registration (immediate recall), spontaneous delayed recall, and assessment of recall with cues and recognition. Evaluating the difference between immediate memory trials and delayed memory provides an index of the efficiency of consolidation (or retention). Assessment of recognition after delayed recall additionally allows for evaluation of retrieval deficits. Relatively preserved recognition in the presence of deficient spontaneous recall implicates faulty retrieval processes with intact encoding. Assessment of memory necessitates evaluation of registration, recent and remote memories. The following is a summary of common practices of memory evaluations:

Registration

The examiner can assess registration via immediate recall of materials presented to the patient. This can be achieved by assessment of forward digit span, and having the patient repeat words immediately after hearing them (for more details see pp. 125–126). Additionally, registration can be assessed by asking the patient to count from one to 100, then the examiner interrupts the patient at 27. After a minute the patient is asked to continue counting. At 42, the examiner interrupts the patient, and asks him/her to restart counting after 3 minutes.

Short-term Memory (recent memory)

Recent memory can be assessed by:

1. Asking the subject about recent personal activities, such as components of their last meal, how they came to the clinic or hospital, and their last activity preceding the interview.
2. After self-introduction, asking the subject to recall your name.
3. Testing digit span (see p. 119).
4. Having the patient recall a word list composed of five unrelated words that are presented three times, and telling them which words they forgot in the immediate recall phase. Patients are notified that they will be asked to recall these words later. Their immediate spontaneous recall across three trials is recorded. Cued recall of the words is attempted if there is difficulty in spontaneous recall (e.g., horse: animal, apple: fruit).
5. Articulating a semantic message containing five elements to the patient and requesting immediate recall. The message is repeated twice, and the subject is told that they will be asked to recall the story precisely later.
6. Visual short-term memory and visual recognition: the subject is shown a collection of pictures (e.g., pen, cow, coin, window, and rose) and asked to look at the picture for 10 seconds and then removed from sight. The patient is asked to spontaneously remember these pictures, followed by recognition of these pictures from a group of other pictures later on.

Long-term Memory (remote memories)

Long-term memory can be evaluated by assessment of episodic and semantic memory (see p. 127).

More comprehensive assessment of memory involves the use of an enormous number of neuropsychology memory tests, e.g., Wechsler Memory Scale, Wide Range Assessment of Memory and Learning, Rey Auditory Verbal Learning Test, and Hopkins Verbal Learning Test—Revised.

Abstract and Conceptualization

Abstraction ability is another indicator of intellectual functioning. Some specific questions will help in this assessment. The "similarities" section of the Wechsler Adult Intelligence Scale lends itself to use in a Mental Status Examination. An illustrative example is given at first, e.g., similarities between a hammer and a screwdriver; both are tools. Then ask the patient about similarities between an apple and an orange, a train and a car, a table and a chair, a coat and a dress.

Abstraction can also be evaluated by assessment of the patient's ability to understand proverbs. The patient is asked about the meaning of certain proverbs, e.g., a stitch in time saves nine. Concrete interpretation includes "sewing prevents more rips" while abstract interpretation includes "taking action today will prevent problems tomorrow." Many other proverbs could be used.

Intelligence

One can get a general estimate of a patient's intelligence simply by talking to him or her. Specifically, the patient's vocabulary will give dues about intelligence, especially if considered in view of educational level. A college graduate can be expected to have a good vocabulary, but if a laborer with a third grade education shows evidence of a rich vocabulary, one may conclude that his intelligence is much above his level of scholastic achievement.

Concrete answers are more likely to reflect lack of education than intellectual impairment. However, the answers to these questions can be revealing at both ends of the spectrum. A patient with minimal schooling who shows a high level of abstraction ability can be assumed to have good intelligence. A patient with a college degree whose answers are concrete (an apple and an orange both have peel; a table you eat at and a chair you sit on . . .) shows significant intellectual impairment.

Another way to test abstraction ability is by asking the patient to interpret proverbs. However, knowledge of the patient's sociocultural background is essential because one cannot assume that the patient has ever heard or understood the proverbs that we take for granted. Proverb interpretation can be approached as follows: "Now I am going to give you a few sayings, and I want you to tell me what they mean. Have you ever heard the saying, 'Don't cry over spilt milk'?" If the patient says yes, ask him or her to interpret. If he or she says no, interpret it for him or her. ("It means that there is no use worrying about something bad that has happened and that can't be fixed.") "Now let's try another one: can you tell me what could be meant by 'a stitch in time saves nine'?" Concrete interpretations should be evaluated in the same way as concreteness in "similarities."

General Fund of Knowledge

The interviewer should always take into consideration the patient's educational background and other training in evaluating answers. *Possible questions include*:

- Who is the president of the United States?
- Who is the vice president?
- Who were the last five presidents, in order?
- What is the state capital?
- Name five of the largest cities in the country.

Insight and Judgment

To assess the patient's insight, the interviewer should ask the patient about his/her illness: "Do you think that you have any illness?" "Do you believe your feelings, thoughts, or behavior show any abnormality?" "Do you need help?" Different types of insight were discussed before.

Judgment is evaluated clinically in light of the entire history. Many patients who have normal intellectual functioning suffer from poor judgment in organizing their personal lives. During the interview, evidence of poor judgment should be noted and documented with specific examples. For instance, walking around city streets wearing a bikini is poor judgment, as is a history of repeated suicidal gestures or of impulsive job changes. Items from the Wechsler Adult Intelligence Scale, such as the well-known "What would you do if you were the first one in a movie house to see smoke and fire? What would you do if you found a sealed letter that has an address and a stamp on it?" can be used to assess judgment.

Though all aspects of judgment (social, vocational, etc.), are important; the most critical to clinical practice is the understanding of the patient to his/her need to treatment. Other aspects of judgment are usually good in most conditions, except those with evidence of intellectual impairment.

Reliability

Reliability refers to a patient's credibility and trustworthiness. Reliable informants carefully present their life histories and current personal information honestly and accurately. In contrast, some clients may be highly unreliable; for one reason or another, they distort, confabulate, or noticeably lie about their life circumstances and personal history. It's often difficult to determine when clients are being untruthful. Persons with good attention to details and who give spontaneous and elaborate responses to your questions are likely to be reliable informants. In contrast, persons who answer questions in a vague or defensive manner or who appear to be obviously exaggerating or storytelling have a greater probability of being unreliable. In some cases, you will have a clear sense that clients are intentionally omitting or minimizing parts of their history (Sommers-Flanagan & Sommers-Flanagan, 2014). For example, a patient who comes to treatment under family pressure may give a very self-serving story that cannot be judged as reliable. A histrionic patient may color his or her own reports by exaggeration, retrospective falsification, and wishful thinking. A patient with antisocial traits may tell bold-faced lies to get out of legal trouble, and a patient with limited intelligence may simply make up facts to avoid embarrassment and to get the doctor "off his back." Psychotic patients and patients with organic mental disorders may be unreliable informants. Whether or not the patient is deemed reliable must be stated explicitly. An example of normal and abnormal mental status examination is shown in Tables 3.1 and 3.2.

Diagnosis and Case Formulation

Case formulation usually describes the interviewer's understanding of why things are as they are. This may reflect one or more theoretical perspectives. The biomedical or psychosocial approach to conceptualizing patients' problems and identifying treatments is a powerfully compelling paradigm that continues to increase in popularity and dominance (Overholser, 2006; Sommers-Flanagan & Campbell, 2009). Using a biomedical approach, interviewers formulate patients' problems as a medical illness and perform diagnostic assessments to identify biomedical treatments. In practice, most psychiatrists recognize that integrating psychosocial and biological treatment-planning approaches is useful and do so to some extent. This is referred to as the biopsychosocial model (Engel, 1980; Engel, 1997). However, when biomedical and psychosocial treatments are combined, the biomedical approach (also known as the medical model) tends to dominate case formulation and treatment planning (Sommers-Flanagan & Campbell, 2009).

The case formulation usually includes information specific to the individual patient that goes beyond what is conveyed by the diagnosis: all relevant areas of assessment including history, and mental state examination, laboratory findings, psychological test results, if available, as well as drugs the patient has been taking including dosage and duration of intake. Based on information obtained in the evaluation, a differential diagnosis is developed. The diagnosis and case formulation together facilitate the development of an initial treatment plan. In many cases, clients qualify for more than one DSM diagnosis. This comorbidity problem makes sorting out appropriate diagnostic labels even more difficult.

Differential diagnosis: although some patients report symptoms consistent with more than one diagnostic entity and are appropriately assigned two or more diagnostic labels, other clients report confusing symptom clusters

Table 3.1 Case Example of Normal Mental Status Examination

Appearance/ Attitude		Normal	Cooperative
Mood		Euthymic	Calm, comfortable, euthymic, friendly, pleasant, unremarkable
Affect	Appropriateness	Normal	Appropriate, congruent
	Intensity	Normal	Normal
	Variability/Mobility	Normal	Mobile
	Range	Normal	Full
	Reactivity	Normal	Reactive, responsive
Speech		Fluency, repetition, comprehension, naming, writing, reading, prosody, quality of speech	Normal
Thought	Process	Amount	Normal
		Form	Normal
	Content	Thoughts	No abnormal content
Perceptions		Normal	No hallucinations or illusions or perceptual distortions
Cognition			
Orientation	Time	Oriented	Specify asked question
	Place	Oriented	Specify asked question
	Person	Oriented	Specify asked question
Attention and Con-centration		Normal	Specify asked question
Memory	Working	Average	Specify asked question
	Episodic	Average	Specify asked question
	Semantic	Average	Specify asked question
Knowledge Base		Average	Specify asked question
Abstract Thinking		Abstract	Specify asked question
Intelligence		Average	Specify asked question
Insight		Good	The patient is aware of his/her symptoms
Judgment		Good	The patient accepts need for treatment
Reliability		Reliable	

Table 3.2 Case Example of Abnormal Mental Status Examination

Appearance/ Attitude		Abnormal	Uncooperative, hostile, guarded, suspicious
Mood (may be one of these moods)		Angry	Angry, bellicose, belligerent, confrontational, frustrated, hostile, impatient, irascible, irate, irritable, oppositional, outraged, sullen
		Euphoric	Cheerful, ecstatic, elated, euphoric, giddy, happy, jovial
		Apathetic	Apathetic, bland, dull, flat
		Dysphoric	Despondent, distraught, dysphoric, grieving, hopeless, lugubrious, overwhelmed, remorseful, sad
		Apprehensive	Anxious, apprehensive, fearful, frightened, high-strung, nervous, overwhelmed, panicked, tense, terrified, worried
Affect	Appropriateness	Abnormal	Inappropriate, incongruent
	Intensity	Abnormal	Blunted, exaggerated, flat, heightened, overly dramatic
	Variability/Mobility	Abnormal	Constricted, fixed, immobile, labile
	Range	Abnormal	Restricted range
	Reactivity	Abnormal	Nonreactive, nonresponsive
Speech		Fluency, repetition, comprehension, naming, writing, reading, prosody, quality of speech	Normal
Thought	Process	Amount	Circumstantiality, flight of ideas, loose associations, tangentiality, word salad
		Form	Clanging, echolalia, neologisms, perseveration, thought blocking
	Content	Delusions	Delusions, homicidal ideation, magical thinking, obsessions, overvalued ideas, paranoia, phobia, poverty of speech, preoccupations, ruminations, suicidal ideation, suspiciousness
		Obsession	Excessive thoughts about themes like dirtiness of hands or doubt and rechecking

continued . . .

Table 3.2 Continued

Perceptions		Illusion	Misinterpret a robe as a snake
		Hallucination	Auditory, visual, or olfactory, etc.
Cognition			
Orientation	Time	Oriented	Specify asked question
	Place	Oriented	Specify asked question
	Person	Oriented	Specify asked question
Attention and Con-centration		Normal	Specify asked question
Memory	Working	Average	Specify asked question
	Episodic	Average	Specify asked question
	Semantic	Average	Specify asked question
Knowledge Base		Average	Specify asked question
Abstract Thinking		Abstract	Specify asked question
Intelligence		Average	Specify asked question
Insight		Poor	Patient has impaired reality testing
Judgment		Poor	Patient refuses treatment
Reliability		Reliable	

requiring extensive questioning for diagnostic clarity. Despite difficulties sorting out these various disorders, diagnostic specificity is important because of treatment implications (i.e., medication type, treatment approach, hospitalization, and prognosis).

Initial Treatment Plan

The initial clinical interview is designed to obtain assessment information that is used to aid in the diagnostic process, which broadly informs treatment. An initial treatment plan usually includes answers to the questions that were posed and/or a plan for obtaining additional necessary information.

The initial treatment plan begins with an explicit statement of the diagnostic, therapeutic, and rehabilitative goals for treatment. In the case of patients who initially will be treated in an inpatient or partial hospital setting, this implies dividing the therapeutic task between a hospital phase and a post-hospital phase. On the basis of the goals, the plan specifies further diagnostic tests and procedures, further systematic observations to be made, and specific therapeutic modalities to be applied.

All potentially effective treatments should be considered. *More detailed consideration of the risks and benefits of treatment options may be needed in the following circumstances:*

1. When a relatively risky, costly, or unusual treatment is under consideration.
2. When involved parties disagree about the optimal course of treatment.
3. When the patient's motivation or capacity to benefit from potential treatment alternatives is in question.
4. When the treatment would be involuntary or when other legal or administrative issues are involved.
5. When external constraints limit available treatment options.

MEDICAL ASSESSMENT OF PSYCHIATRIC PATIENTS

Medical assessment of patients with mental symptoms seeks to clarify the following points:

1. **Physical disorders *mimicking* mental disorders**: numerous physical disorders cause symptoms mimicking specific mental disorders, e.g., thyroid diseases, multiple sclerosis, metabolic encephalopathies, electrolyte disturbance, and connective tissue diseases.
2. **Physical disorders *accompanying* mental disorders**:
    *   Psychiatric patients may present with accompanying physical diseases that need to be considered during prescribing drugs (e.g., cardiac arrhythmias may be aggravated by anticholinergics and some antipsychotics and tricyclic antidepressants; dyslipidemia and diabetes mellitus may be aggravated by atypical antipsychotics; and psoriasis may be aggravated by lithium).
    *   Some physical disorders do not cause specific mental disorders but may result in changes in mood and energy.
    *   Physical disorders (e.g., encephalitis, hepatic encephalopathy, diabetic ketoacidosis) in patients with a mental disorder may result in new or worsened mental symptoms. Thus, a clinician should be aware that the cause of new onset of mental symptoms in patients with a known mental disorder that may result from comorbid physical disorder. The clinician needs to address all possible physical causes of mental symptoms, especially in patients who are unable to describe their physical health because they have psychosis or dementia.
3. **Physical disorders caused by mental disorders or their treatment**: psychiatric patients may develop physical disorders due to their mental disorder (e.g., malnutrition due to lack of appetite in depression) or its treatment (e.g., hypothyroidism due to lithium, or dyslipidemia secondary to atypical antipsychotics).

Medical Evaluation

Evaluation of a medical condition follows the regular methods used in medicine, history, examination, and investigation, but usually necessitates a high degree of caution and suspicion (proficiency) on the side of the psychiatrist. Undiagnosed medical conditions may be the cause of high morbidity and mortality among persons with major psychiatric disorders.

PSYCHOLOGICAL TESTING

Psychological testing refers to the administration of psychological tests, which are an objective and standardized measure of an individual's performance on tasks that have usually been prescribed beforehand.

Goals of Assessment

The indications of assessment vary with the setting in which the assessment is conducted and the typical patient encountered in that setting. In clinical psychiatric settings, assessment is most often requested to aid in reducing uncertainty regarding diagnosis and in evaluating the severity of specific symptoms or symptom complexes (e.g., depression, suicide intent, thought disorder). Such an assessment plays an important role in providing information on patients that can be usefully generalized by facilitating comparisons between patients or by tracking the severity of symptoms under the impact of treatment. This assessment may form the basis for recommended treatments, help in establishing goals for the general treatment plan, or assist in determining treatment progress and the need for further intervention. *In summary, a psychological test may be requested for one of the following goals*:

1. Screening for psychiatric disturbance.
2. Clarification of diagnostic uncertainty following clinical interview.
3. Specification of the severity of symptoms and other difficulties.
4. Assessment of patient strengths.
5. Informing differential treatment assignments.
6. Monitoring the impact of treatment over time.
7. Assessment of barriers to learning for educational planning.
8. Assessment of quality and cost-effectiveness of systems of care.

Forms of Assessment Instruments

Current psychological assessment instruments take many forms. The most common forms of assessment include clinical interview, observational methods, self-reports, or projective techniques.

The Clinical Interview

The clinical interview is a core component of any psychological testing, including clinical, educational, work and organizations, and forensic assessment. The clinical interview can be used to assess varied psychological events whether subjective or objective, motor, cognitive, or physiological.

Before any formal psychological testing is done, a clinical interview is nearly always conducted (even if the person has already gone through one with a different professional). Psychologists conducting the testing will often want to form their own clinical impressions, which can be best done through a direct interview with the person. The clinical interviews could be either unstructured or structured.

Unstructured Interview

The unstructured interview is characterized by the clinician following the flow of questions and answers that come from a more naturalistic conversation between the patient and the clinician. This allows for total freedom in the questions and answers, and may allow the clinician to gather information not touched in a more structured interview format.

This approach allows the clinician to have maximum latitude and flexibility regarding what questions to ask, how to probe symptom patterns, and how much time to spend on different subject matters, resulting in a rich amount of clinical information and a deep understanding of the unique make-up of a client. Such flexibility is thought to greatly aid in establishing rapport with the client, as the client's main concerns are the focus of the interview and little time is spent in questioning other areas or symptoms. However, validity and reliability of information obtained in the unstructured interview format may be inferior to structured and semi-structured diagnostic interviews. In addition, there is some evidence that the unstructured interviewer's own beliefs, definitions of certain clinical constructs, and preconceptions may exert a biasing effect on the interview process itself, affecting what the patient is willing to discuss in the ongoing reciprocal process of selecting seemingly pertinent information, leading finally to confirmatory bias.

Structured Interview

In a structured clinical interview, the interviewer proceeds in verbatim fashion through a predetermined list of questions presented in a predefined order, with tightly defined criteria used for interpretation. In other words, structured interviews require clinicians to do two things: (a) ask questions and follow-up probes in a standardized manner and sequence, and (b) rate client responses using systematized ratings.

Most structured interview formats share some common features. These interviews are typically organized by disorder or syndrome, a system called symptom clustering. Also they typically employ unidirectional scoring, meaning that approval of an item is a sign of psychopathology.

Structured interviews vary considerably across three main dimensions; diagnostic coverage, ease of use, and degree of structure. The level of structure imposed on the clinician varies among structured interviews. There are two types of structured approaches: semi-structured (or interviewer-based) and highly structured (or respondent-based) interviews.

The most prominent standardized interviews are schedule for affective disorders and schizophrenia (SADS), diagnostic interview schedule (DIS), and the present state examination (PSE). SADS is a semi-structured interview for use by clinicians with clinical experience. It is designed to define symptoms of disorders as determined by research diagnostic criteria (RDC), it takes 1–3 hours, and yields information for making both current and lifetime psychiatric diagnoses.

Observational Tests

Psychological assessment may involve the observation of people as they complete activities. Observational assessment is performed either in the subject's natural setting (such as a classroom), in an experimental setting, or during an interview.

Observational assessment may be used to establish diagnosis (as in Autism Diagnostic Observation Schedule), to assess baseline classroom behaviors among hyperactive or aggressive children, or to observe the nature of a parent–child interaction in order to understand a relational disorder. In research, direct observation procedures are also used to explore consequences of behavioral interaction or to study the relationship between intrapsychic variables and specific target behaviors.

Self-reports

Self-report is any test or measure that relies on the subject's own report of their symptoms, beliefs, attitudes, or behaviors without interference from the examiner. Self-reports are commonly used in clinical practice and in research because they are inexpensive and easy to obtain, and can provide information about a lot of domains.

Self-reports can be obtained through questionnaires, inventories, or scales containing a set of relevant verbal statements. The individual can respond with answers such as yes, maybe, or true, false, or cannot say. The best example of these tests is the Minnesota Multiphasic Personality Inventory-2 (MMPI-2).

Self-reports have several sources of bias. Collecting data about thoughts or feelings based on self-reports is only useful in persons who are willing to reveal them to the experimenter. Several conditions can affect the credibility of self-reports; these include the subject's characteristics, length of the question, formulation of the question, and type of answer and response requested.

Projective Techniques

Individuals are usually presented with a series of ambiguous stimuli, and asked to give a description or a story about each, thus projecting their own personality characteristics onto those stimuli.

The best known projective test is the Rorschach test. Ten inkblots are presented to the person on a series of ten cards, and the person's reactions are observed. Three factors are usually considered when interpreting responses; the part of each inkblot to which the subject responds; aspects of the inkblot on which the subject stresses (color, shape, etc.); and what the inkblot represents to the subject (its content).

Thematic Apperception Test (TAT) is another widely used projective test. A series of 20 pictures are presented to the subject. Each picture can be interpreted in diverse ways; the subject is asked to construct a story based on each one. Responses are expected to reflect a person's problems, motives, preoccupations, and interpersonal skills.

Characteristics of a Good Psychological Test

A good test is characterized by its reliability, validity, and having good norms.

- **Reliability**: refers to the consistency of the test results. There are different types of test reliability:

  - *Test–retest*: test yields comparable scores when repeated at two proximate points in time. A test is highly reliable when its results do not vary much along weeks or months; hence results from an IQ test are highly reliable. By contrast, a mood state does not last over long periods of time; thus the reliability of its measurement is low.
  - *Alternate form*: two forms of the same test yield comparable scores.
  - *Split-half*: subgroups of items yield scores comparable with those of other subgroups of items.
  - *Interrater reliability*: the consistency with which the same information is obtained if the test is given by different examiners.

- **Validity**: refers to the ability of the test to measure what it is intended to measure. Simply speaking, validity informs you whether the car is the right tool for transportation, and reliability tells you how good your car is. To explain more, suppose that a test of intelligence is based on eye color, where blue eyes indicate higher intelligence than brown eyes; this test would be highly reliable, because eye color does not change over time, however, it is not valid, because IQ and eye color have little or no correlation with each other. *There are different types of test validity:*

- content: items adequately sample the content area;
- criterion related: test score correlates with other measurements of the same area of activity;
- construct: test measures a theoretical construct and is unrelated to similar but different constructs.

- **Standardization**: all aspects of the testing procedure, including the administration of the test, the scoring, and the evaluation of the results should follow the same pattern each time. This helps to avoid differences in test results resulting from variation of test procedures. One way to standardize a test is to establish norms, which are scores obtained from groups of people who have taken the test. Once norms have been determined, the performances of others taking the test in the same manner can be compared with the norms.
- **Norms**: refer to data concerning group performance on a particular test for which a person can be compared with. Thus, it provides a comparison between an individual and a group. In a good test, the normative sample should be representative of the population that will be tested, considering age, gender, ethnicity, cultural diversity, socioeconomic and educational status.
- **Objectivity**: means that a measurer's prejudices play no role in measurement. That is, all measurements are made in a neutral fashion.

Pitfalls of Psychological Assessment

1. Inappropriate Test

The use of certain psychological tests may not be appropriate in all situations, all cultures, or across all ages. Selecting the appropriate assessment instrument involves choosing tests with good established sensitivity, specificity, reliability, and validity. Suitability for specific culture, age, and purpose should be considered when selecting a test.

2. Confirmation Bias

If a psychologist forms an initial impression about the person being assessed, he/she may tend to seek a test that supports that impression, and ignore tests that do not favor such impression. To guard against such bias, it is useful to search actively for tests that prove and disprove our initial impression, and to find out other explanations of the available data.

3. Confusing Retrospective and Predictive Accuracy

Predictive accuracy refers to the probability that a test is precise in classifying individuals or in predicting whether or not they have a specific condition or characteristic. In other words, when having a test result, predictive accuracy determines the likelihood that a person with these results has condition X (e.g., ability, aptitude, quality, etc.).

Retrospective accuracy questions whether certain condition such as an ability, an aptitude, or certain quality is likely to be present among those showing certain test results. Caution is needed when interpreting the directionality of the inference; the relationship between a certain variable and having a certain test result is bidirectional, it could be cause or effect.

4. Unstandardizing Standardized Tests

Standardization of a test is achieved by empirically establishing its norms, validity, reliability, specificity, sensitivity. Standardization is the source of test power. It makes the measurement process a uniform procedure and decreases the possibility of bias. Failure to abide by test instructions, or the test items themselves, or the way items are administered or scored, is likely to deviate from standardization of the test and make attempts to draw conclusions from such test results questionable. Situational factors can threaten the assessment's validity and endanger assessment results. Psychologists should be aware of these effects and try to handle them effectively.

5. Misinterpreting of Base-rate

Base-rate error refers to the cognitive bias in which one may underestimate the importance of the frequency of the relevant disorder in the appropriate population (the pretest base rate), leading to misinterpretation of the diagnostic significance of test results.

6. Financial Bias

Financial conflict of interest can affect the way in which even the most routine data are collected, interpreted, and presented. To guard against this, formal guidelines prohibit privilege and any form of fee that is related to the outcome of a case.

7. Ignoring Confounding Variables

Testing is complicated by the effect of gender, aging, education, ethnicity and cultural factors, and the presence of psychiatric disorder or substance abuse on neuropsychological functions.

The psychologist should be aware that audio/video-recording, or the presence of third parties can affect the responses of people during psychological and neuropsychological assessment. Ignoring these potential effects can generate misleading results.

Some physical conditions may also affect the examined person and need to be checked for, e.g., having a painful physical condition, forgetting reading glasses or hearing aid, taking medications that affect cognition or perception, forgetting to take needed psychotropic medication, or having trouble understanding the language in which the assessment is conducted.

Major Areas of Assessment

There are thousands of psychological tests that cover a number of different areas with *the main ones being described below*:

- Assessment of Intellectual Functioning (IQ)
- Educational testing
- Adaptive behavior
- Personality assessment
- Specific areas of symptomatology
- Non-clinical assessment.

1. Assessment of Intellectual Functioning (IQ)

Assessment of intellectual functioning usually involves one or more of the different cognitive abilities including problem solving, reasoning, vocabulary, comprehension, and memory. Cognitive tests used for this purpose usually include those referred to as intelligence tests, and are usually used in educational contexts, to provide information about children in need of special help. The most commonly used intelligence tests include the Stanford-Binet and the Wechsler intelligence scales. Specific tests of specific cognitive function, e.g., memory, are also available.

Neuropsychological assessment is a comprehensive evaluation of cognitive processes. It aims at determining all of the cognitive strengths and deficits of the person. Neuropsychological tests are specific tasks designed to measure a psychological function that is linked to a particular brain structure or pathway. It helps in the assessment of possible deficits linked to these parts of the brain. A battery of tests is usually used in which a group of different tests are used together to get more detailed information about a certain brain function.

2. Educational Testing

Psycho-educational testing refers to tests that are used to analyze mental processes underlying a child's educational performance. It helps to identify the strength and weakness of cognitive and academic domains in a way that can be targeted to provide appropriate intervention or additional support. It is initiated when there is a concern about a child's cognitive functioning, learning, attention, and/or behavior at school. Educational testing includes the use of general cognitive tests and specific achievement tests. General cognitive tests include tests of Intellectual Functioning. Specific achievement tests are used to assess how well an individual is progressing in a specific area (e.g., reading, writing, mathematics) along with providing information about difficulties they may have in learning in such areas. Educational testing helps in the educational process and ensures that difficulties are identified and addressed appropriately.

3. Adaptive Behavior

Adaptive behavior refers to a group of conceptual (time, money, numbers), social, and practical skills that all humans develop and use in order to be able to cope and function in their daily lives. Adaptive behavior is usually assessed in combination with other cognitive tests in individuals with suspected intellectual disability.

4. Personality Assessment

Personality assessment usually addresses evaluation of personal characteristics through administration of empirically supported measures. Assessment of personality varies according to the theoretical perspective on which the assessment is based. It includes objective personality tests based on both self-report and informant ratings, projective tests, and behavioral observation. No single method of assessment is superior to others; each of the major methods has both strengths and limitations. By using multiple approaches, psychologists can overcome the limitations of a single method and develop a more integrated view of personality. Examples of personality tests include Minnesota Multiphasic Personality Inventory, Personality Assessment Inventory, The Millon Clinical Multiaxial Inventory. Assessment of temperamental characteristics is closely related to personality assessment. It focuses on characteristics of the individual that are supposed to have a strong biological basis such as general activity level, adaptability, and mood.

5. Specific Areas of Symptomatology

A number of instruments have been developed for the assessment of a wide variety of symptoms. These measures depend on either self-report or interview methods for data collection. Available measures can be used to screen or to assess diagnosis, severity, treatment planning, and to monitor outcome of developmental disorders, depression, mania, anxiety, obsession, thought disorder, psychosis, substance abuse, and many other symptoms and disorders.

6. Non-clinical Assessment

A number of psychological tests are used to evaluate or predict a specific topic, e.g., interest, or aptitude, career or work counseling, management skills, and career planning.

(a) Interest Tests

These are psychological tests that are used to assess a person's interests and preferences in his/her daily activities. It is based on the assumption that persons usually exhibit the same pattern of interests and preferences in all situations. It is used mainly in career counseling.

(b) Aptitude Tests

Aptitude tests refer to tests that are used to measure an individual's capacity in a particular area, e.g., mechanical or clerical skills. These tests are based on the idea that people differ in their special abilities and that these differences can be useful in predicting future achievements. An aptitude test represents a person's level of competency in performing a specific task. It is usually used to assess academic potential or career suitability by determining the extent to which an individual has the suitable characteristics and abilities, e.g., aptitude test to become a fighter pilot, or to study computer programming.

INVESTIGATIONS IN PSYCHIATRY

Psychiatric diagnoses rely primarily on clinical grounds; laboratory and other diagnostic tests do not play a central role in the diagnosis and treatment of patients with psychiatric disorders. *The use of laboratory and neuroimaging studies could fall into one of the following categories:*

1. Routine evaluation of the patient's baseline medical condition.
2. Exclusion of other possible causes of psychiatric symptomatology.
3. Monitoring of drug level and possible side effects of drugs.
4. Screening and monitoring of drug abuse.

Routine Evaluation of the Patient's Baseline Medical Condition

There are no consensus guidelines for the initial laboratory screening of psychiatric patients without known medical illnesses. Clinicians are generally guided by the history, physical examination, mental status examination, and by their own clinical judgment to decide what tests are appropriate to obtain.

In patients without medical problems or complaints, it is sufficient to screen for complete blood count, serum glucose concentration, blood urea nitrogen (BUN) concentration, and urinalysis. Screening laboratory tests will vary according to the patient's clinical presentation, the clinical situation (outpatient clinic vs. emergency department vs. inpatient setting), and concomitant medical illnesses. Any laboratory test may be considered routine for certain patients' categories, e.g., ECG becomes a routine investigation in patients when the history, review of systems, or findings from the physical examination suggest cardiovascular disease, in the elderly, or on initiating treatment with a psychotropic drug.

Exclusion of Other Possible Causes of Psychiatric Symptomatology

Laboratory and diagnostic testing can be used to differentiate neurological and medical illnesses that can give rise to psychiatric symptomatology.

Laboratory tests are indicated in the following patients:

1. Patients of significantly low intelligence may require genetic testing for chromosomal abnormalities and other causes of intellectual disability.
2. New-onset psychosis: there are many causes of psychosis that need to be considered, including central nervous system (CNS) or systemic infections, temporal lobe epilepsy, substance intoxication and withdrawal, metabolic or endocrine disorders, CNS tumors, and heavy metal poisoning. A careful evaluation is important for a patient with a first episode of psychosis in order to rule out the many possible medical and neurological causes of psychosis. Routine screening tests often include serum chemistries such as sodium, potassium, chloride, carbon dioxide, BUN, and creatinine; liver function tests such as total protein, total and direct bilirubin, serum aspartate transaminase/serum glutamic-oxaloacetic transaminase (AST/SGOT), and alanine aminotransferase/serum glutamate pyruvate transaminase (AAT/SGPT); complete blood count (CBC) with platelets and differential; TSH; a rapid plasma reagin for syphilis; HIV serology; serum alcohol level; urinalysis; and urine toxicology screen for drugs of abuse. Other tests to consider during the initial workup include structural neuroimaging (head CT or brain MRI) and electroencephalography. If appropriate, the clinician should also consider ordering a urine pregnancy test and baseline electrocardiogram, especially if he or she is planning to initiate or change antipsychotic medication. If these initial tests do not immediately yield an etiology, the clinician may also consider a lumbar puncture if clinically appropriate, to analyze cerebrospinal fluid (CSF) for the presence of red and white blood cells, protein, and glucose; opening pressure; and bacterial culture, cryptococcal antigen, and viral serologies.

Antinuclear antibodies, rheumatoid factor, erythrocyte sedimentation rate, urine porphyrins, blood cultures, and assays for heavy metals (manganese and mercury) and bromides are other tests to consider.

3. Mood disturbance: a thorough laboratory screening is also recommended for the evaluation of adult patients with new-onset mood symptoms such as depression or mania. Tests might include TSH, serum chemistries, CBC, urinalysis, and urine toxicology screen for drugs of abuse. If appropriate, the clinician should also con-sider ordering a urine pregnancy test and electrocardiogram, especially if he or she is considering starting a mood-stabilizing medication. Measuring levels of therapeutic drugs can be helpful to confirm suitability of the recommended dosage, and compliance on medication. Serum trough levels of mood stabilizers such as lithium, valproate, or carbamazepine and TCAs can be obtained to monitor therapeutic response in accordance with therapeutic levels.

4. Anxiety: the initial workup for anxiety symptoms should include serum chemistries, serum glucose, and TSH and other endocrine measures. Many different medical diseases can also manifest with anxiety, including angina and myocardial infarction, mitral valve prolapse, substance intoxication and withdrawal, and metabolic and endocrine disorders such as thyroid abnormalities, pheochromocytoma, and hypoglycemia. Neurological disorders, such as many forms of dementia, can also present with anxiety. Cardiac workup is important because cardiac symptoms may masquerade as panic attacks and are often misdiagnosed as such, especially in female patients. Therefore, electrocardiography, Holter monitoring, stress test, and/or echocardiography may be necessary. Respiratory function should also be evaluated with a chest radiograph or pulmonary function tests to rule out chronic obstructive pulmonary disease as a contributory factor. Other tests to consider if one has clinical suspicion include electroencephalography, urine porphyrins, and urine vanillylmandelic acid.

5. Cognitive decline and dementia: the American Academy of Neurology (Knopman et al., 2001) practice recommendations for evaluation of reversible causes of dementia include testing for vitamin B12 deficiency and hypothyroidism. Syphilis serology screening is necessary only in patients with dementia who are at risk for neurosyphilis. Other possible investigations include copper levels for Wilson's disease, and HIV testing.

6. Psychiatric disorders have been reported in up to 60 percent of patients with systemic lupus erythematosus (SLE). These patients may present with psychosis, depression, or anxiety. If organic disorder is not considered, a misdiagnosis of schizophrenia may be made. Investigations for SLE may be justified in patients with anemia, leucopenia and a high ESR.

Electroencephalography

The use of electroencephalography in the differentiation of psychiatric disorders is fairly limited. However, an electroencephalogram can be very useful when a patient has altered mental status, such as delirium or encephalopathy. *It can be useful for distinguishing between possible diagnoses, e.g.*:

1. It can diagnose complex partial status epilepticus, in cases of altered consciousness and abnormal behavior. However, normal EEG does not exclude seizure disorder from the differential diagnosis, because 20 percent of patients with epilepsy will have normal EEGs, and 2 percent of patients without epilepsy will have spike and wave formation.
2. The EEG is also useful for distinguishing some specific etiologies of encephalopathy; it might show the di- and triphasic waves characteristic of renal failure, hepatic failure, or anoxia.
3. In comatose patients, the EEG can be very valuable for identifying the level of nervous system impairment; it can show an alpha coma pattern or a theta coma pattern characteristic of brainstem lesions producing coma or it may show a delta coma pattern characteristic of bihemispheric disease. In catatonic patients, the EEG has a normal awake-look.
4. The EEG may detect sleep abnormalities consistent with sleep apnea, rapid eye movement sleep behavior disorder, or narcolepsy.

Polysomnography

A typical polysomnogram will consist of an EEG, electrocardiogram, electrooculogram, and electromyogram and measurement of respiratory airflow and oxygenation, blood pressure, and body temperature.

No definitive guidelines exist as to the usefulness of polysomnography in the clinical workup of the psychiatric patient. A polysomnogram is useful when there is clinical suspicion of parasomnia or hypersomnia (narcolepsy), a breathing disorder such as sleep apnea, or limb movements during sleep. Polysomnography is also a useful technique in the psychiatric patient if a sleep disorder is suspected to be responsible for or exacerbating psychiatric symptoms, e.g., hypnagogic hallucinations, and if there is considerable overlap in symptoms of depression and sleep disorders, such as insomnia, daytime fatigue, or excessive daytime sleepiness.

Evoked Potentials

Evoked potential testing provides clinically useful information about processing of sensory stimuli, which is helpful in discriminating medical versus psychogenic causes of some symptoms, e.g., visual evoked potentials can be useful to differentiate psychogenic blindness from true blindness, and auditory evoked potentials can be used to differentiate psychogenic deafness from catatonia in a mute, unresponsive patient, and in assessing hearing in a mute child suspected to have autism or deafness.

Structural Neuroimaging Examinations

Routine brain imaging is seldom required. The primary use of structural neuroimaging such as CT (computed tomography) and MRI (magnetic resonance imaging) in psychiatric diagnosis is largely limited to the identification of medical causes of psychiatric symptomatology. Structural imaging is helpful to evaluate for evidence of abnormalities such as new or unexplained focal neurological signs, cognitive changes or impairment, cerebrovascular disease, demyelinating disease, brain tumor, trauma, or developmental abnormalities that might underlie psychiatric symptoms.

CT is widely available, less expensive than MRI, has a quick scanning time, and is relatively more comfortable and convenient than other structural imaging modalities. Deep brain structures, including those of the posterior fossa such as brainstem and cerebellum, are poorly visualized with CT because of the surrounding bony structures. Furthermore, discrimination between gray and white matter in the brain is limited due to their similar radiodensities. MRI of the brain has the advantage over CT of being more sensitive. It is much more likely to detect vascular disease and demyelinating disease. It is also useful for detecting mild neurodegenerative changes that might point to degenerative dementias. However, MRI does take longer (about 45 minutes) than CT scans, and it is at least twice as expensive.

Monitoring of Drug Level and Possible Side Effects of Drugs

Some psychotropic drugs are associated with adverse events and necessitate monitoring. It is wise to check blood count, and liver and kidney values before starting a drug, and recheck every 3 months if results are within normal levels. Some drugs necessitates regular monitoring, e.g., clozapine (WBC) or lithium (TSH, electrolytes), and atypical antipsychotics. *The following is a summary of recommendations to follow for different psychotropic categories:*

Antidepressants

Specific Serotonin Reuptake Inhibitors (SSRIs): do not require specific laboratory monitoring. *However, patients experiencing any of the following three rare medical complications of SSRIs need appropriate assessment:*

1. **Bleeding**: the bleeding risk of SSRIs is probably a direct effect of serotonergic stimulation that commonly manifests as GI bleeding. It is not

caused by platelet dysfunction, and hence routine monitoring of bleeding parameters is not indicated. CBC is ordered when a patient presents with symptoms suggestive of blood loss.

2. **Hyponatremia** (below 135 mEq/L): a rare side effect most likely to occur in patients over 65 within 30 days of initiating SSRIs. It does not require routine monitoring, but it should be considered in an elderly patient who reports fatigue, dizziness, or cramping after initiating SSRIs.

3. **Osteoporosis**: a possible side effect in the elderly. Some authors recommend routine bone density screenings in elderly patients on SSRIs.

Venlafaxine: blood pressure needs to be assessed periodically after starting or increasing the dose of Effexor, because of increased risk of rise in blood pressure.

Duloxetine: liver enzyme alanine transaminase (ALT) is elevated in 1 percent of patients; thus checking ALT is indicated after starting duloxetine.

Tricyclic antidepressants: ECG is required both before starting a tricyclic and after reaching a therapeutic dose in patients with pre-existing cardiac disease. A screening ECG is recommended in all patient above 40–50 years regardless of cardiac history.

MAOIs: monitoring of liver function is recommended in cases using phenelzine because of reported cases of liver failure.

Lithium

Dosage of lithium recommended in acute treatment of mania is usually titrated to achieve serum concentrations of 0.5±1.2 mmol/L. Lithium concentrations above 0.8 mmol/L are associated with an increased risk of renal impairment especially in women. So, the target range of biochemical monitoring of plasma lithium concentrations is 0.6–0.8 mmol/L (Goodwin et al., 2016). Older patients may be more likely to develop cognitive impairment with lithium. Many elderly patients tolerate only low serum levels of lithium (e.g., 0.4–0.6 meq/L) and can respond to these levels (Van Gerpen et al., 1999).

Atypical Antipsychotics

Patients taking an atypical antipsychotic may experience an elevation of blood glucose, serum triglyceride, and LDL levels, and a decrease in the HDL level. These effects may occur without an increase in BMI, and can be considered a direct effect of the antipsychotic. Clozapine and olanzapine carry the highest risk of dyslipidemia. Quetiapine and risperidone are considered of intermediate risk; the risk associated with quetiapine is closer to that of olanzapine. Aripiprazole and ziprasidone carry a lower risk of dyslipidemia and glucose elevations (Zeier et al., 2013).

HbA$_{1c}$ and fasting plasma glucose levels should be measured at baseline and throughout the course of treatment. Obtain another set of measurements at 3 months, then annually thereafter, unless the patient develops type 2 diabetes mellitus.

Obtain a fasting lipid panel at baseline and periodically, after 3 months and annually thereafter. BMI and waist circumference should be obtained at baseline and followed throughout treatment.

ECG Monitoring

Thioridazine, and mesoridazine, are no longer available in most countries, and pimozide should be avoided in patients with known heart disease. Ziprasidone should be used cautiously in patients with heart disease, with baseline and follow-up ECG recommended. However, it does not require special monitoring in non-cardiac patients.

Prolactin

Patients receiving dopamine antagonists such as typical antipsychotics and most atypical antipsychotics should be asked about symptoms of elevated prolactin. In women, ask about milk discharge from breasts, and changes in menstruation or libido. In men, ask about changes in libido and sexual dysfunction. Assessment of prolactin levels is ordered when screening questions suggest possible hyperprolactinemia.

Screening and Monitoring of Drug Abuse

Laboratory testing is used to screen for and confirm the presence of a drug or combinations of drugs so that the person can receive proper treatment. Laboratory test results can also be useful in confronting the denial of substance abuse by the patient or his or her family. Clearly, laboratory testing is essential to the evaluation, monitoring, and subsequent treatment of patients who abuse alcohol, prescribed addictive medications, or illicit drugs. Laboratory tests are used also to detect end-organ damage related to the abuse, e.g., liver function tests (particularly γ-glutamyl transferase) can reveal harmful use of alcohol. Laboratory testing can be conducted with blood and urine specimens or with saliva and hair samples. Urine specimens are typically preferred, because the detectable length of time that a particular drug of abuse and its metabolites are present is longer in urine than in blood. However, some substances, such as alcohol or barbiturates, are best detected in blood specimens. The level of toxic dose of a certain drug is usually variable in patients due to difference in their duration and amount of intake and development of tolerance. *The following is a summary of possible toxic levels and duration to be detected in urine for screening:*

- **Alcohol**: toxic level is dependent on individual tolerance and usage, although levels greater than 300–400 mg/dL can be fatal due to respiratory depression; it can be detected for up to 7–12 hours.
- **Amphetamines**: toxic level varies widely, severe reactions have occurred with 30 mg, yet doses of 400 to 500 mg are not uniformly fatal; it can be detected for up to 48 hours.
- **Barbiturates**: plasma level of 35 mg/L for short-acting barbiturates, or 90 mg/L for long-acting barbiturates, carries an unfavorable prognosis. Available urine tests have different cutoff concentration of barbiturates or its metabolite (100, 200, 300ng/mL). It can be detected for up to 24 hours (short-acting), or 3 weeks (long-acting).
- **Benzodiazepines**: quantitative determinations of benzodiazepines are not useful in the clinical management of intoxicated patients since there is no correlation between serum concentrations and pharmacological and toxicological effects; it can be detected for up to 5–7 days of prolonged use of alprazolam, or as long as 5–30 days in case of prolonged use of diazepam.
- **Cannabis**: the median lethal dosage (LD-50) rating has never been established in humans. Considering that a dosage of 3000 mg/kg of pure THC is non-fatal in studies of large animals, an equivalent dosage to an average 70 kg human will be 210 grams. Thus, a person could smoke 2.1 kg of marijuana all at once in order to reach the same levels of THC, given that the average level of THC found in marijuana is approximately 10 percent. Marijuana can be detected in urine for up to 4–6 weeks.
- **Cocaine**: toxic blood level = >1 μg/mL. Common doses of cocaine vary between 10 and 120 mg. The estimated minimal lethal dose of cocaine is 1.2 g, but individuals with hypersensitivity to cocaine have died from as little as 30 mg. Some cocaine addicts with considerable tolerance have reported that they can tolerate up to 5 g of cocaine daily. It can be detected for up to 6–8 hours, and 2–4 days for its metabolites.
- **Opiates**: toxic blood level varies with medication. Heroin: >100–250 ng/mL; Codeine: >1.1 μg/mL; Morphine: >200 ng/mL; it can be detected for up to 2–3 days.
- **Phencyclidine**: toxic blood level = >1 mg/mL; it can be detected for up to 1 week of single use or 2–4 weeks of prolonged use.

4   Special Considerations

ASSESSMENT OF CHILDREN AND ADOLESCENTS

Community studies indicate that a considerable proportion of children and adolescents have significant psychiatric symptoms or disorders, a matter that has its implication on those children and adolescents on achieving their potential and affects their quality of life. Therefore, considerable effort is needed to detect and manage those symptoms and disorders, as early as possible.

Evaluation of children and adolescents may be seen by some medical students or practitioners as a mysterious job, stressing its difficulty, longer time needed, and contradictory views of parents and their children. Indirectly added problems are the controversy about classification and labeling of children and the use of adult classification in children. Difficulties of treatment of childhood disorders and relying mainly on adult strategies of management add to the problem of psychiatric disorders in children. However, all of these concerns about evaluation of children and adolescents are not unique to this age group, but are present throughout psychiatry; this does not nullify the importance of improving skills to interview children and adolescents. Thus, deeply thinking about the assessment of children and adolescents will reveal that it essentially has the same core and framework as that of adults, but some considerations are needed.

Considerations in Working with Children

1. **Children are not just like us as adults**: nor are they like us when we were younger; they are rapidly developing, fully human, deserving respect and age-appropriate communication and information. Interviewers of children need to be familiar with basic cognitive and social/emotional developmental theories and have direct experience with children (i.e., you should have spent some time with children in either a caretaking or emotionally connected manner) (Wilson & Powell, 2001).

2. **Interview environment**: the best interview environment is one that is organized, comfortable, warm, and friendly. The interview room should

be private and free from unnecessary interruptions or distractions. If the child feels threatened or anxious; reduction in formality may alleviate this. Try to have seating available that is appropriate for the size of the child. If possible, you should sit at the same level as the child, with your chair facing the child's chair at a slight angle to maintain eye contact.

3. **Need for multiple data sources**: comprehensive child assessment requires data from other sources in addition to interviews. Other data sources include direct observations in classrooms and other group situations, standardized parent and teacher rating scales, self-reports, questionnaires, and other procedures, as appropriate. It is especially important to recognize that data collected from one method are not inherently better than data collected from others. Information from teachers, child care personnel, and other community agencies can help greatly in the psychiatric assessment of children and youth. However, contact with the school or outside agencies should only occur through, or after signed permission is obtained from, the parent(s). Teachers can provide valuable details about the academic achievement and a description of the child's relationships with peers and school personnel. School information is essential if the child is having difficulties in the school setting. Contact with social workers or access to reports from community agencies is helpful in dealing with children in foster care or adopted children.

4. **Situational variations**: children's behavior is likely to vary across situations and relationships. Because environmental conditions can vary across situations, children's behavior is likely to vary from one situation to the next. Children's relationships with different adults, such as parents versus teachers, are also likely to involve variations in behavior. Good assessment requires identifying patterns of children's behavior that differ across situations and relationships as well as patterns that remain consistent, despite variations in situations and relationships.

5. **Limited cross-informant agreement**: there is low-to-moderate agreement between informants who are in different situations or different relationships with the same child. Low agreement between informants does not mean that one is right and the other is wrong, or that one has a "truer" picture of a child than does the other. Parents may know more than teachers about many aspects of their child's functioning simply because parents spend more time with the child and they have a special, unique relationship with the child. Still, teachers may know more than parents about other aspects of functioning, such as the child's approach to academic tasks or ability to relate to peers, because of the special circumstances of school versus home. Differences in people's perceptions of the child are as informative as are the similarities in perceptions. The challenge is to put all these pieces together to form a meaningful picture of the child's functioning under the given circumstances. By examining similarities and differences in perceptions, practitioners can identify important clues to

factors affecting the child's behavior in different situations and relation-ships. In turn, these clues can lead to intervention strategies that are best suited to each of these special circumstances and relationships.

6. **Caregiver**: a caregiver should be allowed to stay during the interview, if the child expresses this wish. The caregiver is advised not to interrupt the child and not to ask questions or prompt answers. It is a good idea to seat the caregiver behind the child to limit the influence and possible distraction. If the child appears uncomfortable while talking about the abuse in the presence of the caregiver, or if the caregiver appears overly upset hearing about the abuse, then another person who does not have a close interest may replace the parent (e.g., a neighbor or community worker).

7. **Confidentiality**: parents and children should be informed early in the interview about issues of confidentiality. It depends on the child's age and possible danger or risk to the child. It is useful to inform the child in developmentally appropriate terms that what is discussed is confidential unless it involves his/her own or someone's safety.

8. **Use of toys in an interview**: the usefulness of toys, puzzles, and stationery depends on how distracting they are and what they are being used for. Allowing a child to play with toys can be a good way to ease the child into the strange interview environment. However, if the toys are too exciting, they may distract the child. Getting a child to settle down and talk after an exciting game can be very difficult. For preparation and planning of an interview of a nervous child, doing a quiet and relatively easy task together (e.g., a jigsaw puzzle or a card game) may help the child to talk by deflecting the main focus of attention away from him/herself. However, make sure the activity is age-appropriate. The child may be offended if invited to play a game that he/she considers him/herself too old for. Drawings can also be helpful, as most children like to draw. Having a young child draw a person and label the parts of the body can be a useful means of learning what names the child has for various body parts (Wilson & Powell, 2001).

How to Facilitate Engagement of Family in Interview

When interviewing a child, it is not unusual for the child and/or family members to be uncomfortable about the interview. Parents may attend the interview under pressure from the other parent, other family member, or school personnel, without being convinced by its need or value. Parents may also be worried about how they will be viewed during the evaluation. On the other hand, children may have received no advance information about the visit and have little understanding about the need for the assessment, or the child may interpret the evaluation as that others consider him/her crazy.

A priority of the examiner is to focus on establishing alliances with both parents, or at least with the parent who is the primary caregiver. The examiner can gain engagement of the family by displaying respect to each family member, listening attentively to all family members, and respecting the family's culture, customs, and traditions. In other words, the examiner needs to create a sensitive and empathic environment for the child and his or her family. Establishing a friendly atmosphere and clearly outlining the plan for assessment (e.g., explaining who will be interviewed and in what order) helps reduce anxiety and facilitates the gathering of information.

Child and adolescent psychiatrists should support families and be a partner, not to judge or blame. They listen to concerns, and help the child or adolescent and his/her family, define the goals of the evaluation, encourage family members to express their concerns, and ask them why they attended this consultation. Be prepared for responses such as, "Because my family doctor told me to." Such comments should be followed up by asking the family members what they hope to accomplish by this meeting, apart from what others may have suggested.

By paying attention to the larger picture of the family, the examiner is able to observe lines of authority, family coalitions, family subsystems, generation boundaries, and so forth. Furthermore, attending to the whole family gives the examiner the opportunity to find major foci of dysfunction and to attend to forces that undermine parental authority or interfere with the resolution of the problems. On the other hand, the examiner may encounter resources or areas of strength in different family members or subsystems. These resources may be instrumental in solving major conflicts within the family or in solving problems of the family transacting with other systems.

The examiner needs to avoid criticizing or patronizing the members, or entering into power struggles with the families regarding authority or discipline within the family, unless such family practices are questionable or abusive. An unsound practice during initial evaluations is to interject personal views or to challenge the family's philosophy, religion, political views, lifestyle, or composition (Cepeda, 2010).

Do I Need Consent from Parents to Interview a Child?

The best way to obtain the cooperation of the parent(s) is to keep them fully informed of your actions at all times and to ask for their permission before you interview the child. In legal and abuse situations, parental consent may not be sought or obtained. It is also important to seek the child's assent to being interviewed. Although the interview may be compulsory, obtaining the child's assent first will help build the child's trust. Further, if the child does not wish to be interviewed, it can be very helpful to know the reason at the outset.

Characteristics of Child Interview

The arrangements for the interviewing of children and adolescents and their families depend on the characteristics of each, and on the age of children and type of complaints. As a general rule, children and their parents are inter-viewed, at least for a part of the assessment, individually and together with other members. Interviewing of an adolescent in front of his/her parent is better avoided as it is likely to result in the adolescent hiding his/her symptoms and/or risk-taking behavior (such as sexual activity, drug use, suicidal thoughts). Confidentiality issues should be discussed with adolescents, who may be hesitant to disclose drug use, even when their parents are absent, because of concern about possible legal consequences. Contradictory assessment findings among children, parents, and collateral sources are expected about some types of information.

There is no fixed order or manner of conducting the child interview; these vary with the nature of the chief complaint and presenting pathology, the child's age and development status, the interviewer's personal style, and the clinical setting and context (e.g., emergency room, hospital ward, school-based consultation, private office, outpatient mental health clinic). Whatever the variations in format, the interview is organized and guided by the clinician's attention to the various key areas and phenomena and the interviewer's strategic sense of how best to elicit the relevant data in the case at hand. Some data emerge spontaneously, while others require questioning or other deliberate means of eliciting information.

The structure and content of clinical interviews should vary in relation to the informant and the goals of the interviews. By interviewing children, practitioners can understand children's views of their problems and compe-tencies, their desires, fears, and coping strategies, and their reactions to the circumstances and important relationships affecting their behavior. Inter-viewers can also directly observe children's behavior, affect, and coping strat-egies. By interviewing parents, practitioners can understand parents' views of children's problems and competencies, children's developmental and medical history, family circumstances, and parents' reactions to their children's behavior. Parent interviews can also provide clues about parents' own psychological functioning and coping strategies. By interviewing teachers, practitioners can know teachers' views of children's problems, competencies, and academic performance. They can also learn about teachers' instructional strategies, school interventions for academic and behavioral problems, and forms of special help or services that have been provided.

Comprehensive psychiatric evaluations usually require several hours over one or more office visits for the child and parents, to avoid the potential influence of fatigue on the behavior of the young child; a matter that may give rise to an inaccurate mental status examination. This will help to con-firm observations at one session, and also allows time to interview collateral resources to see the problem from different perspectives.

The broad goals of the child interview are often conceptualized under two headings: history taking and the mental status examination. History taking consists of an inquiry into the presenting problem, significant areas of the child's life and functioning, relevant past history, child's developmental level, school and friends, family relationships, and parent and family health and psychiatric histories. The mental status examination is nearly the same as in adults; it consists of assessment and description of the following areas: physical appearance; manner of relating to examiner and parents, including ease of separation; motor behavior (including activity level, coordination, neurological soft signs, cerebral dominance, and presence of tics or stereotypes); affect; mood; content and form of thought, including delusions and obsession; speech and language; perceptual disorders; orientation to time, place, person; overall intelligence; attention; memory; neurological functioning; judgment and insight; and preferred modes of communication (e.g., play, drawing, direct discourse). In the actual practice of the child interview, however, history taking and mental status assessment are not always clearly separable processes and often proceed simultaneously.

When assessing psychopathology, the clinician should adopt a developmental approach to account for differences between children and adults and to consider differences among children at various developmental stages. Developmental consideration of symptoms and psychopathology is critically important to account for changes in mood expression and cognition across life. Just applying adult diagnostic criteria to children's symptoms may result in imprecise assessments and wrong decisions.

When the child or adolescent is uncooperative the clinician gives them more time to calm down before being interviewed. This can be achieved by first introducing himself or herself to the patient, explaining the purpose of the evaluation process, and then proceeding with all other aspects of the consultation, and leaving the patient interview to the end. Alternatively, the interviewer can introduce him/herself as a patient support, e.g., by asking, "What can I do to help you to make things better?" or "I would like to hear your side of the story so I can understand the best way to help you."

When a child or an adolescent continues to refuse cooperation with the interviewer, they may appropriately respond by clearly outlining the available decisions and the consequences of the child/adolescent's refusal to cooperate; e.g., if the available information suggests that the child/adolescent may pose a danger to him/herself or someone else, refusing to speak to the interviewer will make that information the only source of the interviewer's decision. If the patient continues to refuse to cooperate with the interviewer, the clinician should attempt to do a safety assessment and mental status examination and rely on collateral contacts to provide any additional information required for treatment planning.

At the end of assessment, the child and adolescent psychiatrist combines biological, psychological, and social parts of the problem with the developmental needs, history, and strengths of the child, adolescent, and family to formulate the child's problems and explains them in terms that the parents and child can understand. Formulation is used to plan treatments or interventions that will address the child's and the family's needs.

Some Tips for Effective Questioning of Children

1. Explain to the child who you are, what your role is, and why the interview is taking place. The same applies to other people in the interview team. Neutral descriptions of your job may be appropriate, for example, "I listen to children who have worries," "I help kids sort things out." The approach taken, however, will obviously depend on the child's level of understanding and on the circumstances of the concern.
2. Give the child a rough idea of what you will do together; that is, merely talking, and how long this will take.
3. Emphasize to the child that it's better to say "Don't know" than to give an answer that he/she is not sure of.
4. Do not persist with questions that a child is not capable of answering.
5. Be cautious about "Why," "When," and "How" questions with children below six years of age. This is because they require abstract concepts and reasoning skills that children don't acquire until they are much older.
6. Mix specific questions with open or general probes to avoid the interview sounding like a test, and follow up a closed question with "Tell me more about that" or "How do you know?" to check that the child has not made up a response to please the interviewer.
7. Speak slowly and clearly, using short, simple sentences that contain no more than one question. Try to avoid the use of passives and negative questions. Ask "Did you see Joe?" not "Was Joe seen?"; and "Did you tell anyone about this?" not "You didn't tell anyone about this, did you?"
8. Watch carefully for signs of confusion and blankness and assume responsibility for clarifying the child's understanding of the questions and for cleaning up inconsistencies in the child's account.
9. Use the child's own language where possible.

EMERGENCY EVALUATION

The concept of a psychiatric emergency is difficult to define, because mental illnesses tend to evolve relatively slowly, and quite often it is not the patient who thinks that there is an emergency. Emergency psychiatry is usually used to indicate that someone (patient, family member, or professional) is frightened. Alternatively, emergencies can arise when the patient's mental state has shown little change, but someone else has suddenly become aware that it is unwell (Poole & Higgo, 2006).

The emergency psychiatric evaluation may occur in response to emergent or urgent problems. A psychiatric emergency is defined as an acute disturbance of thought, mood, behavior, or social relationship that requires an immediate intervention as defined by the patient, family, or the community.

Urgent problems as opposed to emergencies can be thought of as situations that have some or all of these features but, where the situation is evolving more slowly, the feared outcome is not imminent and attention can be delayed for a short time.

The psychiatric emergency room (ER) is an intense, stressful work environment where psychiatrists must perform rapid assessments and make rapid treatment decisions. During psychiatry residency training, the ER provides critical experience that helps sharpen residents' diagnostic and interview skills, as well as enhance their overall clinical confidence. *Among these skills, the following are essentially of importance* (Brasch et al., 2004):

1. **Prioritization skills**: clinicians should learn how to detect and prioritize the most distressed, dangerous, medical illnesses, emergent medication, and how to use seclusion, restraint, and monitor patients.
2. **Assessment and Diagnostic skills**: clinicians should learn to have rapid, focused assessment, mental status examination, risk assessment: violence and suicide, neurological examination as needed, obtaining collateral information (family, outpatient, or inpatient records, etc.), lab work, diagnosis and biopsychosocial formulation, and accurate, timely documentation.
3. **Medico-legal skills**: clinicians are more subjected to decisions with medico-legal aspects that need awareness with involuntary commitment laws, evaluating competence to give informed consent, public intoxication laws, exceptions to confidentiality, laws on confidentiality, exceptions to confidentiality, and reporting laws on: child abuse, elder abuse, domestic violence, unsafe driving.
4. **Management and treatment**: clinicians should learn how to take decisions about inpatient or outpatient treatment recommendations, and how to justify them, formulating risk reduction plans. Also, clinicians should learn how to provide feedback, counseling, support, and treatment to patients with suicidal or homicidal ideation, acute psychosis, acute intoxication or withdrawal, and other causes of psychiatric emergencies.

The Aims of Emergency Evaluation

These include the following:

1. To assess medical and psychiatric (suicidal or homicidal ideation) risk factors of the emergency situation.
2. To establish a provisional diagnosis of the mental disorder most likely to be responsible for the current emergency, and to identify other diagnostic possibilities requiring further evaluation in the near term, including general medical conditions that represent potential causes of or contrib-

utors to the patient's mental condition. Comorbid psychiatric illness, recent trauma, substance use and substance-related conditions, and cognitive impairment disorders should be considered. In many emergency settings patients initially are examined by a non-psychiatric physician to exclude acute general medical problems. Such examinations usually are limited in scope and rarely are definitive. Therefore, the psychiatrist may need to request or initiate further general medical evaluation to address diagnostic concerns that emerge from the psychiatric evaluation.

3. To identify social, environmental, and cultural factors relevant to immediate treatment decisions.

4. To develop a plan for immediate treatment and management plan, with determination of whether the patient requires treatment in a hospital or other supervised setting and what follow up will be required if the patient is not hospitalized.

Though it is important to develop the skill of brief evaluation, it is important to know that there is a risk of being inaccurate. Information that could not be obtained from the patient in a single setting is better delayed for later settings according to the patient's condition and the clinician's judgment. This will save the patient and clinician time without affecting the diagnosis or treatment plan, or distressing the patient. Patients who are to be discharged to the community after emergency evaluation may require more extensive evaluation in the emergency setting than those who are to be hospitalized.

Common Disorders that Demand Emergency Psychiatric Evaluation

1. Medical disorder causing psychiatric symptoms
2. Substance-induced psychiatric symptoms
3. Mood disorder with psychotic features
4. Acute psychosis
5. Personality disorder
6. Drug-induced EPS
7. Situational problems (acute bereavement and acute trauma)
8. Drug seeking
9. Malingering.

Among all these disorders, violent and injurious behavior directed against self or others needs special consideration.

THE VIOLENT AND AGGRESSIVE PATIENT

Disruptive and aggressive behavior is an everyday problem challenging clinicians in the emergency department. Patients exhibiting these behaviors have a high morbidity and mortality, and represent a medico-legal risk for the clinicians. This medico-legal risk stems from the patients' behavior, injuries they may have obtained, or from the underlying organic illness if it is the cause of their adverse behavior (Rueve & Welton, 2008).

Although the overall contribution of individuals with mental illness to violence in society is relatively small, they are more likely to engage in aggressive and assaultive behavior than people in the general population. Thus, violence among the mentally ill constitutes a serious public safety concern. Particularly vulnerable are the mental health providers who work with those violent patients. Among clinicians, violence toward psychiatrists and mental health professional is common and is an important issue. The risk of violent victimization is greater in clinicians with less experience. So, a crucial aspect of psychiatric training is how to assess and manage the violent patient.

Personal Safety

When confronted with a potentially violent patient, personal safety should be a priority. Consequently, effective training should emphasize the staff member's right to personal safety and places the issue in consciousness. Specific protocols that consider the safety of the medical team and patients should be available and followed in specific situations. Some emergency departments and hospitals adopt very strict prevention policies regarding physical aggressive behavior toward staff. This should not prevent clinicians from having their duty of care to those patients, or providing assessment and treatment.

Confined and overcrowded conditions on a ward have been associated with higher rates of patient violence. Do not enter a closed, private space with a patient unless you feel safe, and further safety measures are available. Suitable numbers of confident-appearing, "but not confrontational" staff or security may deter the patient from acting out. Proper use of the physical space and security personnel increase safety and decrease the potential for violent behavior, e.g., some patients do better when interviewed in a small, private setting. Other interviews must be conducted in a triage area while police companions hold the patient and handcuffs remain on.

Ideally, you and the patient should have equal access to the door if you conduct the psychiatric interview in an enclosed room, and the door should be left open. With high-risk patients, arrange your seating at a 90-degree angle "rather than face-to-face" to limit sustained, confrontational eye contact. Sit at greater than an arm swing or leg kick away from the patient, and require him or her to remain seated during the interview (or you will promptly leave). As the interview progresses, if the patient's control appears to be deteriorating, as evidenced by increased pacing or making threatening gestures, the clinician should communicate to the patient that external controls will be enforced if necessary. If that assurance does not allay the patient's agitation, external controls (e.g., restraint, seclusion, or medication) should be instituted without delay.

In the outpatient practice, terminate the interview or evaluation session if a patient in a negative affective arousal state does not allow verbal redirection. Before you make any movement to exit, announce to the patient, "I am leaving the room now."

When patients with a history of violence are brought to the hospital in high arousal states, let them remain in restraint with security present during the initial interview. If the patient cannot have a back-and-forth conversation with you, keep the security force present until you believe that verbal interactions have a substantial effect.

Patients must be responsive to talking interventions before restraint, security, or other environmental safety measures are removed. Some patients do not reach this point until medication is given.

Indications for Restraining Violent and Aggressive Patients

The use of restraints is not a matter of ease or convenience. Restraining a violent and aggressive patient is indicated when there is a need to prevent the patient from: harming him/herself or other patients, harming care givers and other staff members. It is indicated also to prevent disruption or damage to the environment, and to help in assessing and management of the patient.

Precautions on Using Physical Restraints

- Clinicians should be aware of local policies, laws, and acts before restraining patients.
- The clinician ordering the restraints should document the reason for restraints, what limbs are restrained, how frequent neurovascular observations are needed, and when the indication of restraints need to be reviewed; it is generally reviewed by the treating clinician every 2 hours.
- The shortest period of time and the least restrictive manner should be applied when restraints are used.
- Applying physical restraints needs one person for each limb and a fifth person to lead the restraint and manage the airway.
- The safety of the patient should parallel the restraining control, e.g., applying padding between restraints and the patients to prevent neurovascular injury. Neurovascular observations should be performed regularly every 15–30 mins while the patient is physically restrained. Also, restraints should be easily removed when necessary, e.g., if the patient begins to vomit, has a seizure, or loses control of their airway.
- Using psychotropic drugs should always follow physical restraint.

Confidentiality and Violence

The clinician can make an estimate of threat risk based on careful assessment of potential for violence. When violence is unlikely, maintain the patient's confidentiality and continue evaluation or treatment as clinically indicated. When potential violence is an issue, the clinician's duty to maintain confidentiality may conflict with the duty to protect; it may warrant warning a third party or initiating involuntary hospitalization of the patient, both of which breach confidentiality.

When the clinician has concluded that violence is a real risk, he/she should discuss the implication of such assessment with the patient and discuss the possible expected next steps to treat the risk of violence, e.g., hospitalizing the patient or modifying treatment. If the patient does not agree with the clinician's conclusion or procedures, the clinician has a clear obligation to breach confidentiality to prevent imminent threat of violence. It is mandatory to keep meticulous records that include notes outlining the rationale underlying the clinician's thinking for each of their decisions.

Assessment of the Risk of Violence

The clinician should routinely assess the violence potential, even if the patient does not express thoughts of violence. The evaluator must take into consideration demographic, historical, and environmental factors, and clinical aspects of psychopathology that may be related to an increased risk of violence.

When making a decision about violence potential, the clinician should interview family members, police, and other persons with information about the patient and about violent incidents to ensure that the patient is not minimizing his or her dangerousness. It is also important to contact or attempt to contact the patient's current and past therapists and review old charts for previous episodes of violence, police and arrest reports, and other available records such as judicial proceedings (Simon & Tardiff, 2008).

Identify Arousal State of the Patient

Patients are more likely to become aggressive in high arousal states, but rarely commit violent acts when their anxiety and moods are well controlled. A patient's verbal threatening is considered a red flag alert to the clinician, who should start de-escalation techniques and prepare for a violent incident.

Anger can be easily anticipated by observing signs of escalating tension. The common signs of anger include loud voice, inappropriate staring, knocking things over, clenched fists, agitated pacing, impatience and refusal to comply with the usual intake procedures in the emergency department or clinic, and verbal threats. De-escalation measures should be taken once these signs are observed.

Decrease provocation of the patient by clarification of your behaviors and arrangements in advance, e.g., "I would like to enter the room, sit down, and talk with you for about 20 minutes." Avoid displaying warmth toward paranoid patients, as it may be interpreted as trying to deceive them.

Fear plays a central role in most situations in which patients act violently. Danger signals may be poorly displayed and may be difficult to interpret in a fearful patient. Thus, caution is recommended when dealing with such patients; affording enough personal space to avoid provoking the patient, e.g., a fearful paranoid patient needs an intimate zone that is greater than usual.

Dysarthria, unsteady gait, dilated pupils, tremors, and other signs of acute drug or alcohol intoxication dictate caution and serious consideration of the potential for violence, even though threats of violence may not have been expressed.

It is necessary that clinicians avoid arousing confused patients through explaining their actions, e.g., a nurse dealing with such circumstances can say "Hello Mr. Fred, I am Suzy, I am a nurse in this hospital. I will need to check your blood pressure using this apparatus."

Confusion can be a causal risk factor in patients with delirium and organic brain diseases. Those patients may unexpectedly attack health care providers during routine procedures; caution is always recommended among those working in similar situations.

Patients can react aggressively to loss of self-esteem and feelings of power-lessness, e.g., patients who are brought by police into an emergency detention situation may act violently to restore their sense of self. Staff can reduce a patient's potential response to humiliation by using a therapeutic, esteem-building interview technique, e.g., calling the patient "Mr." instead of by first name.

Demographic Characteristics

Demographic characteristics of patients should be considered in the assessment of violence potential. These include ages 15 to 24 years old, male gender, poverty, non-white race, and low educational level. Other factors that may increase the risk of violence include history of abuse, victimization, family violence, limited employment skills, poor family network, and frequent moves or job changes (Battaglia, 2004).

Past History of Violence

Past violence is the most powerful predictor of future violence. Higher frequency of aggressive episodes, greater degree of aggressive injury, and lack of apparent provocation in past episodes all increase the violence risk. However, not having a violent history does not guarantee that a patient will not become dangerous during a clinical encounter.

The past history of violence should be treated as any other medical symptom. This includes noting the date of onset, frequency, place, and severity of violence, provoking events and possible etiological causes (e.g., because of psychosis or alcohol drinking), and their consequences. Information that should be obtained and recorded about past history of violence includes prior psychological testing, imaging, laboratory testing, and other evaluations, as well as past treatment, hospitalizations, and response to treatments.

Alcohol and Drug Use

Alcohol and drug intoxication or withdrawal can cause violence on its own, or exacerbate the psychopathology in persons with psychiatric disorders. Use of alcohol and drugs can cause changes in the brain that may lead to chronic impairment and psychiatric symptoms related to violent behavior. Alcohol intoxication is accompanied by emotional lability and impaired judgment. In some cases, alcohol withdrawal may lead to delirium, and violence may result from gross disorganization of behavior or as a response to threatening auditory hallucinations or delusional thinking.

Continued use of cocaine, particularly when taken intravenously or smoked in the form of crack, may cause grandiosity, psychomotor agitation, suspiciousness, and, frequently, violence. Suspiciousness becomes first paranoid ideation and then paranoid delusional thinking. Thus, violence results from delusional thinking as well as from the stimulation effect of cocaine.

Violence may occur during intoxication with a number of hallucinogens, but less commonly than it occurs in phencyclidine (PCP) intoxication. Within 1 hour of oral use (5 minutes if the drug is smoked or taken intravenously), PCP often produces marked violence, impulsivity, unpredictability, and grossly impaired judgment. There also may be delusional thinking or delirium.

Intense or prolonged amphetamine use may result in confusion, rambling, incoherence, paranoid ideation, and delusional thinking, which are accompanied by agitation, fighting, and other forms of aggression.

Psychiatric Disorder

Disorders characterized by psychotic symptoms, including schizophrenia, delusional disorder, substance abuse disorders, mood disorders, especially with mania, and neurological and medical disorders, may be accompanied by violent behavior. Risk factors for violence among psychiatric patients include individual history of violence, active paranoid delusions, hallucinations associated with negative affect, manic states, non-compliance with treatment, neurologic abnormalities, alcohol or drug intoxication and withdrawal states, history of abuse, and family violence.

Psychosis, regardless of its cause, increases the risk of violence. In schizophrenic patients violence may stem from delusions of persecution. Command auditory hallucinations may result in violent behavior and homicide. However, some schizophrenic patients are violent because of generalized disorganization of thought and a lack of impulse control accompanied by purposeless excited psychomotor activity (akathisia), or they may inadvertently come into physical contact with other patients, which may lead to fights.

A manic patient may become violent as a result of trials to restrict his/her activity, to stop his/her continuous talking, or to dispute his/her ideas. Persecutory delusions are another cause of violence in those patients.

Personality Disorders

Violence and aggression among persons with antisocial personality disorder is a core feature of the disorder. These patients have no remorse for their actions, and the victim is perceived as deserving the beating. The person with borderline personality disorder can be violent and make suicidal gestures when rejected or feeling rejected by others. The violence and suicide attempts are part of a broader picture of impulsivity and instability of interpersonal relationships. Persons with narcissistic personality can be violent occasionally when angry, such as when they are not given something they think they deserve. The person with paranoid personality rarely attacks those seen as persecutors, but when violence does occur it can be severe, even taking the form of mass murder. The person with intermittent explosive disorder is violent during circumscribed episodes, often with little apparent precipitating cause or out of proportion to any identifiable cause.

Assessment of Violent Ideation and Its Degree

Planning

The clinician should begin by assessing whether the patient has thoughts of violence toward other persons. Evaluation of violent ideation includes assessment of how well planned the ideation or threat is, i.e., the degree of formulation. Vague threats of killing someone, such as "She'll be sorry to see me," are not as serious as the patient's saying, "I'm going to kill my wife with a gun because she had an affair."

Intent

If a patient has thoughts of harming someone, it is important to explore whether he or she really intends to do something or is just having thoughts of violence. This disclosure may arise during an outpatient treatment session, as an offhand comment on the inpatient unit, or during any other contact with the patient. The patient's mere thought of violence may not be sufficient for the clinician to take actions such as warning someone, changing medication, or hospitalizing the patient. For some patients these thoughts of violence may seem intrusive, alien, and disturbing, and they will say that they do not intend to do anything to carry them out.

Available Means

The availability of a means of inflicting injury or death is important in the assessment of violence potential. If the patient is thinking about getting a gun or already has one, the clinician should obviously take a threat of violence more seriously. The clinician always should ask a potentially violent patient if he or she has or has ready access to a gun or other fatal tool. Vigorous efforts should be made to have the patient get rid of the gun or to have it taken from the patient by family members or others. When guns are removed, the potential for homicide is reduced; however, that does not necessarily preclude the patient's attacking the victim in other, less lethal ways. "Available means" also applies to the physical availability of the potential victim. How easily accessible is he or she to the patient? Does the potential victim live in a secluded place or in a city building without a doorman? A schizophrenic patient who threatens his or her father may be an immediate threat if actually living with the father as opposed to living in a different city or state at a distance from him.

Medical History

A lot of medical causes may make a patient vulnerable to violent and aggressive behaviors. These include: head injury, hypoxia, metabolic disturbances/hypoglycemia, CNS infection (meningitis, encephalitis), hyperthermia or hypothermia, seizures (postictal or status epilepticus), cerebrovascular insults (stroke or subarachnoid hemorrhage). All these conditions need appropriate evaluation.

Investigating the Violent and Aggressive Patient

- Routine investigation includes full blood count, blood sugar level, urea, creatinine, urinalysis, electrolytes, and urine drug screen.
- Other investigations should be guided by history and physical examination, e.g., head CT/MRI, and lumbar puncture.

Final Statements about Dealing with Violence and Aggression

1. Recognition of predictors of violence and aggression risk, and early use of de-escalation techniques are aimed at prevention of the spread of a volatile situation.
2. Personal safety and the safety of other patients and their visitors should be considered at all times. This includes ensuring adequate personal space, keeping safe escape route, and never turning your back on the individual.

3. Dealing with the aggressive person: this includes placing him/her in a secure quiet area; allowing the person to express him/herself; providing continuous observation; administration of appropriate medications; repeated evaluation of the patient's condition and recording behavior changes in the patient's notes.

SUICIDE

Suicide is one of the leading causes of death among people of all ages especially young people. For each suicidal death, there are many non-fatal suicidal acts ranging in seriousness from mild overdoses and superficially inflicted cuts to potentially lethal acts such as jumping from a high place or ingesting a corrosive poison. As mental disorders contribute in large part to suicide, it is important to assess suicidal risk accurately in every psychiatric patient (Simon & Hales, 2006).

Clinical Assessment of Suicide Risk

In the case of clinical assessment for suicide risk, risk factors are usually used to evaluate the likelihood of suicide occurrence in the near future. However, risk factors do not predict which person will or will not die by suicide or when they might make a lethal or non-lethal attempt.

Practical Suggestions for Initiating Assessment of Suicidal Persons

The following should be done:

- establish rapport;
- use a calm, patient, non-judgmental, and empathic approach;
- begin with supportive statements and open-ended inquiries;
- start with general and then move toward more specific questions in a sensitive and non-judgmental way that creates an opportunity for dialogue.

The following should not be done:

- allow your personal feelings and reactions to influence assessment and treatment;
- rush the patient or ask leading questions;
- interrogate the patient or force the patient to defend his or her actions;
- minimize the patient's distress;
- undermine the seriousness of the suicidal thought or action.

Acquiring Collateral Information

- A patient may not explicitly admit to suicidal thoughts, behaviors, or history (passive suicidality). Family, friends, health professionals, teachers, co-workers, or others may also provide valuable information to support the assessment.
- If no informants are able to provide collateral information and the patient does not directly answer questions; clinical judgment based on apparent risks, and possible warning signs of hidden suicidal ideation (e.g., presence of psychosis, despondence, anger, agitation; inability to develop rapport, make eye contact, answer direct questions about suicide), and subjective impressions may need to be called upon. Furthermore, the clinician may need to review hospital or clinic records for evidence of past self-harm behaviors, and pay close attention during the physical examination for signs of suspicious injuries.

Assessment of Suicide Can Go through the Following Steps

1. Evaluation of suicide risk factors
2. Evaluation of warning signs of suicide
3. Asking about previous suicidal attempts
4. Assessment of the suicidal ideation, intent, plan, and access to lethal means
5. Identification of targets for intervention.

Evaluation of Suicide Risk Factors

When establishing the presence of suicidal ideation, the overall goal is to determine the risk for death by suicide. Therefore, history taking and a thorough psychological assessment, especially addressing suicide risk factors, are essential. *Risk factors for suicide cover a broad range of variables, it is important to collect information about the following*:

1. **Psychiatric disorders**: suicidal thoughts and behaviors (including suicide attempts and committed suicide) are commonly found at increased rates among individuals with psychiatric disorders, especially major depressive disorder, bipolar disorders, schizophrenia, PTSD, anxiety, drug dependence, and personality disorders (e.g., borderline and antisocial). While patients with chronic schizophrenia or recurrent mood disorders have a greater risk of dying by suicide than the general population, anxiety disorders, organic states, and drug and alcohol abuse also have an associated risk of suicide. Alcoholics commonly attempt suicide while intoxicated. Even delirious patients can kill themselves, usually accidentally. Manic

patients sometimes kill themselves as a result of recklessness, abrupt swings into depression, or psychosis. Schizophrenic patients kill themselves for a variety of reasons, including response to overwhelmingly terrifying delusions, command hallucinations, or concurrent depression. Psychiatric comorbidity increases risk for suicide, especially when substance abuse or depressive symptoms coexist with another psychiatric disorder. Aspects of the patient's personality, such as personality traits or thinking styles, affect how he or she tolerates emotional or psychological stress and what type of coping strategies he or she uses to deal with these stressors. Although these factors do not predict suicide, they may contribute to the overall risk profile through their effect on the patient's ability to cope, and on the support systems available to the person.

2. **Psychosocial factors**: a number of psychosocial factors are associated with risk for suicide and suicide attempts. These include recent life events such as losses (especially employment, careers, finances, housing, marital relationships, physical health, and a sense of hope), and chronic or long-term problems such as relationship difficulties, unemployment, and problems with the legal authorities (legal charges). Psychological states of acute or extreme distress (especially humiliation, despair, guilt, and shame) are often present in association with suicidal ideation, planning, and attempts. Obtaining psychosocial history helps to gain insight into the patient's current living situation and level of functioning, and to investigate the presence of acute or chronic stressors that may be overwhelming the patient's coping capabilities. The psychosocial history also allows for determination of external supports available to the patient, investigation of the presence of risk buffering factors present in the patient's environment, and exploration of cultural or religious beliefs relating to death or suicide.

3. **Physical disorders**: certain physical disorders are associated with an increased risk for suicide including diseases of the central nervous system (epilepsy, tumors, Huntington chorea, Alzheimer disease, multiple sclerosis, spinal cord injuries, and traumatic brain injury), cancers (especially head and neck), autoimmune diseases, renal disease, and HIV/AIDS. Chronic pain syndromes can contribute substantially to increased suicide risk in affected individuals. So, it is good practice to ask and obtain a medical history that identifies the presence of current medical diagnoses or physical challenges that may increase both short- and long-term suicide risk, such as terminal illness, chronic disease, pain, functional impairment, cognitive impairment, loss of sight or hearing, disfigurement, and loss of independence or increased dependency on others.

4. **Traumatic brain injuries (TBI)**: in comparison with the general population, TBI survivors are at increased risk for suicide ideation, suicide attempts, and suicide completions. Increased impulsivity, enduring

motor disturbances, sensory deficits, and psychiatric symptoms (such as depression, anxiety, psychosis, and personality changes) as well as cognitive dysfunction may lead to a life-long increased suicide risk that requires constant attention.

Evaluation of Warning Signs of Suicide

Suicide risk factors are not necessarily closely related in time to the onset of suicidal behaviors, nor does any risk factor alone increase or decrease risk. Population-based research suggests that the risk for suicide increases with an increase in the number of risk factors present at a time.

A history of suicide attempts is the strongest predictor of future suicide attempts, as well as death by suicide. Intentional self-harm (without the expressed intent to die) is also associated with long-term risk for repeated attempts as well as death by suicide. Threatening to hurt or kill oneself, looking for ways to kill oneself, seeking access to pills, weapons, or other means, talking or writing about death, dying, or suicide, should be considered as serious warning signs for impending suicide that indicate the need for immediate medical intervention.

Factors that may decrease the risk for suicide (protective factors) include: positive social support, spirituality, sense of responsibility to family, children in the home, pregnancy, life satisfaction, reality testing ability, positive coping skills, positive problem-solving skills, and positive therapeutic relationship. It is also useful to assess personality strengths and weaknesses.

Asking about Previous Suicidal Attempts

The frequency of previous attempts, the setting at which an attempt occurred (e.g., time, precipitating factors, degree of planning and impulsivity, substance use, and presence of witnesses), lethality and knowledge about the lethality of the method used in the attempt, intent of dying and attitude toward life, and the consequences of the suicide incident (medical consequences, resulting treatment, psychosocial consequences) are important features of past suicidal attempts that should be clarified during assessment.

Assessment of the Suicidal Ideation, Intent, and Plan

Asking questions about suicidal ideation, intent, and plan is not easy. Sometimes the patient will provide the clue to ask about suicide, but does not readily offer related information. Nevertheless, it is important to ask a screening set of questions whenever the clinical situation or presentation warrants it. A great deal depends upon the clinician's familiarity with the key screening questions and the ease and comfortableness he/she has with the topic and the asking of the questions. A good practice when assessing suicidal intent, plan, and access to lethal means, is to introduce statements that pave the way to ensuring an informative and smooth dialogue and reassure the patient that you are prepared for and interested in the answers. Evaluation of suicidal thoughts has already been covered.

Identification of Targets for Intervention

Information gathered in the previous steps should be used to identify specific targets for intervention. From the beginning of the evaluation of a suicidal person, the clinician should focus on the management of risk, not the measurement of risk factors. These include the presence of an underlying psychiatric diagnosis or symptoms, distressing psychosocial situations, and personality difficulties. The clinician's appraisal of the likelihood of impending suicide is used to guide suitable clinical interventions.

FORENSIC ASSESSMENT

Patients having mental disorders may develop troubles with the law due to their illness. Mental disorders may lead a person to act violently and some behaviors can lead those persons to criminal charges that stem from symptoms of mental illness. These symptoms include impaired judgment, lack of impulse control and disinhibition, suspiciousness and delusions, hallucinations, hyperactivity, and irritability. For example, a patient may act violently toward others in response to command auditory hallucinations, or may attack a presumed persecutor when having paranoid delusions. The use of alcohol or illegal drugs by people with serious mental illness can also lead to trouble with the law. Some mentally ill persons may commit crimes as a way to support themselves, such as stealing food or trespassing to sleep in buildings as a way to survive.

People who are charged with an offence are referred to Forensic Psychiatric Services for the following reasons:

1. **Assessment**: a person is referred by the courts for psychiatric assessment to:

   • **Determine fitness to stand trial**: the legal system guarantees that offenders of criminal acts be fit to stand trial. This necessitates the ability of the accused person to: (1) understand the charges against them; (2) understand the possible consequences of the charges; (3) understand the roles of the participants in court (e.g., judge, crown counsel etc.); and (4) the ability to communicate with their lawyer in order to assist them in preparing the case.

- **Assist in determining whether a person should be found not criminally responsible on account of mental disorder**: it is different from fitness to stand trial. Criminal responsibility is related to whether a person was mentally ill at the time of the offence occurrence or not. The periodic nature of some mental disorders may result in some persons suffering from signs of mental disorders at the time of the alleged offence but considered fit to stand trial at the time of the trial. Conversely, symptoms of mental illness may emerge at the time of the trial that were not present at the time of the alleged offence.

2. **Treatment**: patients who have been proved to be unfit to stand trial or not criminally responsible are referred to forensic psychiatric facilities for treatment. This includes the full range of medical and psychosocial interventions.

3. **Monitoring** of the offender to observe for future signs that the person might be moving closer to offending. This will include a range of psychological, social, and behavioral cues, e.g., asking about violent sexual fantasies, drug or alcohol testing, closed-circuit television monitoring of certain areas of mental state.

4. **Victim safety planning**: to protect any potential future victims. This might include making potential particular individuals aware of the risks an offender poses toward them or making local citizens generally aware of how to protect themselves.

Forensic Report

Referral Information

- The forensic report will be submitted to the court and the attorneys involved.

- Current legal situation: this is a summary of the underlying allegations noting: date of arrest, specific charges.

- The referral question and discussion of notices regarding the nature and purpose of evaluation, absence of confidentiality, and any applicable privilege, as well as the examinee's understanding of this notice.

- Evaluator/s: name, degree, title.

- Date(s) of evaluation.

- Date of report: month, day, year.

Defendant Information

Full name: _____ Sex: _____

DOB: _____

Marital status: _____

Informed Consent/Assent:

Confirm that the Defendant/Minor was informed of the purpose of the evaluation. Confirm that the Defendant/Minor was advised that the evaluation may or may not be confidential.

Sources of Information

Provide a list of all sources of information considered or reviewed; e.g., interview (note how much time was devoted to an interview); psychological testing; review of arrest reports or other third party documents such as depositions, medical records, criminal justice records, or school records; interview with others such as family members, arresting officers, jail staff, treating health care professionals.

Relevant History

Describe past events indicative of an individual's psychosocial functioning across time. The evaluator must apply clinical judgment when considering the relevance and accuracy of all sources of information, including the defendant's accounts and third party accounts and records. The evaluator should report the use of third party information, as appropriate, relevant to the referral questions. Findings from previous psychological/psychiatric evaluations are also included.

It is imperative to collect and review as much collateral information as possible. This includes law enforcement records, outside medical and mental health records, education and military records, criminal history, interviews with the opposing attorneys, family, employers, and others. Repeated efforts may be necessary to obtain the material in a timely manner. Some of the documents may not arrive until after the departure of the inmate from the institution. Whenever possible, any conflict between the information provided by the inmate and other sources should be explored and resolved to the satisfaction of the examiner.

Current Clinical Observations

Assessment will include serial interviews of the inmate and behavioral observations. Assessment typically includes all items of mental state examination. The evaluator may select to use a structured or unstructured clinical interview, as appropriate.

The examiner should offer a comprehensive description of the defendant's behavior, cognitions, and emotional functioning at and around the time of the alleged offence, based upon consideration of the defendant's self-report and relevant third-party sources of information (e.g., police reports, witness statements). The examiner should describe the relationship between the defendant's behavioral, cognitive, and emotional functioning and his or her ability to understand the nature and consequence of his/her actions, and distinguish between right and wrong at and around the time of the alleged offence.

Regardless of the clinical evaluation approach, evaluators should provide underlying facts when communicating opinions, e.g., if the opinion is that the defendant is "paranoid," the evaluator should provide the underlying facts, and the statements and behaviors that support this opinion, "the defendant stated and seemed to believe that he was the King of the Universe."

If the evaluator concluded the defendant was depressed, the evaluator should provide the underlying facts or other supportive facts, e.g.:

> The defendant reported a sad mood, which was consistent with his presentation which included a sullen facial expression, some crying, self-blame, a lack of eye contact, and a paucity of speech. Records in the jail indicate that he sleeps approximately 16 hours each day.

When individuals refuse to participate in the process of evaluation, clinicians may rely on observational data or other data as appropriate.

Psychological Testing

The evaluator shall report the results of relevant testing and assessments completed by the examiner or referenced in third party documents. The evaluator should typically describe the purpose of each test or assessment instrument prior to presenting results and interpretations to the court. Relevant assessments may include but are not limited to estimations of intelligence, cognitive functioning, neurological functioning, personality style, etc. The evaluator should remain aware of the applicable ethical standards of his or her profession and the legal standards regarding the use of tests.

Medical Evaluation

A medical evaluation is essential to a forensic study. Organic conditions can cause any number of psychiatric symptoms, including psychosis and dementia. This evaluation should include relevant laboratory and radiologic studies. Performing specific tests and diagnostic studies is usually guided by the history, physical, and mental health evaluation;

however, pregnancy testing should be performed in all females in the child-bearing period. Additional studies may be indicated in inmates with special medical or psychiatric findings, or from areas where certain significant conditions are endemic (such as cysticercosis, or HIV). Any abnormal findings should be immediately addressed.

Conclusions and Recommendations

This statement includes general finding(s) and recommended disposition (e.g., competent to proceed, incompetent to proceed, insanity opinion) as guided by referral request. A brief but accurate rationale supporting the opinion should be included. The evaluator should provide a more extensive explanation or rationale for an opinion of competency in the context of recent symptoms/behaviors that appear to inconsistent with the opinion. For example, the evaluator should explain why she believes the defendant is competent, notwithstanding his or her continuing paranoid thoughts.

Evaluator's Signature _____

EVALUATION OF CAPACITIES IN PSYCHIATRY

The evaluation of capacities requires a great deal of conceptualization and speculation about the interaction of many biological, psychological, and social variables. The task is often confounded by the presence of insufficient data, possible moral and legal consequences, and fear of fraud by those included in the evaluation and informants. Capacities could be conveniently classified into:

I. Past Capacities

The significance of past capacities is almost entirely legal. Forensic psychiatrists are called on to evaluate the defendant's capacity for choice at a time when he or she committed a crime (the insanity defense) and sometimes to speculate about the competence of a deceased person at a time in the past when making a will. More rarely, forensic psychiatrists deal with past capacities to manage affairs or to make contracts.

II. Current Capacities

The assessment of current capacities usually involves an evaluation of the patient's capacity to choose. Patients have the opportunity to make a number of choices related to their treatment and to the management of their affairs.

The assessment of the capacity to choose may have legal and clinical implications. Some patients elect to refuse a psychiatric or medical treatment, including the need for hospitalization. They must be determined to be incompetent before they could be treated without consent. Also, patients who cannot make self-protective choices in managing their financial affairs may need to have a legal guardian appointed to take over this function.

III. Future Capacities

Future capacities refers to predictive statements about how the patient is likely to respond to a variety of tasks imposed by different environments. This kind of evaluation depends on observation of the patient's capacity to deal with situations without acting in a deviant or socially unacceptable manner, and the patient's capacity to deal with the demands of a new environment or situations.

Assessment of dangerousness and assessment of possible suicidality are the commonest examples of prospective capacities assessment that face residents in their beginning years.

Prospective evaluations of capacity have the potential for moral consequences. These are determined by the extent to which the physician's recommendations either excuse or fail to excuse the patient from an obligation, e.g., a patient who is told that he/she is capable of returning to work may be judged blameworthy (by themselves or others) for not following such obligation.

How Is the Patient's Capacity to Choose Evaluated?

One immediate moral and legal problem in evaluating the capacity to choose is determining what standard will be used to judge whether the patient's choice is right. Words such as adaptive and appropriate are usually used in evaluating the capacity to choose, but these are hardly sufficient. The determination of what is adaptive or appropriate for a given individual depends a great deal on value judgments, i.e., these are decisions that someone else makes about what is best for that person. The term appropriate also does not account for situations in which altruistic motivation influences motivation.

1. Assessing the capacity to choose could be summarized in the following steps:

    - determining exactly the choices the patient is being asked to make;
    - ascertaining the risks and benefits of a particular choice and the alternatives;
    - communicating the risks, benefits, and alternatives to the patient;
    - assessing whether the patient has perceived the information provided;

- assessing whether the patient understands the information provided;
- determining whether there are disturbances of emotionality or think-ing that lead to distortion in the risk–benefit alternative assessment;
- assessing the patient's capacity to weigh alternatives.

2. Assessing the capacity to respond to a future environment. The capacity to respond to a future environment is the patient's ability to meet expectations without behaving aberrantly or experiencing excessive suffering, i.e., this is an evaluation of the patient's capacity to perform a task successfully. Such evaluation has two components: the capacity to perform the task, and the capacity to perform the task successfully, that is, without being disruptive and without experiencing serious suffering or distress. *Evaluation of these two components could be summarized in the following*:

(a) The patient's ability to perform the task involves the following steps:

- determining the exact nature of the task to be performed. This will also involve an assessment of the demands of the environment in which it is performed;
- determining what skills are required for performance;
- determining whether the patient has the requisite skills and is free from impairment that will compromise performance.

(b) The capacity to perform the task successfully: it necessitates that per-formance is not distressing to the patient and that it is not associated with disruptiveness. The evaluation involves the following steps:

- determining whether the patient is likely to experience unusual distress if the task is attempted (based on the history and the patient's own predictions);
- determining whether disruptiveness may be reasonably predicted (based on history, demographics, patient's current behavior, patient's own predictions, patient's motivations regarding future behavior, and sometimes patient's diagnosis);
- assessing the probable environmental contingencies that will favor or diminish disruptiveness;
- prediction of whether the patient's current mental status will remain constant or will change. These in turn allow one to speculate about how current impairments may influence the patient's capacity to choose non-disruptive conduct in some future prospective situation. The patient's diagnosis may help the clinician make this prediction.

Bibliography

Ackerman, S. J., Benjamin, L. S., Beutler, L. E., Gelso, C. J., Goldfried, M. R., Hill, C., . . . & Rainer, J. (2001). Empirically supported therapy relationships: Conclusions and recommendations of the division 29 task force. *Psychotherapy: Theory, Research, Practice, Training, 38*(4), 495–497.

Akhtar, S. (Ed.). (2007). *Listening to others: Developmental and clinical aspects of empathy and attunement.* Lanham, MD: Jason Aronson.

Amador, X. F., & Gorman, J. M. (1998). Psychopathologic domains and insight in schizophrenia. *Psychiatric Clinics of North America, 21*(1), 27–42.

American Psychiatric Association (1990). Guidelines regarding possible conflict between psychiatrists' religious commitments and psychiatric practice (official actions). *American Journal of Psychiatry, 147,* 542.

American Psychiatric Association (1993). Position statement on bias-related incidents (official actions). *American Journal of Psychiatry, 150,* 686.

American Psychiatric Association (1995). Position statement on the role of psychiatrists in assessing driving ability (official actions). *American Journal of Psychiatry, 152,* 819.

American Psychiatric Association (2006). *Practice guideline for the psychiatric evaluation of Adults* (2nd ed.). Arlington, VA: American Psychiatric Association.

American Psychological Association (2010). Ethical principles of psychologists and code of conduct. [September 8, 2017]. www.apa.org/ethics/code.

American Psychiatric Association (2013). *Diagnostic and statistical manual of mental disorders* (5th ed., DSM-5). Arlington, VA: American Psychiatric Association.

Andreasen, N. C. (1984). *The scale for the assessment of negative symptoms (SANS).* Iowa City, IA: The University of Iowa.

Anfinson, T. J., & Kathol, R. G. (1992). Screening laboratory evaluation in psychiatric patients: a review. *General Hospital Psychiatry, 14,* 248–257.

Anfinson, T. J., & Kathol, R. G. (1993). Laboratory and neuroendocrine assessment in medical-psychiatric patients. In A. Stoudemire, & B. S. Fogel (Eds.). *Psychiatric care of the medical patient.* New York: Oxford University Press.

Appelbaum, P. S., & Gutheil, T. G. (1991). *Clinical handbook of psychiatry and the law.* Baltimore, MD: Williams & Wilkins.

Applegate, W. B., Blass, J. P., & Williams, T. F. (1990). Instruments for the functional assessment of older patients. *New England Journal of Medicine, 322,* 1207–1214.

Barnhouse, R. (1986). How to evaluate patients' religious ideation. In L. Robinson (Ed.). *Psychiatry and religion: Overlapping concerns.* Washington, DC: American Psychiatric Press.

Barrett, D. H., Abel, G. G., Rouleau, J. L., & Coyne, B. J. (1993). Behavioral therapy strategies with medical patients. In A. Stoudemire, & B. S. Fogel (Eds.). *Psychiatric care of the medical patient*. New York: Oxford University Press.

Bassuk, E. L. (1985). The diagnosis and treatment of psychiatric emergencies. *Comprehensive Treatment of Schizophrenia, 11*(7), 6–12.

Battaglia, J. (2004). Is this patient dangerous? 5 steps to assess risk for violence. *Current Psychiatry, 3*(2), 14–21.

Baumeister, R. F. (Ed.) (1999). *The self in social psychology*. Philadelphia, PA: Psychology Press (Taylor & Francis).

Benjamin, A. (1987). *The helping interview with case illustrations*. Boston, MA: Houghton Mifflin.

Birdwhistell, R. L. (1970). *Kinesics and context: Essays on body motion communication*. Philadelphia, PA: University of Pennsylvania Press.

Bleuler, E. (1972). *Lehrbuch der Psychiatrie* (12th ed., revised by M. Bleuler). Berlin: Springer-Verlag.

Bloch, M. H., Bartley, C. A., Zipperer, L., Jakubovski, E., Landeros-Weisenberger, A., Pittenger, C., & Leckman, J. F. (2014). Meta-analysis: Hoarding symptoms associated with poor treatment outcome in obsessive-compulsive disorder. *Molecular Psychiatry, 19*(9), 1025–1030.

Bordin, E. S. (1979). The generalizability of the psychoanalytic concept of the working alliance. *Psychotherapy: Theory, Research & Practice, 16*(3), 252–260.

Bordin, E. S. (1994). Theory and research on the therapeutic working alliance: New directions. In A. O. Horvath, & L. S. Greenberg (Eds.), *The working alliance: Theory, research, and practice* (pp. 13–37). Oxford, UK: Wiley.

Brasch, J., Glick, R., Cobb, T., & Richmond, J. (2004). Residency training in emergency psychiatry: A model curriculum developed by the education committee of the American Association for Emergency Psychiatry. *Academic Psychiatry, 28*, 95–103.

Buyukdura, J. S., McClintock, S. M., & Croarkin, P. E. (2011). Psychomotor retardation in depression: Biological underpinnings, measurement, and treatment. *Progress in Neuro-Psychopharmacology and Biological Psychiatry, 35*(2), 395–409.

Cameron, N. (1964). Experimental analysis of schizophrenic thinking. In J. Kasanin (Ed.), *Language and thought in schizophrenia*. New York: W.W. Norton.

Casey, P., & Kelly, B. (2007). *Fish's clinical psychopathology: Signs and symptoms in psychiatry* (3rd ed.). Cambridge: RCPsych Publications.

Cepeda, C. (2000). *Concise guide to the psychiatric interview of children and adolescents*. Washington, DC: American Psychiatric Press.

Cepeda, C. (2010). *Clinical manual for the psychiatric interview of children and adolescents* (1st ed.). Washington, DC: American Psychiatric Publishing.

Chambless, D. L., & Ollendick, T. H. (2001). Empirically supported psychological interventions: Controversies and evidence. *Annual Review of Psychology, 52*, 685–716.

Chang, C. K., Hayes, R. D., Broadbent, M., Fernandes, A. C., Lee, W., Hotopf, M., & Stewart, R. (2010). All-cause mortality among people with serious mental illness (SMI), substance use disorders, and depressive disorders in southeast London: a cohort study. *BMC Psychiatry, 10*, 77.

Cheyne, J. A., & Girard, T. A. (2007). Paranoid delusions and threatening hallucinations: A prospective study of sleep paralysis experiences. *Consciousness and Cognition: An International Journal, 16*(4), 959–974.

Cormier, L. S., Nurius, P. S., & Osborn, C. J. (2012). *Interviewing and change strategies for helpers: Fundamental skills and cognitive-behavioral interventions* (7th ed.). Belmont, CA: Brooks/Cole.

Cox, A., Holbrook, D., & Rutter, M. (1981). Psychiatric interviewing techniques, VI-experimental study: Eliciting feelings. *British Journal of Psychiatry, 139,* 144–152.

Cox, A., Hopkinson, K., & Rutter, M. (1981). Psychiatric interviewing techniques, II-naturalistic study: Eliciting factual information. *British Journal of Psychiatry, 138,* 283–291.

Cox, A., Rutter, M., & Holbrook, D. (1981). Psychiatric interviewing techniques, V-experimental study: Eliciting factual information. *British Journal of Psychiatry, 139,* 29–31.

David, A. S. (1990). Insight and psychosis. *British Journal of Psychiatry, 156,* 798–808.

de Clérambault, G. G. (1942). *Les psychoses passionelles. Oeuvre psychiatrique.* Paris: Presses Universitaire.

DeLassus Gress, C. (2014). Dysarthria. In M. J. Aminoff, & R. B. Daroff (Eds.). *Encyclopedia of the Neurological Sciences.* London: Academic Press.

Dickstein, L. (1991). New perspectives on human development. In A. Tasman, & S. Goldfinger (Eds.). *American Psychiatric Press Review of Psychiatry, vol. 10.* Washington, DC: American Psychiatric Press.

Dubovsky, S. L. (1998). *A concise guide to clinical psychiatry.* Washington, DC: American Psychiatric Press.

Engel, G. L. (1980). The clinical application of the biopsychosocial model. *American Journal of Psychiatry, 137*(5), 535–544.

Engel, G. L. (1997). From biomedical to biopsychosocial: I. Being scientific in the human domain. *Psychotherapy and Psychosomatics, 66*(2), 57–62.

Escobar, J. I., Burnam, A., Karno, M., Forsythe, A., Landsverk, J., & Golding, J. M. (1986). Use of the Mini-Mental State Examination (MMSE) in a community population of mixed ethnicity: Cultural and linguistic artifacts. *Journal of Nervous and Mental Disease, 174,* 607–614.

Fish, F. (1967). *Clinical psychopathology.* Bristol, UK: John Wright.

Flaherty, J. A., Gaviria, F. M., Pathak, D., Mitchell, T., Wintrob, R., Richman, J. A., & Birz, S. (1988). Developing instruments for cross-cultural psychiatric research. *Journal of Nervous and Mental Disease, 176,* 257–263.

Fogel, B. S., & Summergrad, P. (1991). Evolution of the medical-psychiatric unit in the general hospital. In F. K. Judd, G. D. Burrows, & D. R. Lipsitt (Eds.), *Handbook of studies on general hospital psychiatry.* New York: Elsevier.

Fok, M. L., Hayes, R. D., Chang, C. K., Stewart, R., Callard, F. J., & Moran, P. (2012) Life expectancy at birth and all-cause mortality among people with personality disorder. *Journal of Psychosomatic Research, 73*(2), 104–107.

Garfinkel, P. E., & Dorian, B. (2000). Psychiatry in the new millennium. *Canadian Journal of Psychiatry, 45,* 40–47.

Garrick, T. R., & Stotland, N. L. (1982). How to write a psychiatric consultation. *American Journal of Psychiatry, 139,* 849–855.

Gaw, A. (1993). *Culture, ethnicity, and mental illness.* Washington, DC, American Psychiatric Press.

Gelder, M., Gath, D., & Mayou, R. (1983). *Oxford textbook of psychiatry.* Oxford: Oxford University Press.

Gilboa, A., & Verfaellie, M. (2010). Telling it like it isn't: The cognitive neuroscience of confabulation. *Journal of the International Neuropsychological Society*, 16(6), 961–966.

Gold, L. H., Stuart, M. D., Anfang, A., Drukteinis, A. M., Metzner, J. L., Price, M., . . . & Zonana, H. V. (2008). Practice guideline: Evaluation of psychiatric disability. *Journal of the American Academy of Psychiatry and the Law*, 36(4), 2008 Supplement.

Goldstein, K. (1944). Methodological approach to the study of schizophrenic thought. In J. S. Kasanin (Ed.), *Language and thought in schizophrenia*. Berkeley, CA: University of California Press.

Gonzalez, C.A., Griffith, E. E. H., & Ruiz, P. (1995). Cross-cultural issues in psychiatric treatment. In G. O. Gabbard (Ed.), *Treatments of psychiatric disorders* (2nd ed.). Washington, DC: American Psychiatric Press.

Goodwin, G. M., Haddad, P. M., Ferrier, I. N., Aronson, J. K., Barnes, T., Cipriani, A., . . . & Vieta, E. (2016). Evidence-based guidelines for treating bipolar disorder: Revised third edition recommendations from the British Association for Psychopharmacology. *Journal of Psychopharmacology*, 30, 495–553.

Group for the Advancement of Psychiatry. (1991). The Mental Health Professional and the Legal System, report no. 131. New York: Brunner/Mazel.

Gruhle, H. W. (1915). Self-description and empathy. *Zeitschrift fuer Gesundheitswesen Neurologie und Psychiatrie*, 28, 148.

Halleck, S. L. (1991) *Evaluation of the psychiatric patient: A primer*. New York: Plenum Publishing.

Hamilton, M. (1985). *Fish's clinical psychopathology: Signs and symptoms in psychiatry* (2nd ed.). Bristol, UK: John Wright & Sons.

Harrington, R., Hill, J., Rutter, M., John, K., Fudge, H., Zoccolillo, M., & Weissman, M. (1988). The assessment of lifetime psychopathology: A comparison of two interviewing styles. *Psychologial Medicine*, 18, 487–493.

Hartley, J. (2002). Notetaking in non-academic settings: A review. *Applied Cognitive Psychology*, 16(5), 559–574.

Hays, P. A. (2013). *Connecting across cultures: The helper's toolkit*. Thousand Oaks, CA: Sage.

Herman, J. L. (1992). *Trauma and recovery*. New York: Basic Books.

Hill, C. J., & Garner, S.J. (1991). Factors influencing physician choice. *Hospital and Health Services Administration*, 36(4), 491–503.

Hopkinson, K., Cox, A., & Rutter, M. (1981). Psychiatric interviewing techniques, III-naturalistic study: Eliciting feelings. *British Journal of Psychiatry*, 138, 406–415.

Hyman, S. E. (1988). *Manual of psychiatric emergencies* (2nd ed.). New York: Little, Brown.

Iverson, G. L. (2004). Objective assessment of psychomotor retardation in primary care patients with depression. *Journal of Behavioral Medicine*, 27(1), 31–37.

Jaspers, K. (1962) *General psychopathology* (trans. J. Hoenig & M. W. Hamilton from 1959 book). Baltimore, MD: Johns Hopkins University Press, reprinted in 1997.

Joseph A. B.(1986). Focal central nervous system abnormalities in patients with misidentification syndromes. *Bibliotheca Psychiatrica*, 164, 68–79.

Katz, S. (1983). Assessing self-maintenance: Activities of daily living, mobility, and instrumental activities of daily living. *Journal of the American Geriatric Society*, 31, 721–727.

Kendler, K. S., Glaser, W. M., & Morgenstern, H. (1983). Dimensions of delusional experience. *American Journal of Psychiatry*, 140, 466–469.

Kiran, C., & Chaudhury, S. (2009). Understanding delusions. *Industrial Psychiatry Journal, 18*(1), 3–18.

Knopman, D. S., DeKosky, S. T., Cummings, J. L., Chui, H., Corey-Bloom, J., Relkin, N., . . . & Stevens, J. C. (2001). Practice parameter: Diagnosis of dementia (an evidence-based review). Report of the Quality Standards Subcommittee of the American Academy of Neurology. *Neurology, 56*(9), 1143–1153.

Kovess, V., Sylla, O., Fournier, L., & Flavigny, V. (1992). Why discrepancies exist between diagnostic interviews and clinicians' diagnoses. *Social Psychiatry and Psychiatric Epidemiology, 27*, 185–191.

Kozak, M. J., & Foa, E. B. (1994). Obsessions, overvalued ideas, and delusions in obsessive-compulsive disorder. *Behavior Research and Therapy, 32*, 343–353.

Kraepelin, E. (1905). *Lectures on clinical psychiatry* (3rd ed.) (transl. T. Johnstone, 1917). New York: W. Wood.

Kroll, J., & Sheehan, W. (1989). Religious beliefs and practices among 52 psychiatric inpatients in Minnesota. *American Journal of Psychiatry, 146*, 67–72.

Kurt, P., Yener, G., & Oguz, M. (2011). Impaired digit span can predict further cognitive decline in older people with subjective memory complaint: A preliminary result. *Aging and Mental Health, 15*(3), 364–369.

Lewis, M. (1990). Self-knowledge and social development in early life. In L. A. Pervin (Ed.), *Handbook of personality*. New York: Guilford.

Lopez, S., & Nunez, J. A. (1987). Cultural factors considered in selected diagnostic criteria and interview schedules. *Journal of Abnormal Psychology, 96*, 270–272.

Lowenstein, R. J. (1991). An office mental status examination for complex chronic dissociative symptoms and multiple personality disorder. *Psychiatric Clinics of North America, 14*, 567–604.

Macbeth, J. E., Wheeler, A. M., Sither, J. W., & Onek, J. N. (1994). *Legal and risk management issues in the practice of psychiatry*. Washington, DC: American Psychiatric Press.

MacKinnon, R. A., & Yudofsky, S. C. (1988). Outline of a psychiatric history and mental state examination. In J. A. Talbott, R. E. Hales, & S. C. Yudofsky (Eds.), *Textbook of psychiatry*. Washington, DC: American Psychiatric Press.

Mackintosh, N. J. (2011). *History of theories and measurement of intelligence*. New York: Cambridge University Press.

Maier, W., Philipp, M., & Buller, R. (1988). The value of structured clinical interviews. *Archives of General Psychiatry, 45*, 963–964.

March, J. S. (1993). What constitutes a stressor: The "Criterion A" issue. In J. R. T. Davison, & E. B. Foa (Eds.), *Posttraumatic stress disorder: DSM-IV and beyond*. Washington, DC: American Psychiatric Press.

Margulies, A., & Havens, L. L. (1981). The initial encounter: What to do first? *American Journal of Psychiatry, 138*, 421–428.

Markkula, N., Härkänen, T., Perälä, J., Partti, K., Peña, S., Koskinen, S., . . . & Saarni, S. I. (2012). Mortality in people with depressive, anxiety and alcohol use disorders in Finland. *British Journal of Psychiatry, 200*(2),143–149.

McConaughy, S. H. (2005). *Clinical interviews for children and adolescents: Assessment to intervention*. New York: Guilford Press.

McGoldrick, M., Pearce, J., & Giordano, J. (Eds.) (1982). *Ethnicity and family therapy*. New York: Guilford Press.

Meier, S. T., & Davis, S. R. (2011). *The elements of counseling* (7th ed.). Belmont, CA: Brooks/Cole.

Miller, N. E. (1983). Behavioral medicine: Symbiosis between laboratory and clinic. *Annual Review of Psychology, 34,* 1–31.

Moor, A., & Silvern, L. (2006). Identifying pathways linking child abuse to psychological outcome: The mediating role of perceived parental failure of empathy. *Journal of Emotional Abuse, 6*(4), 91–114.

Morrison, A. (1848). *Cases of mental disease.* London: Longman and S. Highley.

Murray, R., Hill, P., & McGuffin, P. (1997). *The essentials of postgraduate psychiatry* (3rd ed.). Cambridge: Cambridge University Press.

Norcross, J. C., & Lambert, M. J. (2011). Psychotherapy relationships that work II. *Psychotherapy (Chic), 48*(1), 4–8.

Notman, M., & Nadelson, C. (1991). *Women and men: New perspectives on gender differences.* Washington, DC: American Psychiatric Press.

Nurcombe, B., & Fitzhenry-Coor, I. (1982). How do psychiatrists think? Clinical reasoning in the psychiatric interview: a research and education project. *Australia and New Zealand Journal of Psychiatry, 16,* 13–24.

Osatuke, K., Ciesla, J., Kasckow, J.W., Zisook, S., & Mohamed, S. (2008). Insight in schizophrenia: A review of etiological models and supporting research. *Comprehensive Psychiatry, 49*(1), 70–77.

Othmer, E., & Othmer, S. C. (2002). *The clinical interview using DSM-IV-TR: Vol 1: Fundamentals.* Washington, DC: American Psychiatric Publishing.

Oulis, P., Konstantakopoulos, G., Lykouras, L., & Michalopoulou, P. G. (2013). Differential diagnosis of obsessive-compulsive symptoms from delusions in schizophrenia: a phenomenological approach. *World Journal of Psychiatry, 3*(3), 50–56.

Overholser, J. C. (2006). Panacea or placebo: The historical quest for medications to treat depression. *Journal of Contemporary Psychotherapy, 36*(4), 183–190.

Panagiotis, O., Konstantakopoulos, G., Lykouras, L., & Michalopoulou, P. G. (2013). Differential diagnosis of obsessive-compulsive symptoms from delusions in schizophrenia: A phenomenological approach. *World Journal of Psychiatry, 22*(3), 50–56.

Perry, S., Cooper, A. M., & Michels, R. (1987). The psychodynamic formulation: Its purpose, structure, and clinical application. *American Journal of Psychiatry, 144,* 543–550.

Pinderhughes, E. (1988). *Understanding race, ethnicity and power.* New York: Free Press.

Pipes, R. B., & Davenport, D. S. (1999). *Introduction to psychotherapy: Common clinical wisdom.* Englewood Cliffs, NJ: Prentice Hall.

Poole, R., & Higgo, R. (2006). *Psychiatric interviewing and assessment.* Cambridge: Cambridge University Press

Powell, G. (Ed.). (1983). *The psychosocial development of minority group children.* New York: Brunner-Mazel.

Roberts, R. E., Rhoades H. M., & Vernon, S. W. (1990). Using the CES-D Scale to screen for depression and anxiety: Effects of language and ethnic status. *Psychiatry Research, 31,* 69–83.

Robins, L. (1989). Diagnostic grammar and assessment: Translating criteria into questions. *Psychological Methods, 19,* 57–68.

Rogers, C. (1959). A theory of therapy, personality and interpersonal relationships as developed in the client-centered framework. In S. Koch (Ed.), *Psychology:*

A study of a science. Vol. 3: Formulations of the person and the social context. New York: McGraw Hill.

Rudd, M. D. (2006). *The assessment and management of suicidality.* Sarasota, FL: Professional Resource Press.

Rueve, M. E., & Welton, R. S. (2008). Violence and mental illness. *Psychiatry (Edgmont), 5*(5), 34–48.

Sadock, B., & Sadock, V. (2007). *Kaplan & Sadock's synopsis of psychiatry: Behavioral sciences/clinical psychiatry* (10th ed.). Philadelphia, PA: Lippincott Williams & Wilkins.

Santín, J. M. López, & Gálvez, F. Molins. (2011). Overvalued ideas: Psychopathologic issues. *Actas españolas de psiquiatría, 39*(1), 70–74.

Sattler, J. (1988). *Assessment of children.* San Diego, CA: Jerome Sattler.

Scheiber, S. (1988). Psychiatric interviewing, psychiatric history, and mental status examination. In *The American Psychiatric Association textbook of psychiatry.* Washington, DC: American Psychiatric Press, 1988.

Schiffer, R. B., Klein, R. F., & Sider, R. C (1988). *The medical evaluation of psychiatric patients.* New York: Plenum.

Schneider, K. (1957). Primary and secondary symptoms in schizophrenia. *Fortschritte der Neurologie-Psychiatrie, 25,* 487–90 (transl. Marshall H). In S. R. Hirsch & M. Shepherd (Eds.) (1974), *Themes and variations in European psychiatry.* Bristol: John Wright.

Sederer, L. I. (1992). Brief hospitalization. In A. Tasman, & M. B. Riba (Eds.), *American psychiatric press review of psychiatry, vol. 11.* Washington, DC: American Psychiatric Press.

Serby, M. (2003). Psychiatric resident conceptualizations of mood and affect within the mental status examination. *American Journal of Psychiatry, 160*(8), 1527–1529.

Shea, S. C. (1998). *Psychiatric interviewing: The art of understanding.* Philadelphia, PA: W. B. Saunders.

Siassi, I. (1984). Psychiatric interview and mental status examination. In G. Goldstein, & M. Hersen (Eds.), *Handbook of psychological assessment* (pp. 259–275). New York: Pergamon Press.

Simon, R., & Hales, R. (2006). *Textbook of suicide assessment and management.* Arlington, VA: American Psychiatric Publishing.

Simon, R., & Tardiff, K. (2008). *Textbook of violence assessment and management.* Arlington, VA: American Psychiatric Publishing.

Sims, A. (1995). *Symptoms in the mind: An introduction to descriptive psychopathology* (2nd ed.). Philadelphia, PA: W. B. Saunders.

Skre, I., Onstad, S., Torgersen, S., & Kringlen, E. (1991). High interrater reliability for the structured clinical interview for DSM-III-R axis I (SCID I). *Acta Psychiatrica Scandinavica, 84,* 167–173.

Sohlberg, M. M., & Mateer, C. A. (1989). *Introduction to cognitive rehabilitation: Theory and practice.* New York: Guilford Press.

Sommers-Flanagan, J., & Campbell, D. (2009). Psychotherapy and (or) medications for depression in youth? An evidence-based review with recommendations for treatment. *Journal of Contemporary Psychotherapy, 39*(2), 111–120.

Sommers-Flanagan, J., & Sommers-Flanagan, R. (2007). *Tough kids, cool counseling: User-friendly approaches with challenging youth* (2nd ed.). Alexandria, VA: American Counseling Association.

Sommers-Flanagan, J., & Sommers-Flanagan, R. (2014). *Clinical interviewing* (5th ed.). Hoboken, NJ: Wiley.

Stein, T. (1993). Changing perspectives on homosexuality. In J. Oldham, M. Riba, & A. Tasman (Eds.), *American psychiatric press review of psychiatry, vol. 12.* Washington, DC: American Psychiatric Press.

Stone, T., & Young, A. W. (1997). Delusions and brain injury: The philosophy and psychology of belief. *Mind and Language, 12,* 327–364.

Strupp, H., & Binder, J. (1984). *Psychotherapy in a new key: A guide to time-limited dynamic psychotherapy.* New York: Basic Books.

Talley, B. J., & Littlefield, J. (2009). Efficiently teaching mental status examination to medical students. *Medical Education, 43,* 1200–1202.

Tardiff, K. (1992). The current state of psychiatry in the treatment of violent patients. *Archives of General Psychiatry, 49,* 493–499.

Taylor, M. A. (1981). *The neuropsychiatric examination.* New York: S. P. Medical and Scientific Books.

Tombini, M., Pellegrino, G., Zappasodi, F., Quattrocchi, C. C., Assenza, G., Melgari, J. M., . . . & Rossini, P. M. (2012). Complex visual hallucinations after occipital extrastriate ischemic stroke. *Cortex: A Journal Devoted to the Study of the Nervous System and Behavior, 48*(6), 774–777.

Trzepacz, P. J., & Baker, R.W. (1993). *The psychiatric mental status examination.* New York: Oxford University Press.

Van Gerpen, M. W., Johnson, J. E., & Winstead, D. K. (1999). Mania in the geriatric patient population: a review of the literature. *American Journal of Geriatric Psychiatry, 7,* 188–202.

Veale, D. (2002). Over-valued ideas: A conceptual analysis. *Behaviour Research and Therapy, 40,* 383–400.

Watson, C. G., Juba, M. P., Manifold, V., Kucala, T., & Anderson, P. E. (1991). The PTSD interview: Rationale, description, reliability, and concurrent validity of a DSM-III-based technique. *Journal of Clinical Psychology, 47,* 179–188.

Wernicke, C. (1906). *Fundamentals of psychiatry.* Leipzig: Thieme.

Westermeyer, J. (1989). *Psychiatric care of migrants: A clinical guide.* Washington, DC: American Psychiatric Press.

Westermeyer, J. J. (1993). Cross-cultural psychiatric assessment. In A. C. Gaw (Ed.), *Culture, ethnicity, and mental illness.* Washington, DC: American Psychiatric Press.

White, A. J., & Barraclough, B. (1989). Benefits and problems of routine laboratory investigations in adult psychiatric admissions. *British Journal of Psychiatry, 155,* 65–72.

Wilson, C. J., & Powell, M. (2001). *A guide to interviewing children: Essential skills for counsellors, police, lawyers and social workers.* Crows Nest, NSW: Allen & Unwin.

Witlox, J., Eurelings, L. S., de Jonghe J. F., et al. (2010). Delirium in elderly patients and the risk of postdischarge mortality, institutionalization, and dementia: a meta-analysis. *JAMA 304*(4), 443–451.

Woods, D. L., Kishiyama, M. M., Yund, E. W., Kalisvaart, K. J., Eikelenboom, P., & van Gool, W. A. (2011). Improving digit span assessment of short-term verbal memory. *Journal of Clinical and Experimental Neuropsychology, 33*(1), 101–111.

Wright, J. H., & Davis, D. (1994). The therapeutic relationship in cognitive-behavioral therapy: Patient perceptions and therapist responses. *Cognitive and Behavioral Practice, 1*(1), 25–45.

Yassini S. M., Harrazi, M. A., & Askari, J. (2010). The study of most important factors influencing physician choice. *Procedia Social and Behavioral Sciences, 5,* 1945–1949.

Zeier, K., Connell, R., Resch, W., & Thomas, C. (2013). Recommendations for lab monitoring of atypical antipsychotics. *Current Psychiatry, 12*(9), 51–54.

Zohar, J. (2012). *Obsessive compulsive disorder: Current science and clinical practice* (1st ed.). Hoboken, NJ: Wiley-Blackwell.

Index

Page numbers in *italics* refer to figures. Page numbers in **bold** refer to tables.